THE MIDDLEBURG MYSTIQUE

Cheers
&
Tally Ho!,
JAM

The Middleburg Mystique

A Peek Inside the Gates of Middleburg, Virginia

Vicky Moon

ISBN 978-0-9617683-1-7

Library of Congress Cataloging-in-Publication Data
Moon, Vicky.
    The Middleburg mystique : a peek inside the gates of Middleburg, Virginia / Vicky Moon.
        p. cm.

    ISBN 978-0-9617683-1-7

1. Middleburg (Va.)—Social life and customs. 2. Middleburg
(Va.)—Biography—Anecdotes. 3. Celebrities—Virginia—Middleburg—Anecdotes. 4.
Upper class—Virginia—Middleburg—Anecdotes. 5. Middleburg (Va.)—Buildings,
structures, etc. I. Title.

F234.M48 M66 2001
975.5'28-dc21   2001025923

Printed in the United States of America

Second Edition

10 9 8 7 6 5 4 3 2

Photos by Howard Alien, Janet Hitchen, June Hughes, Vicky Moon and JeffYorke

CONTENTS

In memory of those who have
lived, loved, and laughed and
added to the mystique: (from top
left, clockwise) Virginia Gunnell,
Jim Jenkins, David "Peaches"
Lee, Gary Gardner, Mary Howe
diZerega and Mary Moore
deButts, Buck Nalls, Madelyn
Marzani, Barrick Groom and
Marsyl Hammond, John Levis,
and Bettina Ward.

CHAPTER I

20118

"In this town everybody has to be forgiven for at least one thing."

Elizabeth Taylor called Middleburg home
while married to her sixth husband
Senator John Warner.
(Photo by Jeff Yorke)

*L*inda Tripp, White House administrative aide turned Department of Defense
political appointee and confidante turned consummate snitch, walks across the
street with the mail under her arm. Some friends are in my office across the
street and we lean over the desk to peer out the window as she slides into her
Chrysler mini-van (which still has Maryland tags). It wasn't until several hours
later that a detail occurred to me and I swear this is true. There was a Big Gulp
on the dash.

Middleburg, Virginia and the surrounding crossroads, hamlets and villages
has captivated many well-known personalities from the Kennedys (Jackie came

to fox hunt here for many years), Averell and Pamela Harriman, Elizabeth Taylor, Dick Smothers, Liz Whitney, Tab Hunter, Robert Wagner and Oliver North. Places with names such as Upperville, Delaplane, Unison, Aldie, Philomont, Bluemont, The Plains and Rectortown are loosely included. And smaller spots such as Frogtown, Halfway and Atoka are known only to the locals.

Linda Tripp sought the tranquility of the horse country after the Monica Lewinsky fiasco and rented a cottage on a larger farm. Her reviews here were mixed, at best.Actually, if the truth were known, the neighbors were in a snit worried that the press (God forbid) would be up and down the road all the time. The town has always included a cast of local characters. As one resident aptly says, "we have one of everything here."

The 1787 Act of the Assembly of the Commonwealth of Virginia establishing the town, described it as "50 acres of land lying in the county of Loudoun, the property of Leven Powell," who is now considered the founding father. I often tell people that I have my finger on the pulse of Middleburg. From my second floor office on West Washington Street, I can see the simple civic Federal style brick post office out my front window.Right next to it, I can see the architecturally detailed Georgian Revival style bank. And...from my side window, I can see the liquor store.

The post office is the heartbeat of this village. Here, the news of the day originates (good news and bad, some of it true and the rest vaguely true).The well-to-do pass by the not so well off, retrieving everything from dividend checks to welfare checks to even baby chicks. (More on that in a minute.)You might call it checks and chicks.

"In a sense, life revolves around it," says Jim Jenkins, who worked as a clerk for 25 years from 1968-93. "If you're not around the post office you lose out on a lot." Foot traffic ebbs and flows throughout the day and into the late night, with the peak around late morning when all the mail is "up" as they say.

There are 1,856 mailboxes, yet the official population of the town is 650.In the surrounding countryside of farms and estates, the mail is delivered on the rural route. So how does this account for the inflated number of box holders?

It's very simple...the 20118 zip code is highly sought after. According to sources inside the post office, at least one third or more of the box holders are people from outside the area.Many that have no business or property in the area pay the $14-44 annual fee for what they perceive to be a coveted address.

According to Postmaster Norris Beavers, there is a waiting list at any time from 20-60 names. "I get requests from California and Connecticut," he says, adding. "It looks good on the letterhead for a small business. The people getting the letter don't know that it is actually [coming from] a home/office in some little lean-to in Millwood."

Besides Linda Tripp, watching from my window, a typical day might go something like this...Carol Bowersock, mayor of Middleburg from 1992-96 walks over from her home one block over on Marshall Street. She has her prized dog, P. Zechariah, a Welsh Corgi, in tow. "That's his registered name," she says, adding, "That way we can call him Prozac for short."

For years, Bowersock and her twin sister Frances, both 50ish, shared a house that they called "Headquarters." They ran errands for clients. In the garage, their close friend Markey Love operated an elegant floral business focused on weddings and parties in big white tents and things like that.Not to complicate matters too much here, but Markey's sister, Allie Love, was formerly the town manager.

But back to the Bowersocks. Before moving out to Oregon, their main mission in life was with the Middleburg Rescue Squad. They were volunteers for 20 years. Night and day they jumped in an ambulance to assist with a horse-riding accident, kidney stone attack or even labor pains.

The call of their life came through when their parents, the esteemed Justin and Betty Bruce Bowersock, made their final exit by committing suicide together. (But much more on that later.) Miss Bowersock and Prozac greet Sally Godfrey and Stella (as in *A Street Car Named Desire*, I am told).The dogs sniff each other while their owners chat. Ms. Godfrey runs a flower service called Centerpiece from her home/office across the street from the Bowersocks. She does essentially the same thing that Markey Love does, but everyone is friendly and there are more than enough parties for the four florists in this town, which by the way is four blocks long. (Maybe five if you want to stretch it.) Customers arrive in a variety of vehicles and the SUV is definitely the car du jour. A vanity license plate is optional but one proud citizen displays the "20118" zip code. And on the hood of many cars, a colorful hood ornament, a fox or favorite dog or other animal--everything from a goat to a pig. Cost of these adornments range from $45-300.

Regular customers at the post office fall into a couple of categories. First are the commuters, those poor souls who have to drive 50-plus miles into Washington, D.C. to work every day. Thornton "Doc" Saffer commutes with his current wife, Carolyn. He wrote a self- published book called *It Was Mostly Fun* about growing up in Middleburg. It was then recreated into one of the most popular musical productions ever staged by the Middleburg Players.

Rob Banner, publisher of *The Chronicle of The Horse*, a weekly magazine that has been based in this town for 63 years, doesn't have to commute far, just to the corner of town. He zooms up in his sapphire bright blue BMW with the top down. A regular in the owner rider timber races at the point-to-point races, he seems to prefer anything that moves to be fast.

Jeff Gable, the hunky owner of Hunt Country Pools, comes to town each morning in his red truck and sits and reads his mail. He is now known around town as "The Pool Man" since he ran off with the wife of actor Robert Duvall in the summer of 1995. And even though he doesn't live in Middleburg, one employee inside the post office points out that "he got his mail here before he became known as The Pool Man." (And p.s. much more on all that later.)

Then you might see one of the local horse veterinarians, who travel in specially equipped trucks with portable equine x-ray machines, endoscopes and ultrasound machines. They are all early risers, like Willie McCormick, a Middleburg native (his great grandmother was born here) whose mail includes not just the run-of-the-mill trade publications but also The New Yorker. And then there's Ron Bowman, who also travels the countryside throughout the day (and sometimes the night) making "house calls" to the many stables and barns tending to sick and lame race, show jumping and hunting horses.

The post office parade also includes several blacksmiths, also known as farriers. Greg Ramsay has a large red truck (license plate "4 Hooves") decked out with the equipment he needs in his line of work--horseshoes, anvil and propane forge. His truck also has a mini microwave oven and computer.

Bob Mueller, also a blacksmith, has a lovely yellow lab, Bailey, that rides up in back on his navy blue truck. Or Sandy Young, a gentleman farmer and long time resident, who goes to the Middleburg Fitness Club first and then stops by for his mail.

This is followed by the Hill School drop off group. Fathers and mothers have driven their children into town to take them to private day school and then stop by to pick up the mail. Like Robyn Yovanovich, a drama teacher at Foxcroft, now married to horse trainer Don Yovanovich. She drops off daughter Clancy, picks up her mail and proceeds to work.

Later in the morning, some of the ladies who play tennis come by in their white skirts and warm-up suits. Occasionally someone will walk down the street in riding attire, but it's really not the thing to do around here.

One Monday morning finds a local hostess in tears in the corner of the post office lobby. It seems that a number of recent guests around town are trotting instead of their horses. (A bad batch of seafood.)

Folks are very forgiving in this community..."It's olay," a friend tells the hostess. "My husband lost two pounds." Nevertheless, the hostess intends to write all the unfortunate party-goers a note.

Andy Fenton, who serves as the corporate pilot for Ritz Camera, which parks the company jet at the nearby Leesburg airport, comes to town. Horseman Bobby Powell is like clockwork each morning at 10.

Mark Buchanan, an architect up the street, comes to get his mail. Real Estate broker Paul McMahon always stops to chat with a friend. Mortgage banker Jack Schock has just returned from a horse show and has a box full of mail. Ken Tomlinson, former Editor-in-Chief at Reader's Digest, is a fairly new resident in the area, now director at The National Sporting Library, also up on the corner next to The Chronicle of the Horse.

Eugene Howard, a freelance bartender at many of the parties around town and an employee at the Mellon estate in Upperville, shows up. Helen Wiley, a major force behind several charity events from the Hill School Auction to the Trinity Church Stable Tour, cruises up in her maroon BMW station wagon with her Jack Russell terrier, Thorn, at her side.

A bright red vintage Jaguar pulls up and Tully Rector, a multi-talented artist and former advertising executive gets out. (Vanity license plate: Tully.) He now owns two businesses in town--a cosmetics shop, "Tully's Beyond The Pale" and (guess what?) "Tully Rector's Men's and Women's Wear," a sportswear boutique. His daughter, Kelly, once was married to Calvin Klein and from time to time, Tully proudly boasts about his buddy, actor Robert Duvall. (Stay tuned for the scoop on him too.)

Pam Dickson, a Brit who came to town 30 years ago and started the Fursman dog-boarding kennel, comes to collect her mail. Her "clients" now include Buster, Elvis and Cara Scott, a motley group of canines of mixed ancestry owned by the affable *Today Show* television personality Willard Scott and wife Mary, who live not far away in Delaplane. "I tell you what," Dickson offered one day, "the richer people usually have mixed breed dogs."

Don't tell that to Steve Wolf, the head of USAirways. His purebred Labradors: Pierre and Coco, are Fursman regulars. And while their names are not exactly in keeping with that hunt country image, consider that Wolf and his stunning blonde wife, Delores, live on 220-plus acres in a 17,170-square foot house that could very well be the largest one built in the area in recent years. It includes a ten-car garage, pool and large entrance room, but alas, no airstrip. They do like to jet off to faraway places and also maintain a home in Paris. (By the way, their mail is picked up daily by his personal assistant, Jan Johnson.)

Max (a German Shepherd cross) and Blondie (a Collie type) are fairly new visitors at Fursman. When their owners, Nancy and Doug McCorkindale, first came to visit, they spotted a photo of Treasure Chest, Dickson's highly trained German shepherd jumping through a hoop of fire with a copy of *USA Today* in his mouth.

"He asked me about the photo and if the newspaper was rubber," Dickson related. "I told him no, it was real and then I asked him, 'why, do you work there?' I was thinking he was maybe a reporter or something. He sort of hemmed a bit and then told me he had just been named CEO of Gannett."

And speaking of Gannett, it is also very likely that Jan Neuharth Keusch, daughter of *USA Today* founder Al Neuharth, could stroll into the post office at any minute. She and husband Joseph operated Paper Chase Farms, a riding school and training stables complete with indoor arena just on the east side of town. They sold it and it's now known as Fox Chase Farm and they continue with Paper Chase on a smaller scale.

Regulars like Sally and Steve McVeigh, horse breeders and horse owners, venture into town every morning, first for breakfast at the Coach Stop and then a trip to the post office.Close behind the McVeighs would be Claudia Young, who also dines with them each morning. Her husband, Sandy (see above) has already checked the mail, but she stops in from time to time, too.

Seymour Hall shows up almost every day in the same threadbare tweed jacket that has patches on the elbows that are falling off. It can be 93 degrees outside and he's still wearing that jacket. He has at least five dogs of all sizes hanging out of the back of his old navy blue Jeep.

Leffert Lefferts (that's right, that's his name) stops in Middleburg to mail a letter from his 140-acre farm, Horsefeathers, in Upperville. Mosby, his yellow Labrador "type" dog, sits up in the front seat of his oversized silver Ford Expedition just as if he were any well-respected passenger or member of the family. In case you haven't noticed, the dogs are just as important around here as the children and the horses.

Bill Casey, an exceedingly affable man who once owned the BP gas station on the western side of town, stands for 23 minutes in front of the post office one morning. He chats with John Levis and turns to open the door three times for three different attractive women and ignores all others. His wife, Judy Casey, owns the Finicky Filly up the street near the Safeway.

The procession continues: Custer Cassidy, who draws pen and ink cartoons for *The Chronicle of the Horse*, stops by following his daily run around the countryside.The slim and somewhat quiet gentleman jogs at least ten or more miles a day down all the back roads. He is usually wearing jeans and an old hat that only be described as looking like something Popeye would wear. At other times, he is a daily communicant at St. Stephens the Martyr Catholic Church, where he also acts as a Eucharistic Minister.

Inside the post office, the ten employees work to get the morning mail put in all the boxes. Things are not always smooth. "I tell people here, 'do not guess at last names,'" says Postmaster Beavers. "There are lots of divorces around here and people can have the same last name." There are two older women in particular famous for pitching a fit when the mail of the first wife is confused with the mail of the second wife. Their well-known contempt spreads beyond the post office to the beauty salon they both patronize. Their appointments are appropriately staggered so they do not collide. Unlike other areas of the country, when couples divorce here, one of them doesn't move away. And while some may think that could make planning a party a challenge, it doesn't. Although such a notion did cause one person to tell me he could make up a whole luncheon table with women of the same last name, but that included not just several wives but also a mother-in-law and at least one sister-in-law.

Jack Kent Cooke, the late owner of the Washington Redskins and a long time Middleburg resident, went through several highly publicized divorces. During his break with Suzanne, wife number three of four, he would personally call the postmaster. It seems that Cooke was concerned that Suzanne would get some of his mail. According to several sources, "they fought like cats and dogs all the time."

"Mr. Cooke would call and tell me, 'I just had lunch with my friend Tony,'" Beavers relates, "He wanted to remind me that he was friends with Anthony Frank, the Postmaster General at the time."

Another customer (who just so happens to own the post office building) was overheard giving employees a hard time, when he was informed that his copy of *Playboy* magazine could only be forwarded to his winter address in Delray Beach, Florida for two months. Evidently, the rules dictate that mail can only be forwarded for 60 days and the patron intended to be there longer.

In the summer of 2000, word of the suicide of Virginia Bradshaw, former owner of a now defunct shop called The Iron Jockey, shocks those who knew her. And while she and her husband Charlie (once the mayor of Middleburg) no longer live in the area, they still hold the coveted P.O. Box 1.

There is also news that Nancy Lee, an 80ish woman of long standing in the community and owner of Lee Advertising, has recently had surgery. Her husband, David "Peaches" Lee, was postmaster in Middleburg from 1939-1976. Their only daughter, "Punkin" (because she was the only pumpkin in the patch) Lee, runs the highly successful Journeyman Saddlers, a ladies sportswear shop with an adjoining tack repair business. They also make custom-made riding chaps in every color from gray to tan to red at anywhere from $325 to $1,000 per pair shipped to riders all over the country.

In one of those many coincidences around this town, Punkin Lee's first cousin, Berk Lee, runs The Tack Box owned by her father Chubb Lee (brother of Peaches, if you can follow all these Lees). The Tack Box is one of three such establishments in town, where the many equestrians can buy saddles, bridles and blankets for their horses. (Take note, though if you are considering buying a horse. You will need not just one but several blankets. A waterproof turn out rug will cost $190, a waterproof turn out sheet will put you back $160, then there's a stable sheet for $80, and a stable rug $105. And just for matters of good taste an Irish knit--something to throw on them after they have a bath--will be $60 and of course, a Polar Fleece throw when it's a bit nippy after the bath is $120. And that's just the beginning.)

Sitting on the porch of the local bakery (the aptly named Upper Crust), Peaches Lee enjous his coffee and a donut around 8 each morning.He recalls that there were only 125 box holders when he first started as postmaster.

It was located up near the main intersection of town, in the building now occupied by Aliloo Oriental Rugs, just behind the old bank at Washington and Federal Street. The garden shop called Devonshire now occupies the stately stone Greek Revival style bank building. There is a cornerstone on the front west corner dated 1924, the year the bank was built.If you look carefully across the frieze you can still see the words Middleburg Bank faintly under the white paint. Also in this building, the private Hill School first held classes on the upper balcony in 1926.

The price of postage on a postcard when Peaches Lee first started was a penny and a letter was three cents. From time to time, a shipment of 100 baby chicks would come through the post office. "They would always arrive C.O.D.," Lee recalls. "It was $5." Occasionally, they would go unclaimed and he would be burdened with unloading the chicks. But it was no problem for this mild-mannered gentleman, now closer to 90 than 80. "I would sell them off in batches and collect the money." He never had to take in any stray chicks.

When a customer who couldn't read or write came into the post office, Lee would assist them. "Every year, I had to help one man fill out his tax forms. And then there was another woman. She could sign her name but didn't know how to fill out a check in her checkbook, so I helped her do that."

Lee also recalls the day when a very wealthy woman came in on her way to Washington to catch a flight to Paris. "A few hours later, I noticed something on the radiator. It was her jewelry case and inside a diamond as big as a hen's egg. It had been there for hours."

Lee called the lady's home and informed the farm manager that her jewelry was at the post office.

"Do you have a safe down there?" they asked.

Lee told them that wouldn't be possible. "Well then just take it next door to the bank and tell them to put it in her safe deposit box."

No problem.

Ed Wright worked for the post office for two weeks in the summers of 1953 and 1954. His father, Turner Houston Wright, was a rural letter carrier from 1930-58. "I grew up riding around with him while he would deliver the mail," Wright says. "He would sort the mail first and then set out about 7:30 in the morning and be finished by 11:30. He couldn't wait to get home and tend to his farming."

While young Ed Wright rode with the mail, he came to appreciate some of the homes in the area. "I really loved to look at some of the slate roofs," he says. And indeed, Wright was able to more than realize his own slate roof on his home, Strawrick just east of town, where he has lived for "all but 18 months" of his life.

Wright went on to work for the Middleburg Bank. He started in 1957 and his first task was to assist in transferring the various accounts to machine posting. The notes were color-coded. "Real estate loans were green note forms--the color of land," Wright says. And livestock notes were salmon--the color of Hereford cattle. "The loans secured by stocks were blue forms--for blue chip stocks--and unsecured loans were white forms."

When the bank and the post office moved to their present locations in 1958, it was no accident that they remained side-by-side. Shipments of money were still sent by registered mail. "I can recall walking the short distance to the bank with $1,000 of quarters on one shoulder, $200 in nickels on the other shoulder, and a bag of currency under my arm," says Wright, who retired in 1998 after working his way up to senior vice president.

That small amount of currency doesn't hold a candle to the $5,000 the wife of one well-to-do horse farm owner now fetches at the bank each Friday. She brings the money home to their farm, so all the help can be paid in cash. (You figure it out.)

And all day long while this post office procession continues, there is one other person taking it all in. Richard Holmes has worked at the Middleburg bank for over 30 years. He washes the windows, spruces up the garden and polishes the brass on the front door as customers come and go and occasionally greet him or merely nod.

Jim Jenkins worked for Peaches Lee. He is sitting on his porch just outside of town. His ranch style brick rambler house on three and a half acres sits on what the locals call "The Halfway Road." He now tends to a lovely flower garden and remembers his years in the post office.

"Mrs. Iselin used to come in and I was frightened to death of her. I think she tested me out every time she came in," he says. "But once I got to know her, there wasn't a better lady. She gave a little gift each year. A pound of sausage, it was little, but it meant a lot."

Jenkins also says that Peaches Lee used to give a ham to "the poor people in town" each Christmas. As Jenkins talks, he refers to all the women as "Mrs." and never by the first name. Like "Mrs. Arthur White" or "Mrs. Pettibone." Two of the grandest dames the town has ever known.

Mrs. Pettibone used to come into the post office each week and request five crisp one-dollar bills. "She wanted to give them in the plate at the Catholic Church each Sunday," he says, not able to answer why she couldn't make her request next door at the bank. "After a while I would set them aside for her. And I still have the fifth of whiskey she once gave me as a gift."

Other great names of times gone by include: Missy Sipes and Harriet Wadsworth Harper who was well known in fox hunting circles and rode in a custom made side-saddle on the off side. Jane McClary--a writer whose novel *A Portion For Foxes* was a roman a clef of the area--and equine artist Jean Bowman also called Middleburg home.

When actress Liz Taylor was married to Senator John Warner, she would mail a package and use up all kinds of spare stamps. "She would have one cent stamps all over the package," Jenkins says. "I don't think she liked to waste anything."

Heiress Joan Irvine Smith, who used to call Middleburg home but still maintains a farm here, would mail some of her very valuable antique paintings to her home in Irvine, California. "We would have to call a special guard,"

Jenkins relates.

And horse owner Dorothy Jackson, heiress to the National Cash Register Company fortune, and her husband, Howell Jackson, gave $250,000 toward the land for the Community Center. According to Jenkins, she gave everyone at the post office a $10 bill at Christmas.

"People just work for the paycheck nowadays," Jenkins says. "People don't realize that you work for the public and they pay your check."

But don't tell this to Phillip Hamme, 35, a clerk in the post office, who now holds the same position as Jim Jenkins. He would tell you that other than the increased number of people in Middleburg, not that much has changed.

As this is written, I watch Scott Stine, who owns The Upper Crust bakery with his father, Jim Stine, deliver a tray of just-out-of-the-oven cookies to the post office. And they still get baby chicks in the mail over there.

Not that long ago a shipment of full-grown swans came through at 20118. "Forty pounds each and boy do they reek to high heaven," Hamme says.

Actually an attorney was expecting the delivery, and when the package was late, Hamme was threatened within an inch of his life. But needless to say, the fine-feathered friends arrived safe and sound—just one hour late.

There is more bad news, the deaths of Jim Fannon, a publisher in Alexandria, and Harry Sinclaire, a physician who was medical director for the Mobil Oil Corporation for 30 years. Both former residents of Middleburg, it says something of this town, that even those who no longer live here are considered cherished friends.

Not all news at the post office is passed along the grapevine. A small sandwich board with multi-colored letters sits out front to inform the residents: Trash Info Tuesday regular trash Wednesday-Recyclable Yard waste every other Wednesday.

Anna Beavers, 78, is the beloved aunt of the current postmaster, Norris Beavers. Most refer to her has "Mrs. Beavers."She's been collecting clothing for poor children for close to 50 years. Right out of central casting for the classic little old lady, Beavers drives slowly to town in her dated blue sedan and parks in the handicapped spot in front of the bank. She then shuffles to the post office on swollen legs and ankles, mailing packages to seven families and 21 children, ages 2-20.

A retired third grade teacher, she taught a total of 757 children and has recorded all their names. Mrs. Beavers started her mission in 1954 when her daughter was in the first grade at Middleburg Elementary School. "I was a member of the PTA," she says, "and they asked if someone could sew and patch some clothes for the clothes closet."

And while the number of recipients of her generosity has fallen back a bit from peak years, her enthusiasm has not. Her nephew Norris Beavers says, "all I know is that she's been doing this forever or longer than that. I do say now, I sometimes take the donated clothes to her house because she doesn't get around like she used to."

What many may not know about Mrs. Beavers is that her charity is driven by her perception of the disparity of incomes in this town. According to Mrs. Beavers, many of the well to do landowners pay the farm workers a poor wage.

"Anybody who would keep a man and wife and six kids in a house and pay them $20 a week…" she says, her voice trailing off in disgust.

When her outspoken thoughts on the gap of income were printed in the local paper several years ago, someone said something to her.She was quick to respond. "I never have named names," she says while sipping coffee in a local restaurant. "But I have said if this bothers you then your sins have come home to roost." Her mind and memory are sharp. She recalls dates and phone numbers with certainty.

She's a little old lady with an agenda.Her nephew adds, "as far as her agenda, I can see her saying that. She is a fighter." She has a sense of humor and without that, she says, "I'd die tomorrow." She reminds one of the little old lady of "Where's the beef?" Mrs. Beavers would be perfect on Leno or Letterman because she comes right out with whatever's on her mind. And while she never did make it on late night television, she did have her 15 minutes when she went on both the Rosie O'Donnell show and then Oprah after an article appeared on her good deeds in *People* magazine.

She comes to town to chat dressed in pink wool suit (circa 1960s or earlier) that is just a smidge too tight. She has a nice flowered blouse that is held together at the very top button with a cameo. Her shoes are sturdy, school matronly. She is overweight, but pleasantly plump. She has jowls, and her dark hair is held together with a thin, almost invisible hair net. She wears glasses.

She has a standing 9 a.m. appointment at Lil's Grapevine, one of five local beauty parlors. (And, in these parts, they are beauty parlors, not beauty salons.) "Child do you know how old this suit is? I bought it 22 years ago when my son got married in Newport News.

"I just couldn't see a child dirty and ragged and needy," she says. "I would even buy pencils and paper and school supplies for them. The others would make fun of them.Some of them would even need a bath, they would smell bad. I ran them through the bathtub in the back of the school kitchen in a little room. I gave them a shopping bag full of clean clothes and then I sent them up town for a haircut." One mother, she says, didn't even recognize her son when he came home one day.

She is also careful not to offend these children and families.

"When they took their old clothes off, I would put them in a bag and send them home with them. It wasn't my place to get rid of the old clothes. I figured it was up to the mother to burn them." She will also not give names of families currently receiving her good will, but does share names of appreciative children from years ago.

"I was trained at home to do it all," she recalls of her childhood on her father's tobacco farm in South Hill, Virginia. "I cut hair, washed dishes, made bread when I was five and at 12 I learned to sew and make clothes. It all goes back to God put us in this place to do something good."

She is a regular at the Unison Methodist Church and says she never had a drink of whiskey in her life. And, "If I can't spell it, I don't drink it," she says, recalling the time someone offered her a glass of Chardonnay.

She has also put her sewing skills to work to support her one-woman cause. She makes quilts and sells them. "I live on a fixed income now," she says. "I don't have the money that I used too." Although she does live on a 300-acre farm in the middle of this land of the rich and famous, she stresses that it is a working farm, left to her by her husband, a true farmer. She says the county is threatening to raise her real estate taxes and, "If they do, I'm going to court and fight them."

So she makes quilts: $150 for king size, $125 for full size and $100 for single. "The material is expensive," she says half apologizing. She uses the money to buy shoes and underwear for the children, because these items are not acceptable as second hand.

Through the years, she has seen many kids succeed. If they were falling behind in school she would have them over to her home on Saturday and pick them up for summer school. "I never had a child I couldn't manage and couldn't teach to read. I kept with them."

Mrs. Beavers is a bit of a Steel Magnolia, part Mary Poppins and part Miss Hannigan, the stern head of the orphanage in the musical "Annie." She is Southern to the bone, not just with her accent but also with her vocabulary. She uses words and phrases not often heard like: "preacher" and "kin" When she talks about her nephew Norris Beavers, she says he "carries the mail." And she refers to Thanksgiving baskets as "a turkey and all the trimmings".

She lives in a circa 1868 frame house. The "newer part," as she calls it, was added in 1904. It has eight rooms, including five bedrooms. But Mrs. Beavers confines her living to only four rooms, "To cut down on the heating bill." She uses oil stoves that work "just like a hotel." She has a very large and protective German shepherd, "Max."

"He was given to me at two months old by three former students. The family was selling them for $75 each and these children insisted on giving him to me. They brought him in a shoebox and he was all legs and ears."

Indeed, Max is so protective that when a photographer from People magazine brought her dog to a photo shoot, Beavers says, "Max played with the visiting dog only to a point. He protects me tooth and toenail." All hell broke loose and Max tried to attack the visiting dog.

And if anyone else tries to come around uninvited, beware not only of Max. "I keep a double barrel shotgun in a certain place," Mrs. Beaver says.

Sam Huff, still carrying himself with the swagger of the great athlete he once was, walks to the post office from the other end of town. The Hall of Fame pro football player has special privileges at the post office. He likes to use his famous number "70" as part of his address, actually 7070, but there is no such number in Middleburg. So, when letters arrive addressed that way, they are actually forwarded to his real box number.

Huff started Middleburg Broadcasting, syndicating horse related radio programs to local and national stations following an illustrious 13-year career in the NFL.

He played first with the New York Giants and then with the Washington Redskins from 1956-1969. In '69, he was a player coach in Washington on the staff with the great Vince Lombardi. Now 64, Huff grew up in the heart of West Virginia coal country, the son of a coal miner, and was determined not to follow his father's career path. Instead, he became the first member of his family to attend college, at West Virginia University, where he was an All-American defensive lineman.

He arrived in the training camp of the N.Y. Giants in 1956 on a team that included Lombardi as the offensive coordinator and Tom Landry as the defensive coordinator.

When a homesick Huff walked out of camp in the first week of his rookie season, it was Lombardi who got to the bus station and talked him out of it and convinced him to return to the team. Huff is best remembered as a fearsome middle linebacker on one of the great defensive teams of that era. He was named to five Pro Bowls and played in six NFL championship games before there was a Super Bowl, including the Giants' famous 1958 overtime loss to the then Baltimore Colts in what has always been considered the greatest game in pro football history.

He was the subject of a significant documentary, "The Violent World of Sam Huff," aired on CBS's "20th Century" shows, a precursor to "60 Minutes."

Many people believe that show, which included pinning a microphone on Huff during an exhibition game, helped cause the American public to take more notice of the NFL. He also was on the cover of Time Magazine in 1959, another coup for the league.

He was traded to the Redskins in 1964 in a controversial deal that still bothers him, mostly because he had become one of the Giants brightest stars before being shipped off to a woeful team. As it turned out, the trade may have been the best thing ever to happen to him.

While still a player, he was hired by the Bethesda-based Marriott Corporation and eventually assumed a vice president's role in the organization. His main focus was getting sports teams to stay in Marriott hotels on the road, along with their fans, cheerleaders and pep bands.

Huff moved to Middleburg in the early 1980s and became heavily involved in the community and the horse business, while also developing a series of races in his native West Virginia. The highlight of the year is The West Virginia Breeders Classic held at Charles Town Race Course each September.He has a 22-acre place just outside of town called Sporting Life Stables, where he breeds and runs thoroughbreds.

He's still a widely known and popular figure in the Washington area, mostly due to his work as one of the broadcasters on the Washington Redskins radio network. He wrote his autobiography Tough Stuff with Leonard Shapiro, a sportswriter from *The Washington Post*, who also lives in Middleburg.

He was elected to the Pro Football Hall of Fame in 1982, but around Middleburg, he's simply known as 'ol Sam."

There is word that architect Avery Faulkner and his wife Alice have sold their house in Delaplane. And in a case of revolving doors, Valli Arader, divorced mother of four children, has bought the property. She in turn has sold her lovely home near Rectortown to architect Charlie Matheson and his wife Bonnie. Their five children are now grown and gone and they have decided to downsize from their 65-acre farm Heathfield. And Bonnie is busy running an internet business called Childbirth Solutions.

There are also whispers of a very recent divorce, a swift and decisive move on the part of the wife. And now, apparently a new romance has already begun to blossom. She has been spotted at several parties.

A form letter from the Middleburg Fire Department arrived in all the mailboxes and tongues are wagging about this one. It reads, "On Wednesday, August 30, 2000 a warrant was issued for the arrest of our former Treasurer for felony embezzlement. We have every hope and belief that the missing funds will be recovered. The case is still under investigation, but the evidence suggests that the theft occurred over a period of years, and is believed to be in an amount of $25,000 or more."

Life goes on in Middleburg.Word travels fast and furiously: births, divorce and even death. And…from time to time the post office will receive a package of cremated ashes. There is the story of one ever-so-wealthy widow who tried to ship her husband's ashes back to his hometown of Chicago in a coffee can.

But it's not always someone's dearly departed spouse. "We get more animal ashes than we do people now," whispers a post office source. "People want to have their favorite horse cremated. But if you have the money, why not?"

CHAPTER 2

Jackie Onassis in the Piedmont Hunter Pace event. *(Photo by Janet Hitchen)*

JACKIE, PAUL, AND PAM

*F*rom the time President John Fitzgerald's Kennedy's helicopter touched down in Middleburg for the first time on February 11, 1961, things would never be the same.

Mrs. Kennedy's love of horses brought them to the Virginia countryside. It proved to be a challenge for the secret service agents, who at first tried to ride along. Evidently that didn't work, so they followed in cars.

To this day, there are horse people who still recall the time their child rode in the pony club with Caroline or when Mrs. Kennedy came to their hunt breakfast. At The Pink Box, the information center in Middleburg, a gazebo was erected as a memorial to "Mrs. Onassis" and the many happy years she spent here.

At the time of her death in May, 1994, James L. "Jimmy" Young, a master of the Orange County Hunt, recalls that "the people here respected her privacy very much. She could wander the streets. She enjoyed that aspect of it."

In 1961, the President and Mrs. Kennedy first leased a 200-acre estate called Glen Ora, just two miles from town. The next year, they built a house on 39 acres of land purchased for $26,000 from the late Hubert Phipps. It was named Wexford after the County Wexford, the Irish birthplace of the Kennedy ancestors. (Ronald Reagan later leased this very same place in 1980 prior to his successful presidential bid.)

As a young girl, Jackie had been to Middleburg for horse shows or other sporting events, especially when she spent time at Merrywood, the McLean, Virginia home of her stepfather, Hugh Auchincloss.

On that first February weekend, White House press secretary Pierre Salinger held a news conference upstairs at the Red Fox Tavern in the J.E.B. Stuart room, named after the well- known Confederate soldier who was said to have once stopped at the inn for a drink. There were representatives from every major news organization, Including *The Washington Post, Evening Star,* AP, UPI, ABC, NBC, etc.

The arrival of the Kennedy family not only caused a stir in town and in the horse world but also on Sundays. Their association with the Catholic Church created something of a dilemma, since at the time there was no Catholic church here.

Services back then were held at the Community Center, and they attended for the first time in February, 1961. The Bishop had offered to hold a private mass at the farm, but the Kennedys rejected that idea.

This also created a Secret Service nightmare. On one particular Sunday, a red-headed man entered and proceeded up the aisle. Since the ushers did not recognize him, he was detained briefly at the entrance and only later did the members of the church learn that it was Undersecretary of the Navy Paul Fay.

St. Stephens Catholic Church was built and completed in April, 1963. A number of architectural amenities were included to accommodate Kennedy. The usher room adjacent to the confessional was reserved for the president's use. It was bulletproof and soundproof and a direct telephone to the White House was installed. To this day, visitors can find a tiny plaque that marks the pew where the President and his family sat.

As a family, the Kennedys last attended the service at St. Stephens on November 10, 1963, twelve days before their fateful trip to Dallas. Father Pereira's sermon that day was on the meaning of death for a Christian. Father Pereira had loaned President Kennedy a bible, the same bible that was used by Lyndon Johnson when he was sworn in aboard Air Force One after the assassination. Somehow it disappeared and Father Pereira later received an official letter of apology from a member of the Johnson administration.

Photographer Howard Allen recorded many of the Kennedy moments in Middleburg: attending church, out riding, playing with the children. His daughter, Page Allen, vividly recalls those days in the country with the Kennedys.

"Caroline was a little bit younger than me but every Sunday when we went beagling, they would assign one of us older ones to be her [Caroline's] buddy," Page Allen recalls. "And apparently she took a shine to me, and so they called up one day invited me to come over to Glen Ora. They sent a van for my pony and we rode and went in the house and played. Caroline wanted me to be her pony and I was running around on my hands and knees and we were in the den and her mother and father were in there, too. I think her mother might have been reading or something. It was a cold winter day, and there was a fire going and JFK was in the wing chair.

"Later we had dinner and it was just the children and Maude Shaw, the nanny or nurse or whatever you call her. Jackie came through a couple of times and John was making a mess, pouring milk into his food and mixing it all around. He was tiny, maybe two, just a little thing. Later on their way back to Washington, they took me home in a caravan of limos.

"Caroline was out a lot with the pony club and I remember the Secret Service men. She did a lot of the same stuff we did, going to the different little pony shows and some of the clinics, like watching the blacksmith and things like that. Her mother was always there. She would lead her around on the pony for the class or watch her in the walk-trot."

Caroline Kennedy inherited a love of horses from her mother. It was a love her mother nurtured and a love Caroline continues to foster for her own daughters, Tatiana and Rose. They have returned to the area on several occasions for riding weekends.

A local horseman, Clay T. "Barney" Brittle, had a nice and quiet fat little chestnut and white spotted pony named Macaroni. Caroline rode the pony and sometimes her mother would lead her around. The Kennedys eventually bought the pony. And according to Brittle and others, Caroline also enjoyed riding and playing with other children in the area who loved ponies, including Brittle's own children, Shawn, Skip and Gould.

"They would all ride and then have a picnic at the horse shows, Jackie would work like the dickens," Brittle says. They cooked hot dogs and the President was there several times.

Brittle also arranged to meet Mrs. Kennedy and her children at Madison Square Garden for the National Horse Show, where he gave them a backstage tour.

Many ponies are not very accommodating, but Macaroni would tolerate anything. One time, according to Brittle, Jackie called him up and told him that Caroline had gotten into her red nail polish one afternoon and painted the pony's hooves in bright red. On another occasion, Brittle took Macaroni and some other ponies to The White House for all the kids to ride. Caroline was about three at the time.

The Kennedys also had a dun colored pony called Tex that was given to them by Lyndon Johnson. And according to most of the horse people around Middleburg, they kept both ponies long after they moved away.

According to Peter Winants, the former editor of *The Chronicle of the Horse*, Caroline and her mother had "a genuine love and closeness to their ponies. There wasn't any BS, because it was the proper thing to do. They did it because they loved it."

One aspect of Caroline's horse interest included the Middleburg-Orange County Pony Club, where young children learn to ride and take care of ponies. She was a regular at these events. She started out in lead line classes and then went on to walk and trot and soon went on to jumping over logs.

At one event, Caroline entered the costume class and won a prize dressed as "Best Tiger Killers in India" as a send up on a trip her mother had made to the Far East. She rode on a tiger skin and was led around the ring by Skip Brittle. His sister Shawn played the part of a rajah, wearing a colorful robe and turban.

Eve Fout (her husband Paul built Wexford for the Kennedys) was a lifelong friend of Jackie and shared her love of fox hunting and horses. They would often ride together when Jackie continued to visit Middleburg.For years until her death in 1994, Fout's son, Doug, also was a playmate of Caroline's.

"When John died I wrote a note to Caroline," Doug Fout says. "She wants them [her daughters] to have the pleasure of riding outdoors. I think it's quite wonderful that she carries on this tradition. They live in New York and it's just not available. It's like tennis. You learn to play and you keep it up. She has grown up with riding and is totally familiar and comfortable with it."

Jackie's forays into the foxhunting field made worldwide news when she took her first somewhat serious spill in November, 1961. A local photographer, Marshall Hawkins, was there to capture her now famous head first fall over a post and rail fence. The photo was printed around the globe.

Ambassador Charles S. Whitehouse first met Jackie in the summer of 1946, right after World War II when his parents and her parents were friends. He dated her before she was married. "I rode with her up in Newport and down here," he recalls. "She was an enchanting young lady."

Jimmy Young first got to know her in the early 1980s when he was a substitute partner with her in the Piedmont races. "Her partner from New Jersey had a horse that was lame and we ran together," he says. "She was keenly competitive. She loved it when a newspaper article said 'who is this new mystery man?'"

After that, Young became the master of the Orange County Hunt. "She started to come down more often. She would ship her horse down and stay here with the Mellons for October and November and then go back to New York and come back in the spring." She had two horses, Be Frank, a gray Irish hunter, and Midnight, a black thoroughbred.

"After two or three years of that schedule, she felt she was wearing out her welcome with the Mellons and found a place to rent," he recalls.

Jackie's longtime friendship with Bunny Mellon included a shared passion for flowers. Mrs. Mellon designed some of the gardens at the White House, now used as a sculpture garden, and later assisted the First Lady with the design of her husband's gravesite at Arlington Cemetery.

She kept coming to the area until the fall before she died. She loved to go antiquing in the nearby Shenandoah Valley. Her cottage here was described as "charming and simply furnished."

Through knowing her in the hunt field, Young became good friends with Jackie. "Every year, in January, I would visit her in New York" when he went up for the Master of Foxhounds meeting. "She and Maurice Templesman took me to a show and dinner." One summer, Young spent a week in Martha's Vineyard and said it was "very, very informal and pleasant, basically boating and sightseeing. They respected her privacy very much up there, just like here, and she could wander the streets. She enjoyed that aspect of it."

When Diana Vreeland orchestrated the "Man and The Horse" exhibition at the Metropolitan Museum of Art in New York, Jackie got Charlie Whitehouse and Young to come to the opening in their scarlet riding attire. "She couldn't go," Young recalls, "It would have been a circus, so she said she would watch."

When Young wrote a book called *A Field of Horses*, Jackie wrote the forward and advised him on publishers and designers. The book is a compilation of equine photos by Marshall Hawkins, the very same man who captured Jackie taking that famous tumble.

"The most important thing she did for me, at one point I got mind-boggled over which pictures to include and which to throw out," Young says. "She came over and pushed the pictures around on the floor. She was in riding clothes, crawling on the floor. She had quite a good eye and an instinctive appreciation for what would look good."

On November 20, 1993, Jackie took a very bad fall while out with the Piedmont Hunt, suffering a mild concussion and spending the night at the hospital in Leesburg. "She didn't see the trappy fence in front of her," her groom, the late Jimmie Mason, recalled at the time. "The person in front had trouble and she tried to swerve and landed on top of it and fell."

"She had her share of falls just like any other fox hunter. But she was a very athletic rider and it wasn't a social thing with her," recalls another friend. "She wasn't just out for an hour and go in. She was a stayer. She was not a fair weather fox hunter."

Diana Muss was hunting one day the last season Jackie came to Middleburg. "It must have been one of the last times Jackie was out. We came up on this stone wall. It was the biggest thing I'd ever seen, very solid. I turned to the girl with me and said, 'No way.' So we turned around to go back and here comes Jackie Onassis, and she just trots up to it and then as gracefully as you can imagine, jumps it easily."

Horse trainer Don Yovonovich recalls "I took one of the young girls who works for me hunting one day, sort of as a gift. I pointed out Jackie to her and this girl was so impressed with her because I guess her mother had talked about her a lot. I kept saying 'go up and introduce yourself,' but she wouldn't do it.

Finally at the end of day, I rode up to her and said, 'Jackie do me a favor, would you please go and talk to this girl Michelle.' Jackie didn't just do that, she spent twenty minutes talking to her, asking her about school. Was she in college? What did she want to do in the future? It was just idle chit chat, but she spent twenty minutes doing it. It made her life, when Jackie said, 'Hi Michelle, I understand you work for Donnie.' It's something Michelle will never forget.

"She was so thoughtful," says Yovonovich, who has been Trainer of the Year ten times on the point-to-point circuit. "She sent me little notes, handwritten congratulations notes whenever she read something about me, that I won a race or when my daughter was born. I have an armful of them. Every time I got a note from her I was overwhelmed. I thought it was just, nice, nice, nice."

So many folks in Middleburg had fond stories to tell when she died, like Alice Edwards, who knew everybody and everything. She owned the B and A, a mom and pop grocery store on the east end of town, now the upscale "The Piedmont Gourmet" under new ownership "She came in here all the time when she was First Lady," Edwards says. "The children came in with the English nanny and she continued to come in." She maintained a charge account at the tiny store and paid her last bill on Jan. 15, the year she died.

Alice Thuermer, manager of Devonshire, the chic garden accessory shop, says Jackie frequently visited. "I sent her a letter when I read about her being treated for cancer. I told her I was a five-year survivor and that I knew she could make it, too. I got a form letter back. It was on nice pale blue stationary and she had written a little note on the bottom, 'Hope to see you soon.'

"She liked JoAnn Shea's arrangements [at Devonshire]," Thuermer says. "She did open style country arrangements that Jackie liked. And even when she went back to New York she would phone or her girl would phone and order flowers for any birthday or special occasion that the Kennedys had. I remember once she called and wanted an all blue arrangement. I can't remember whether it was for Ethel or Teddy."

Another time, Thuermer was in the shop alone and the classical music station was on the radio. "Jackie walked around for about ten minutes. I left her alone and then she said in a very kind of peaceful way, 'it's so wonderful here-- the flowers, the fragrance, the music, the books, just like being in church.'"

"She was so sweet and soft spoken, always very concerned about you," said Fay Wyne of the Plaza Hair Designs Jackie frequented when she visited Middleburg. And here's how Jackie went out of her way to say nice things to everyone around this village. "She would talk about how nice it was to be in the shop and she said the magazines were nicer than in her New York shop."

Another shop owner recalled the rainy fall day several years ago when Jackie wandered in and bought a few horsey Christmas ornaments. The Visa bill came to $22. The date was Nov. 22, the bitter anniversary of her husband's assassination in Dallas. "I just wanted to be alone today," she told the clerk.

"The hardest thing I had to come to grips with when I was with her was the unwanted intrusion by pure strangers," Young recalls, not necessarily of her visits here but elsewhere. "Everyone felt they had the right to come up to her and talk. If she even acknowledged them, it opened things up to an in-depth conversation and she couldn't get away. You can't imagine the attention that surrounded her all the time. It never stopped."

But in Middleburg that was not the case. "It was almost like she had a zone of immunity around her when she came here," said former Mayor Anne Lackman. "When she came to the Christmas bazaar each year, she would come late in the day, dressed in her riding clothes and no one bothered her."

"I guess it was her ground rules or someone told us but whenever she came in, [to The Fun Shop] we would just say hello to her, and not use her name, like 'Hello Mrs. Onassis.' She never wanted any attention drawn to her. We always used to see her just before Christmas because she would buy tons of ornaments and gifts for the grandchildren."

She visited the shop in December, 1993 and they shipped a huge carton of purchases--stocking stuffers and ornaments and gifts for her grandchildren. "She used to buy a lot so I assumed it was for others, too, because there would be way, way too much for two children. It must have been for other little people, as well," according to Pandora Rohlmeier, a sales associate at the shop.

Toby Merchant, owner of The Plains Pharmacy, will always remember the day Jackie walked into his drug store and almost immediately picked up one of those trashy supermarket tabloids on display down a side aisle.

"There was a headline about someone in the family that must have caught her eye," he said. "It was just after Onassis had died. She sat right down on the floor and kept saying 'I can't believe they're writing all this, I just can't believe it.' People were just walking around her while she was sitting there."

But her aversion to the paparazzi was rarely evident when she was in Middleburg. When local photographer Mary Coker took a picture of Onassis on her horse with a trophy in her arms and it appeared on the cover of *Middleburg Life*, Jackie called and ordered two copies. "It's funny but I would see her handing the grooms a camera and having them take a picture of her on the horse," said Marian Becker, a regular alongside her in the hunting field.

Her groom confirmed this fact. "She always liked to have a picture of herself on the horse, especially the jumping. She brought along a camera and gave it to me to take pictures. She wanted to see how she could improve in her riding."

On another occasion, Jackie came into the same drugstore to pick up a prescription and asked to put it on a house charge. "She asked for me, and I wasn't in," Merchant recalls. "The girl at the counter didn't recognize her and asked if she had an account. She said 'no' and the girl gave her a credit application. She took it across the street to the restaurant and started to fill it out. This girl had no idea who it was, but someone else heard about it and ran across the street and told her she could charge."

Merchant also adds that all his employees knew not to bother her when she came into the store and that asking for an autograph was almost grounds for dismissal.

"This community gave Jackie Onassis the private life she wanted," Merchant says.

———————

This community also gave Paul Mellon a sense of a private life. He, too, was a horse lover and a gentleman of profound wealth with an abiding passion for philanthropy. (At the time of his death in February, 1999, it was estimated that $1 billion had been donated to such patrician causes as the National Gallery of Art, the National Museum of Racing and The Yale Center for British Arts, as outlined in his 84-page will.

Mellon's home is called Oak Spring and the farm is known as Rokeby. He acquired a place in Upperville when he bought his first 400 acres from his mother, who had received Rokeby in 1931 as a "gift" from his father, long after they were divorced.

Mellon fox-hunted frequently while a young man when his mother lived at Rokeby. He continued to hunt for 50 years and served as joint master of the Piedmont Foxhounds with his neighbor, Theo Randolph, a legendary horse owner in her own right.

His land holdings in the area eventually grew to 3,600 wide open acres and included a private fire brigade, a boatload of security personnel and a landing strip to accommodate his jet for commutes back to Pittsburgh and his offices at the Mellon Bank.

The stables at Rokeby are magnificent. Once a year, on Memorial Day weekend, they would be open as part of the Hunt Country Stable Tour, which benefited The Trinity Episcopal Church, which the Mellons built and where he is buried. (More on that in a bit.)

It was home to some of the finest racehorses in the world. He raced six champions, bred 100 stakes winners and was the only owner in the history of the sport to win the Epsom Derby, the Prix de l'Arc de Triomphe and the Queen Elizabeth II Diamond Stakes with Mill Reef.

A bronze sculpture by John Skeaping honoring Mill Reef, who was raised at Rokeby, casts a mid-morning shadow in the courtyard of the broodmare barn. That barn, designed by Cross and Son in New York and built in 1949, is British inspired. Not only was Mellon one of the country's most generous philanthropists, he also was a well-known anglophile.

The mares and foals languish in the spacious 15 X 15 stalls, where a mare can look out a window on one side and her foal can peek out the double Dutch doors. The sliding glass windows, which may seem somewhat perilous, are intentionally set back 18 inches from the walls. Overhead heat lamps provide added warmth for newborns in the winter.

The overhang in front of the stalls, known in horse lingo as "the shed row," is covered with a rubber floor, to provide flexible footing and facilitate cleanliness. Brass name plaques indicate the sire and dam of each horse. One person on the farm is responsible for polishing the brass fixtures in the stables. The wooden buckets and wheelbarrows are handmade on the farm, designed to fit perfectly in place.

Now back to that landing strip, which often comes in handy when one is jetting back and forth to the Kentucky Derby in a single day. In May, 1993, the gray and yellow Rokeby racing colors greeted Mr. Mellon as he arrived back in Virginia after an afternoon at Churchill Downs.

It was indeed a sight to drive down his road, which the locals call "The Rokeby Road." In the middle of a field, where cattle meander during the day, two long strips of white runway lights stretched out and glowed in the early spring darkness.

Mellon's horse, Sea Hero, had captured the Kentucky Derby earlier that day, the one victory that had always eluded him, and everyone on the farm gathered around a bunch of balloons.

Ernie Bugg, farm manager for Mellon for 18 years, was among the employees on the scene that night and was quoted in *The Blood Horse* as saying, "Mr. Mellon was the type not to say much win or lose, but you could tell by the look on his face that he had won the Kentucky Derby and was satisfied."

Mellon also participated in competitive trail rides. He won the Virginia 100 Mile Ride five times on one of his favorite horses, a gray called Christmas Goose.

He also liked to write poetry, often focusing on his experience with this horse. He printed on elegant paper with woodcut prints and distributed it to friends.

HOW TO COOK YOUR CHRISTMAS GOOSE

With eyes half-open, mind half-shut,
We stagger from the weighing hut,
And climb upon our equine friends
Like divers suffering from the bends;
Erect upon our weary horses,
Like images of rigor mortis.
Up all these hills we huff and puff,
Could horses talk they'd cry, "enough!"
And when The Homestead comes in sight
And all their passengers alight,
They'd say, with ill-concealed contempt,

"You call this fun? Good God! Good night!"
And yet each year we keep returning
Like Moslems for their Mecca yearning.
Forgotten last year's vale of tears,
That emptiness between the ears.
Forgotten all those mountain humps,
And last year's corrugated rumps.
Forgotten last year's aching back,
Pains seeming like a heart attack,
Forgotten last year's bleeding stern,
We ask for more- we never learn.
And so I sing our well-earned praises.
Before we all push up the daisies,
Let's all continue bright and smiling
This love-hate thing-this hundred-miling.
In blinding rain or broil sun,
God bless us all and every one."

Paul Mellon
12 April 1979
Hot Springs, Virginia

He also was a man of detail. He never forgot anything, a minute detail of a fox hunt or a brief encounter. He always carried a small pen and pad of paper in the pocket of his shirt or jacket. He would make notes, if necessary.

Horseman Don Yovonovich has told the story about the time he won the Rokeby Bowl Steeplechase in 1989 for the third time and retired the $30,000 trophy. But in horse racing, the owner gets to keep the trophy, not the trainer or rider.

"So as Mr. Mellon presents the trophy, he turns to me and says, 'Don, this doesn't seem fair, what can I do for you?' I told him I would really like to have some of that rye whiskey that he used to carry in his flask out hunting. He wrote it down on his little pad in his pocket and said 'No problem, consider it done.'"

Yonvanovich waited and waited, and months passed. "I figured he had forgotten somehow, but I knew that wasn't his style. Then nine months later on Christmas Eve, a large package, wrapped in plain brown paper, is delivered to my door. "On the package he had written, 'I didn't forget. Merry Christmas.' It was a case of his private label rye whiskey, Overholt 1911."

Both Paul Mellon and his father, Andrew, held stock in the Overholt Distillery. Paul Mellon was hardly a big time drinker, but one story involves his love of a good martini. While riding in that 100-mile event in Hot Springs, Virginia, he carried his martini in a witch hazel bottle in the pocket of his raincoat.

"We were taking a break at the trap and skeet field at the Homestead," said the friend. "And he wanted to break out the martini.It was a lovely sunny and very warm day. He asked his groom, who also happened to be a part time preacher, to hand him his raincoat. When he didn't hand it to him, he asked him again. 'But Mr. Mellon it isn't raining,' the groom said."

Pamela Harriman's love of horses also brought her to Middleburg in 1977. "She was in Washington, D.C. and overseeing Pam's PAC, a Democratic fund raising political action group. She wanted a house in the country, she had fox hunted all her life," says Millicent West, who owned the 65-acre estate at the time.

Averill Harriman bought the place for her. The former governor of New York and an elder statesman who had been advising presidents for 50 years, he was 86 years old. The name of the farm at that time was called "Journey's Rest." And by the way, it included 20 acres of dazzling gardens that are a style to be envied. The rest of the grounds were devoted to the horses.

"Well, he said he would buy it for her, but she had to change the name," says Jimmy Hatcher, who rode horses with Pamela and had maintained a stable there before she moved out to the country. So, she renamed it Willow Oaks.

West says Hatcher can best be described as "an extra man about town. He kept a black tie in the tack room at the barn."

Pamela "hadn't jumped since 1939," Hatcher says. "Her father had been master of the hunt back in England. But his sister, Mary Harriman Ramsey, who actually started the Junior League, was killed out riding and he had a niece that was paralyzed. So jumping was not on top of the list at first."

She started out with the Middleburg Hunt. After all, the kennels were right next door to the property. They didn't jump at first. "Then one day she asked me 'does this thing jump?'" Hatcher continues.

And from that moment on, "she hunted as much as she could, mostly weekends."

Of course Mr. Harriman's roots in this part of Virginia are well documented and most revered by the foxhunters. It was Averill Harriman's father Edward Henry, known as EH, who started the Orange County Hunt when the family would travel down from Orange County, New York by train to The Plains. The would stay the weekend, fox hunt and then return to New York.

Olympic equestrian Katie Monahan also came to know Pam while fox hunting. "I was out riding with Orange County one time," she says, "and I was riding a little brown mare and she came up to me and admired my horse, which, as it happened looked very much like her horse. She told me she loved the horse and would I like to sell it to her? Well she came over to my barn and that one didn't work out, but we became friends."

What did work out became a long business relationship, with Katie riding a number of high level show jumpers for the Harrimans.

The first horse they bought was called The Governor. "I needed a sponsor," Katie recalls, "and when you're desperate you put your pride on the line and I asked her if she would be interested in owning a grand prix jumper. I remember she asked Mr. Harriman if it would be okay if we named him The Governor. And he told her 'Okay, but it better be a damned good horse.'"

The Governor went on to be Horse of The Year on the American Grand Prix circuit in 1985.Katie also rode Special Envoy for the Harrimans and won The President's Cup at the Washington International Horse Show. "They all had royal sort of names," she says.

But Mrs. Harriman was not the only one with a keen eye for horses. According to Katie, her husband also had a wonderful sense for a horse.

"He came over to the barn one day and we turned one of his horses out in the field and the horse galloped out. Most people would oooh and aaah at the sight. But he turns to me like most horsemen would and said 'ugh, there goes a tendon.' He knew what could happen if the horse took a bad step."

When Pamela was ambassador to France, Katie (who speaks fluent French) and her husband, an equestrian and a French citizen, visited her in Paris.

"I know she had a checkered past. She was a dream owner. She never interfered."

When Pamela Harriman died in 1997, she left The Governor to Katie in her will. The great horse died not long after that.

Pam's participation in the Democratic Party is well documented. She entertained on many occasions at the farm. According to Jimmy Hatcher, "when she had her first big party "Democrats for the 80s," Mr. Harriman later told Pam, 'my pool was wall-to-wall people.' He swam almost every day, you know. Anyway, he said 'next year if you have this party, can we have someone I know?'"

She usually had two groups, the political types and the horsey set for a hunt breakfast or cocktail party. Through the years, there were many guests, including Cyrus Vance, who was Secretary of State at the time, or Kitty Carlisle or Richard Holbrook and Diane Sawyer. Her political fundraising efforts on behalf of Bill Clinton gathered the most attention out here in the early 1990s.

It also should be noted that this was not the first time so many Democrats had walked over the threshold at Willow Oaks. When Millicent West, a grand lady in the most delightful sense of worldliness (well-traveled, well-read and so on) was married to Donald MacKinzie from 1978 to 1986, she too, entertained a number of distinguished politicians. Senator Paul Laxhalt and Senator Chuck Robb and many others were guests.

Once she had invited President Johnson for the Middleburg steeplechase races. She thought she should call ahead and alert the officials at the event in case they needed to make security plans.

" I told them I was having The President over for a tailgate," she says. "And they asked, "The President of what?'"

CHAPTER 3

Jeff Gable, also known as The Pool Man, has been frequently spotted at many social events through the years.

ℱAME AND ℱORTUNE

𝒯here's always a little bit of truth in any rumor. Such was the case in July 1995, with the buzz around town regarding Robert Duvall's wife running off with The Pool Man.

So I called Garry Clifford, then the Bureau Chief of *People* Magazine, where I work from time to time as a reporter. I told her I was off to the Fauquier County Courthouse to investigate.

Of course, I really didn't know what I was looking for. I had never been to the record room or the clerk's office or anything like that. I didn't even know what was available.

But I do now. Just on a lark that late summer day, I hit pay dirt. It was truly a hunch. Dumb luck. All I did was ask around. I told the ladies behind the courthouse counter that I was looking for some documents that might relate to Mr. Duvall and a possible domestic situation.

One of them leaned over and whispered "you might want to ask for copies of a Bill of Complaint." It turns out these papers had been filed several weeks before I came around. And it turns out I was the first one to get them.

It also turns out that one Jeffrey Harmon Gable, the buff owner of Hunt Country Pools, was doing more than sucking the debris from the bottom of The Great Santini's cement pond.

In an area with more than its share of manure, this is how it all hit the fan...

It was a drama that eerily resembled the plot of the film the Academy Award-winning actor was working on out of town. The movie, "Something to Talk About," was set on a southern horse farm. It entailed the account of a wife (played by Julia Roberts) who discovers her husband is cheating. The intricacies of marriage betrayal are played out against the backdrop of the horse show circuit.

Flashback to real life... Meet Sharon Brophy Duvall, the then 30-something third wife he met while taking tango lessons in the late 1980s. They were married in nearby Leesburg on May 1, 1991 and again a week later in Buenos Aires, a city Duvall visits frequently.

The Duvalls first lived at Butcher's Run, a 33-acre farm with an 1820s Quaker inspired five-bedroom fieldstone manor house. This house was set in a valley designed to ward off storms, in the old Quaker manner. This area near Butcher's Run has some Quaker roots and at a nearby Quaker Meeting House, Duvall was reportedly a visitor. From this house, there was a majestic view of the Blue Ridge Mountains. There was also a two-bedroom guesthouse, a fitness studio, stocked pond and an eight-stall barn with a tack room. By all accounts, he enjoyed the countryside and even bought a Jack Russell Terrier, the dog of choice in Middleburg, from Gwen and Bob Dobson over in Delaplane.

In January, 1994, Duvall purchased the 200-acre Byrnley Farm for just over $3.5 million. The place has what Virginians worship above all else; it had a history. Originally part of a land grant made in 1731 by Lord Fairfax, it was later owned and named after William Byrne, thought to have been a drafting and surveying instructor to George Washington.

It also happened to be once owned by Jack Kent Cooke, the legendary and colorful owner of the Washington Redskins (See chapter 11, Real...Estates). Cooke had purchased the place for his son, John Kent Cooke, at the time a vice president of the football team.

The house dates to the 1750s and into the early 1800s. The three-story Georgian farmhouse was meticulously renovated in the 1980s. It consists of a master suite, four guest bedrooms, six full and two half baths a separate guest suite over a three-car garage and eight fireplaces. The kitchen has been described as "ultra modern with every convenience."

And what else did their farm have for $3.5 million?

Well... it had French hand painted bath fixtures, a wine cellar, recreation room, tenant houses, greenhouse, machinery shed, stables, feed room and office.

There was just one thing missing…a pool. So on June 22, 1994 Robert Duvall was issued a building permit and guess who was hired to build the pool?

The Pool Man, Jeff Gable.

Col. Brooks (left) chats with Jim Gable

Meanwhile, Sharon Duvall started giving dance lessons to many Middleburg area citizens in the renovated hayloft in one of the cow barns at Byrnley. People lined up to get in step on Wednesday nights. Those taking part included real estate and Insurance agents, a dentist and his wife, a member of the Secret Service who worked at The White House, a few shop owners and The Pool Man.

She would teach the men, and when her husband was in town, he taught the women. And another note, when he was not off filming a movie or working on a project they would often frequent a local down-home restaurant called The Rail Stop, where sources say he would order the oysters no matter what the season.

A bit more on The Pool Man before we move on. Jeffery Harmon Gable, now in his 40s, grew up in Maryland. He is frequently described as a hunk, with some describing him as the Fabio of Middleburg. One client referred to him as chiseled and says he often arrives in short shorts and no top. She says he's frequently flirtatious and leans into her when he talks.

He once turned down a seasonal maintenance contract with some friends and neighbors of mine saying their pool was too small. That was just fine with the husband, who to this day says, "I didn't want him tip-toeing around here anyway,"

The Pool Man's list of clients includes half the countryside.

In addition to building the pool, Gable attended those Wednesday night dance classes. And according to sources, when The Great Santini was out of town, Mrs. Duvall and The Pool Man were spotted at several Thursday morning breakfasts at The Rail Stop with fresh-from-the-shower wet hair. It seems he was doing much more than sliding across the dance floor…

In the papers filed in Fauquier County Courthouse, the 60-something Duvall alleged that on or about July 14, 1995, at Byrnley Farm and again on

July 15 and 16, 1995 at the Gable residence, "the said Sharon Brophy Duvall did commit adultery with the said Jeffrey Harmon Gable. That all of said adultery was committed without consent, connivance, privity or procurement of your Complainant; and that your Complainant has not cohabited with the said Sharon Brophy Duvall since obtaining knowledge of the fact of said adultery; which adultery occurred within five years from the time of the institution of this suit."

The story first broke in the September 4, 1995 issue of *People* Magazine. The Duvalls eventually settled their differences, the marriage went down the drain and they were divorced. But the story wasn't quite over.

The Pool Man continued to eat a hearty country style breakfast (you know, eggs, sausage and grits or potatoes) at his favorite spot, The Rail Stop. He also continued to keep company with the former Mrs. Duvall. But it turns out Mr. Duvall liked the restaurant, too. So in the fall of 1998, Duvall and Chef Tom Kee bought the place. And Lucciana Pedraza, the dazzling new young Argentinean lady friend of Mr. Duvall, stepped in to run things.

Folks from all around flocked to the tiny town of The Plains. The locals weren't so happy. Breakfast no longer consisted of the high cholesterol fare and was replaced with bran muffins and espresso.

The Pool Man and Mrs. Duvall were married. And she kept the catchy last name of Duvall. She continues to teach the intricacies of the rumba, cha-cha and, of course, the tango. (Many say she should offer a sure fire Middleburg favorite, The Fox Trot.)

Two years later Duvall sold his stake in The Rail Stop to Kee. As part of their agreement, he urged that the transaction not be released to the press. Within 24 hours, friends were calling to tell me the latest news, that Robert Duvall had sold the restaurant. I found myself back in the record room at the courthouse. You see, there's always a little bit of truth in every rumor.

So much for fame, what about the fortune?

Middleburg has always been a magnet for those who are fortunate. And for good reason, most are here because they are interested in horses.

Joseph L. Albritton came to the area in the early 1980s. He was looking for a smallish horse farm of 50 acres. They ended up with over 1,700 acres, now known as Lazy Lane Farm. Part of it, once called Brookmeade, was owned by the famed sportswoman and horse owner, Isabel Dodge Sloane.

He has an impressive band of thoroughbred broodmares and breeds for the commercial markets as well as taking some to the races under his own green and yellow checkerboard racing colors. His horse, Hansel, won the 1991 Preakness and Belmont and was three-year-old champion.

Albritton, 70-something, was a Mississippi native and later called Texas home. He's chairman and CEO of Riggs Bank, one of the oldest banks in Washington, D.C. He owns over thirty percent of the company. In the mid-

1970s, he bought and within three years sold *The Washington Star* newspaper to Time, Inc. He also owns a number of television stations, the most notable being the Washington ABC affiliate that bears his initials…WJLA.

Through the years, he has served on a number of prestigious boards, including the John F. Kennedy Center for the Performing Arts, the National Geographic Society and Georgetown University.

The varied pursuits he shares with wife, Barbara, include collecting fine art. *Very* fine art. In the spring of '99, they purchased Vincent van Gogh's "Canal With Washerwoman" for over $19 million.That's okay; his reported net worth is $1 billion.

Arthur Windsor Arundel is also involved in the media business.Like Albritton, "Nick" was once in the radio business. He started the all-news station WAVA in suburban Washington in 1962 and sold it and five other stations in the 1970s.

First and foremost, he's a newspaper publisher, the founder and chief executive officer of ArCom Publications, Inc. He publishes just about every local weekly paper in the surrounding area, from the highly successful *Loudoun Times Mirror* in Leesburg to the *Fauquier Times Democrat* in Warrenton and the *Rappahannock News* in the somewhat remote spot of Rappahannock, 40 minutes west of Middleburg. There are 16 newspapers in all.

Arundel is a Harvard graduate and a decorated U.S. Marine Corps combat officer in both Korea and Vietnam. His journalism background is strong, having served as a UPI correspondent as well as working in the Washington bureau of CBS.

He and wife Peggy have five grown children and entertain frequently at their sprawling retreat, Merry Oak Farm near The Plains. They count among their friends many political types, from former Senator Chuck Robb, John Warner to Oliver North, who happily joined a friendly game of horseshoes during one Fourth of July celebration. And by the way, many private Arundel happenings feature fireworks over their enormous lake.

Arundel was the founder of the Great Meadow Outdoors Foundation, the 500-acrepreserve and setting for the annual Gold Cup Steeplechase near The Plains the first Saturday of May. He has been instrumental through the years in obtaining not just corporate sponsorships, but also national press attention for the event.

He also serves on the Virginia Racing Commission and has been a director of the George C. Marshall Foundation in Lexington, Va. as well as the National Steeplechase Association. His estimated net worth is $190 million, more than enough for many, many fireworks.

Magalen Bryant has been in the publishing business, too, as a member of the Ohrstrom family, which owns *The Chronicle of the Horse*, the bible of the horse show, event and steeplechase crowd for over 60 years.

Known as "Maggie" around town, she favors the color purple and can be spotted in various shades while exercising, playing tennis or working on any number of projects at her farm, Locust Hill.

One recent adventure involved building and backing the first privately owned toll road in Virginia. The road from nearby Dulles Airport to Leesburg first faltered financially but later became a whopping success. So successful that it had to be widened.

Maggie Bryant is a major stockholder in the plastic company called O'Sullivan Corporation located in Winchester, not far away. She also has other investments with her family in the Dover Corporation and Carlisle Companies in New York.

No problem buying more purple outfits: her estimated net worth is about $400 million.

Elizabeth Busch Burke has lived in the Middleburg area off and on for more than 30 years and also maintains a farm near Charlottesville and a home in Wellington, Florda.She is the daughter of August A. Busch Jr., and the granddaughter of August A. Busch Sr., the co-founder of Anheuser- Busch.

Now in her late 60s, Liz, is affectionately known as "Luv Luv." She first lived at Twin Willows Farm when married to horseman Robert "Bobby" Burke, at the time the leading rider in America. They later divorced.

She maintains an interest in show horses, first with her two daughters and a son and now as the owner of a number of international show jumpers. She's also on hand at major horse shows to present the trophies on behalf of Budweiser.

In the mid-1990s, she purchased Fox Lair Farm. "I named it that because there is a fox's den on this land," she says. She is now close to her grandchildren who live in the area with her daughter Lysa and son-in-law Tony Horkan.

Lysa serves as color commentator for ESPN and Fox Sports for their show jumping coverage. She sings the National Anthem at many major horse shows, steeplechase events and some baseball games. And Tony, a native of the area, sells real estate and teaches Tae Kwon Do.

Luv Luv serves on the board of directors for 15 organizations, including the Devon Horse Show and Country Fair, the Upperville Colt and Horse Show and The Hill School.

Andrea Bruce Currier and her sister, Lavinia Currier, both 40ish, were orphaned before they were teenagers. As a result, they inherited a fortune when the plane their parents, Audrey and Stephen R. Currier, disappeared in the Bermuda Triangle in 1967.

Their great-grandfather was the financial genius, Andrew Mellon, who served as Secretary of the Treasury under three presidents--Warren Harding, Calvin Coolidge and Herbert Hoover. Paul Mellon was their great uncle. Their grandfather, David K.E. Bruce, was a well-known diplomat and ambassador to four countries.They also had a brother Michael, who lived in Santa Fe. He died from a fall in September, 1998 in yet another family tragedy.

Andrea Currier takes an agrarian outlook on life. At her Kinloch estate, plant life takes a preference. A vegetarian (and some would say bohemian) lifestyle is supported not just with the magnificent, prolific show quality gardens, but also by becoming the driving force In the revitalization of the Archwood Barns near The Plains.

Once a decrepit barnyard, she bought the corner lots just off Interstate 66 and it now serves as a weekend Farmer's Market, with locally grown produce. She also donated nearby land to the private Wakefield School.

Married and divorced twice, for a while she also owned an upscale restaurant in The Plains called Leathercoat.She and her sister both retain the maiden name. She serves on the board of the Friends of Bull Run, to protect open space. "The area would be dotted with houses if it weren't for her," says one friend.The Curriers have a number of foundations, including one called A Wrinkle in Time. Together they have donated over $2 million to the Virginia Outdoors Foundation.

Andrea has a home on the Hudson in New York. Her published net worth is estimated at $320 million. For her part, Lavinia has taken an artistic approach to life at her adjacent Roland Farm. Married and divorced, she is currently married to Joel McCleary, one of the joint masters of the Orange County Hunt.

While a student at Harvard, she studied poetry.She has made a number of movies and films. Her 1983 work about growing up in Virginia inspired the cable movie "Heart of the Garden," for which she won a Cine Golden Eagle prize for the hour-long feature.

In 1998, she drew upon her own African safari experiences in producing, writing and directing the film "Passion in the Dessert." Set against the framework of Napoleon's doomed Egyptian battle, it's the tale of a French soldier who gets lost in the desert and is befriended by a leopard. The intimate scenes with the actor and the animal were inspired by a short story by Balzac.

The actor, Ben Daniels, had been chosen by Lavinia because during an interview, she put a puma in the room and he seemed to communicate with the cat. The film was shot in Jordan and Utah. At one point, while dancing with a leopard, Daniels was injured.

"He squeezed Ben around the waist and Ben just kind of froze. Suddenly, he could feel its power," she told a writer. "The cat went for his leg and bit him. It was just a puncture wound, and the trainer knocked him off immediately, but after that Ben was shaken a bit."

She has a ranch in Colorado and a sizeable chunk of an island in Hawaii. All together, "Passion in the Desert" took five years and $5 million before a successful debut. Lavinia has plans for future animal-related films on fox hunting and bull fighting. Financing should not be an issue, according to *Virginia Business* magazine. Her net worth is $320 million.

The 50sh John Derby Evans bought Waterford Farm in the mid-1990s and became interested in breeding cattle.This followed an illustrious career in telecommunications in Washington. He was the co-founder and past chairman of C-SPAN, starting out in the business of cable television. He now serves as Chairman and CEO of Evans Telecommunications, a consulting and operating company.

Divorced with two grown children, he also spends time in Key West and has had a home in Wintergreen, a Virginia ski resort area near Charlottesville. As a pastime, he has taken several motorcycle trips through Europe.He sits on the board of the National Cable Television Association, the Washington Metropolitan Cable Club and Falcon Cable Holdings.

His charity related duties include the University of Maryland-Baltimore's Institute of Human Virology, The Eisenhower World Affairs Institute, and the Hollings Cancer Center.

As a graduate of the University of Michigan, in 1997 he instituted the John D. Evans Fund for Media Technology, which includes financial support for the John D. Evans Chair in Media Technology and annual conferences and lectures for scholars and professionals for discussions on issues in the field of media studies.

Dorette Louise Fleischmann lives at Over The Grass Farm with her current husband, Ambassador Richard Viets. A member of the family best known for producing margarine, she has maintained her maiden name through several marriages and even bestowed the name upon her children.

She is very much an Anglophile, clearly visible in her style of decorating. She has a number of oversized birdcages in her dining room and those who have visited say her feathered friends squawk constantly. She is dog-lover with a fondness for Jack Russell terriers and Labradors and keeps exotic chickens and a number of milking cows. Her love of British country life can also be seen in the horse fields where she had Colin McGee, a Scottish artisan, build authentic thatched roof sheds.

Neighbors describe her has "peckish." When they ride across her property one says "she will welcome us with open arms one day and then the next time, she gets on us for coming through."

Named for her late mother, Dorette K. Fleisschmann, she signs her thank you notes and is referred to as "Dielle." Her sister, Joan Fleischmann Tobin, is married to Maurice Tobin, and they are very much in the social swirl of Washington.

Through the years, Dielle, 70-ish, and her sister have reportedly been at odds with one another. But in 1998, the family was embroiled in turmoil when the attorney handling the estate of their mother pleaded guilty to defrauding heirs of more than $1.1 million and evading income taxes as well. The lawyer, Barrett N. Weinberger of suburban Cincinnati, pleaded guilty to mail fraud, tax evasion and interstate transportation of money in execution of fraud.

The case was investigated by the IRS and the FBI for a year and among the financial irregularities they found were $394,953 in credit charges, political contributions of $139,525, a Florida condo for $85,871, payments on personal loans for $59,436, several cars and a $26,500 donation to the Democratic National Committee.

With a plea agreement, Weinberger was sentenced to forty-one months. And, according to *Regardie's Power* magazine in Washington, D.C., the sisters are not spread too thin. They are still listed in Washington's top 100 wealthiest residents with a net worth between $150-200 million. "There is still some old money around town," the magazine wrote.

The Graham family owns a place in the country called Glen Welby Farm. It was first owned by Philip and Katharine Graham and is now owned by Donald Graham.

The Graham name is synonymous with The Washington Post Company, a powerful publishing empire started by Katharine's father, Eugene Meyer, when he purchased the paper in an auction in 1933.

Leadership at the paper was passed down to Katharine's husband Philip, but when he committed suicide at the farm in 1963, Katharine took over the reins. The paper prospered and led the way on the reporting of the Watergate scandal with Pulitzer Prize winning investigative journalism. Don Graham has served as publisher, president, CEO and chairman of The Washington Post Company, which owns not just the paper, but also *Newsweek* magazine, six television stations and much more. Katharine and Don's collective estimated net worth is over $1 billion.

Referred to as "Donnie," he and wife Mary, an attorney, have four grown children. Despite the tragic death of his father, Donnie and family have enjoyed the farm, spending time in the summers when the children were young, riding horses, playing tennis or swimming in the pond while slapping away the snakes. Donnie has a love of trees and has planted and tended to a stand of pin oaks through the years.

Glen Welby operates as one of the area's few genuine cattle breeding facilities. A herd of over 150 black angus cattle are bred, raised and sold at auction each year under the watchful eye of Carl Raymond "Buck" Nalls. Buck has been with the family for over 40 years. He was there in 1963 to clean up after Philip Graham shot himself. "I was supposed to meet with him that day and go and buy some equipment," Buck says. He annually delivers firewood to Mrs. Graham at her home in Georgetown each winter.

Buck and his sons, Larry and Sonny, plant corn and hay and harvest it for the cattle. The highlight of the year comes when all that beef on the hoof goes to auction, usually at a select sale on a Tuesday at the nearby Marshall Livestock yard. (Hint, this is a must visit for everyone.)

Word gets around that the Glen Welby cattle are going on the block, they usually bring well over $1 a pound. And, although Donnie has never been there for the big day, Buck says, "I hope sometime he will."

No doubt if Buck asks, Donnie will show up. The two men have been close friends and Donnie visits the farm often. "He once said to me, 'You took care of me when I was young and now I'm going to take care of you,'" Buck says.

Alice Francis duPont Mills is the grand dame at the 1,600-acre Hickory Tree Farm. She is the daughter of A. Felix duPont, with a net worth of over $500 million. Now in her 80s, she is a graduate of Oldfields, the tony girl's school outside of Baltimore. She made her debut in Philadelphia and married the late James Paul Mills in Wilmington in 1935. He died in 1987 and she now divides her time between her home on the farm called Burnt Mill and La Tenderette in Hobe Sound, Florida.

In 1932, she flew over the Amazon River with her brother Richard duPont in a Waco with pontoons. A pilot at heart, she received advanced instrument ratings and taught recruits on a Link Trainer for ferry command during World War II. In 1946, the Mills' then flew one of the first single engine airplanes, a Nordwyn Morseman, from New York to Buenos Aires.

Her equine, environmental and political associations and memberships are impressive. They include The Jockey Club, a founding member of the National Thoroughbred Association and Advisory Trustee of the National Museum of Racing. She also was a founding member of the Piedmont Environmental Council and has done duty with the Council for Citizens Against Government Waste. She is a former member of the Planned Parenthood National Board.

As the president of Hickory Tree Farm, she has watched many beautiful and well-bred thoroughbreds get their start and go on to the races. Their brilliant colt, Devil's Bag, was a stakes winner and went undefeated in five races in 1983. He was syndicated for a then-record $36 million as a two-year-old.

The Mills moved to the area in the 1950s, purchasing a number of properties and combining them into one large farm. According to Mrs. Mills, the place was named by her "for the lovely old hickory tree used by General John S. Mosby's soldiers as a rendezvous spot halfway between the village of Middleburg and their camp during the Civil War." Unfortunately, lightning has since destroyed that tree.

Part of this farm was a land grant from King George II to Leven Powell, the founding father of Middleburg. Later, one of his descendant's daughters, Charlotte Noland, had a summer school here. She went on to start the private girl's school Foxcroft, just outside of town.

During the 1920s, William Ziegler, a baking soda magnate from Chicago, owned the farm. He built the barns, which were designed by William Lawrence Bottomley. In the 1940s it was owned by a well-known sportswoman from Boston, Eleanora Sears.

The section of the farm known as Burrland Farm Historic District was placed on the Virginia Landmarks Register in 1997. It's here where a guest will visit the historic Confederate Hall for a viewing of yearlings, a party or perhaps a fundraising event.

Originally built in 1907 as the headquarters for the Travelers Protective Association at Jamestown, It commemorated the 300th anniversary of the first permanent English Settlement in North America. It was purchased by the Middleburg chapter of the United Daughters of the Confederacy in 1907, taken apart and shipped by train to The Plains. Horse-drawn vehicles brought it to Middleburg.

For years, it stood at the corner of Washington and Jay Streets on the edge of town. The ladies had their meetings and Miss Charlotte Noland, as headmistress of Foxcroft staged plays here. By the way, she was a founding member of the United Daughters of the Confederacy.

Then the Exxon station came to town and the building was moved one block back. The Daughters meetings fell by the wayside and the building was near ruin. For a time, it was a boarding house. The Mills family purchased Confederate Hall in 1972. A great deal of renovation took place and they hired Barbara Robinson to do the redesign. Now with abbreviated columns, the windows have been dropped to floor level. The pediment is built as it was at Jamestown and the cornices, columns and windows are all original.

One of Mrs. Mills daughters, Phyllis, is married to artist Jamie Wyeth. Her other daughter, Mimi, and son-in-law William "Billy" Abel-Smith look after the daily operations of the farm.

And, oh we forgot to mention, there's a landing strip at Hickory Tree. Those aviation genes were no doubt passed along. Son James P."Jimmy" Mills Jr. can be spotted buzzing by and doing flyovers in one of his two airplanes, a Cessna 182 RG or a twin engine Aztec. His wife, Debbie, a former airline attendant, also has her pilot's license but most of time can be found out riding.

Marland is now owned by Albert Van Metre, a wealthy real estate developer. His Van Metre Companies have built thousands of homes in the Washington area, bringing the 70-something-year-old a net worth of over $100 million.

But around Middleburg, Marland will always be known as the old Mars place. The fieldstone manor house was designed in 1933 by William Lawrence Bottomly, the very same architect who did some of the design work at Hickory Tree. The house is surrounded by a formal garden and swimming pool, with a stone pool house. (And although no official word on who maintains the 25 x 60-foot pool here, it is very likely The Pool Man. His mother, Joan, is currently married to Al Van Metre.)

The house features a library, living room, butler's pantry, dining room, breakfast area, laundry room and servant's quarters with four bedrooms. And of course, a master bedroom and three additional bedrooms.

There are stables, kennels, offices and an indoor riding arena. And EIGHT tenant houses. Unlike many in the area, Van Metre's passion is not horses. He likes to take to the ocean, often on his new racing yacht *Running Tide*. When last heard from, he was putting together a group to try to win back the America's Cup.

Perhaps it was the years she spent at Marland with her very private father Forrest Mars, Sr. that also captivated Jacqueline Mars. When he passed away in 1999, he left an estimated $4 billion to each of his three children. "Jackie" now lives at Stonehall Farm. There's a two-story stone manor house with foyer, living room, den and master suite. Add to that pantry, country kitchen, sun room and guest bedrooms. And of course, the other amenities such as heated swimming pool (no word on who maintains it here) and a pool/guest house with dressing rooms, kitchen and sauna. There are also a number of stables and outbuildings.

Jackie is more than generous with the profits off not just the M&M's and the Milky Ways. The corporation also owns Kal-Kan and Uncle Ben's. She is the major sponsor of the husband and wife three-day event equestrian duo Karen and David O'Connor. When they were part of the bronze medal winning U.S. Olympic team in Sydney, she threw a party Down Under for everyone. And, on top of that, David brought home the individual gold medal.

She was described in a 1995 article in the *Sunday Telegraph* of London as "an energetic ex-debutante with a passion for horses and the outdoor life and goes virtually unrecognized on her rare excursions into the frontline of Washington society. Disdainful of politics and above money, she is said to be happiest hacking through the muddy fields that surround her horse farm in the prime Virginia hunt country. The trademark reclusiveness of the Mars kin is compounded in Jacqueline's case by a personal shyness that keeps her a safe distance from the high-gloss networking of the party circuit. For most of her life she has been content to remain equally detached from the family business, allowing it to be run by her shadowy, bespectacled brothers."

Jackie's 1986 marriage to Harold A. "Hank" Vogel Jr., the tweed-clad owner of an exclusive boot and shoe company in New York City, drew national attention when they divorced in 1994. He attempted to stake a claim on the chocolate heiress's assets, alleging she had not been forthright at the time they signed a prenuptial agreement. He claimed she assured him that he would be taken care of upon her death or if they divorced. She accused him of extreme cruelty and verbal abuse. They both denied each other's charges.

"I'm not asking to live the life of a billionaire, I just want to be comfortable and I don't think that's asking too much," he told *The Washington Post* in January, 1994.

They were both involved in the horse world. He follows the major horse show circuit, measuring people for custom-made boots. She was an active rider at the time and they met when she was ordering boots. Eventually their paths went in opposite directions. He liked to play golf in his down time and she continued with her horse interests.

Part of the acrimony surrounded a 60-acre farm in New Jersey called "Hickory Corner, not far from the Forbes and De Lorean estates, as well as property in Middleburg totaling $5 million in value. Vogel took over the mansion in New Jersey. She moved to Middleburg, but before leaving she padlocked her office, fired all the help and hired a security guard to watch things.

At one point, he refused a $1 million settlement offer. Then in June, 1996, they were quietly divorced in Superior Court in Somerville, New Jersey. The prenuptial agreement was upheld. Vogel was given thirty days to leave the property.

According to an article in the *Newark Star Ledger*, "It was short and sweet, as Mars took the witness stand for all of three minutes to answer perfunctory questions from one of her lawyers and Judge Graham T. Ross."

A chauffeur-driven car was waiting and she departed with two of her attorneys and an unidentified friend. She soon found herself back in Virginia. There's a stream that runs through Stonehall Farm along the east side called Laughing Brook. But this is no laughing matter. Jackie Mars' net worth is $4 billion.

Sandra Payson's love of horses brought her to the area where she maintains a place called Ashley. She formerly owned a well-known thoroughbred farm in Kentucky called Green Tree Stud. Much of her wealth comes from old money made in the oil and railroad business. Her mother was Joan Whitney Payson and her uncle, Jock Whitney, was best known as the financial backer of the movie, "Gone With The Wind". He in turn owned the Llangollen estate in the 1930s while married to Mary Elizabeth Altemus. He built the famous horse show barns and later turned the entire estate over to "Liz."

Payson's interests evidently include politics, a subject scrupulously avoided in pleasant company out here. However, public records reveal she was one of the largest single contributors to the Democratic National Committee during the tumultuous period of January of 1999 to March of 2000, with a check for $250,000.

Abe Pollin, the 70-something son of a Russian immigrant, is a major player in the business world of Washington. He started out in the construction industry building apartments and took to naming them after family members and friends. Such is the case of the "Irene" named for his wife of more than 50 years. One of his projects had the first ever rooftop pool.

He made his real mark when he bought the Baltimore Bullets basketball team and brought them to the Nation's Capitol, building an arena in suburban Maryland with easy access to the beltway. Then he was awarded a team In the National Hockey league and named them the Capitals. The arena first called the Capital Centre and later the USAir Arena had the first ever oversize telescreen for replays and scores. He eventually built the much hailed $200 million state-of-the-art MCI Center smack in the middle of downtown Washington.

Pollin sold the Capitals to AOL executive Ted Leonsis for $200 million and the basketball team is now known as the Washington Wizards. He has served as a board member on the National Jewish Hospital, United Jewish Appeal and the John F. Kennedy Center. His net worth is over $500 million.

The house on his country estate, Cloverland, was designed by none other than architect William Lawrence Bottomley (by now a favorite Middleburg designer). It's been said to be in the style of a grand English country home with a formal entry hall, living room and formal dining room with an original Adams mantle.

Things are so formal here that there was a private wing originally designed for children and a governess. The estate's outbuildings include a three-bedroom house, which was the original circa 1850 farmhouse. There are stables, but no horses. On the kitchen side of the house, there's a four-room apartment above a two-car garage. Perhaps a perfect place for a pick-up game against the backstop, but alas not a basketball hoop in site.

Robert Rosenthal made a fortune in car sales. He started in the business in the mid-1950s, when his father mortgaged his house to start a Chevrolet dealership in suburban Washington. Business boomed and he was off the races. He now has nineteen dealerships, with sales of $800 million. He later put together a REIT (real estate investment trust) called Capital Auto, which owns the real estate of more than two hundred dealerships. All of which leaves him an estimated worth of over $200 million. He and wife Marion own a number of homes in Washington, California, Nantucket and Middleburg.

Boxwood, their 120-acre country estate, is a National Historic Landmark dating to 1826 and is the largest farm within the Middleburg town limits. It was once owned by the late Stephen C. Clark, an heir to the Singer Sewing Machine Company. His father also founded the National Baseball Hall of Fame and Museum in Cooperstown, New York.

Before he died, Clark donated an adjacent 130 acres to The Hill School, the 75-year-old private K-8 country day school, thereby affording a much needed campus expansion. His widow, Kathryn "Kats" Clark, lives at Woodbox in Middleburg and is an active owner on the national horse show circuit. She follows her champion conformation hunters from Palm Beach to Madison Square Garden.

But back to Boxwood. The house is a classic Federal-style of native fieldstone and with sixteen rooms and 10,000 square feet, there's more than enough space to relax in the country. And oh, a three-car garage. The only question would be which one to drive.

Roger Sant is a partner in the world's largest global power company. His AES Corporation has 137 plants in twenty countries, including India, Brazil,

Argentina and Australia.

He and wife Vicki own the former Edes Home in Georgetown. They bought it after the National Symphony Orchestra had the decorator show house there one year. They also own Persimmon Tree Farm and spend quiet weekends in Middleburg. The main house is frame with four bedrooms and four baths and six fireplaces. There's also a guesthouse and a tenant house, and a small stable.

But Roger Sant is a busy man. The company he co-founded has produced not just 40,000 megawatts each year but more than enough money to light up his life with a net worth of $2.2 billion. His charitable service finds him as Chairman of the Board of the World Wildlife Fund.

Others are equally fortunate. Joan Irvine Smith first came to Middleburg when she was married to Morton W. "Cappy" Smith, a legendary horseman. She spends most of her time in "Irvine" California as the heiress of a real estate fortune of $350 million. She's a patron of the arts in California with the Joan Irvine Smith Fine Arts, which in turn sponsors the annual California Art Club Outdoor Painting Festival. She has also been supportive of Middleburg equine artist Wally Nall, whose horse portraits grace a number of walls.

And then there's Mary Lewis Wiley, a scion of Henry Flager, the railroad and oil magnate. She quietly goes about her business in the village picking up mail and going to the grocery store.

Which brings us to the best story of fortune in Middleburg...Barbara Wright. A native of the area, she and husband, Joe live at Hickory Tree Farm, where he works for Jimmy Mills. She has worked at the Middleburg Safeway for twenty years. "I work as the third person," she explains, "I usually close up at night."

She has been a fixture in the village shops, first at the pharmacy where she worked during high school and later at Middleburg Hardware. She's waited on Liz Taylor and Jackie Onassis. And when Willard Scott comes in the Safeway, "he always gives me a big kiss." She recalls once when he came in the hardware store because he had a Japanese Beatle problem in his fruit orchard. "He came back in and told me they were all over the place after I sold him the traps," she says. "It was no wonder, he had hung them in the trees and you're supposed to hang them away from the trees."

She's helpful beyond the call of duty, carrying bags for older citizens and keeping an eye out so the checkout lines move smoothly. Then there was the time a customer came in the Safeway and asked her for some K-Y Jelly. "I took him to the aisle with the grape jelly and I kept saying, 'Oh this sounds familiar.' He told me we were in the wrong place."

Barbara Wright was not in the wrong place in 1999. First she and eight others won the Middleburg Lion's Club raffle at the Community Center. That was worth $10,000, which they all split. Her take was $1,100.

Then one night she found herself in front of the Jackpot machines at the

Charles Town Race Track not far off over in West Virginia. She hit eight out of nine numbers for $8,000.

Still feeling lucky, she went back a few nights later and ended up on the same machine. This time she really hit it…nine out of nine numbers. "That machine jumped out those numbers so quick it was unbelievable," she says. "We had just taken out a vehicle loan and we had 38 more payments."

She brought home $38,000. Her take for the year was $50,000. "I paid off the loan, bought my mother a used car and paid some bills," she says. And like everyone else, "I paid some taxes."

She's gone back for more, too. She's won $6,000 since her biggest score. Not only that, she adds, "I keep playing the lottery pick five every day. I'm hoping I'll win one more time."

The amount of generosity in Middleburg is overwhelming. It includes Robert Duvall, who has loaned his name to a number of good causes, such as the Chukkers For Charity to benefit Robert Duvall's Children's Fund for an afternoon of polo and tango. Benevolence cuts across all income levels. As early morning athletes drag themselves into the Middleburg Fitness Club, they need only look across the parking lot to the back entrance of the Middleburg Methodist Church.

There, a group called Seven Loaves, a consortium of local churches, operates a food bank. It's a sobering moment and stark contradiction. Those who are well off try to shed unwanted pounds from overeating. Yards away, they can watch as Thanksgiving turkeys and Easter baskets go out that back door.

Many who give do so quietly. It's the Middleburg style. When one local man was diagnosed with cancer and went to the bank to check on a savings account, knowing the cost of treatment would be staggering, there was a surprise. Someone had quietly deposited money into the account, wishing to remain anonymous to the recipient. And while that generous and considerate donor will remain nameless here, his identity did not remain unknown to the cancer patient. Years before, the patient had himself done a good deed for his anonymous benefactor. The original act of kindness had been repaid…$10,000 fold.

CHAPTER 4

STYLE

Viviane Warren and Charles T. Matheson define
Middleburg style.

*I*t's about style, not stylish. It's all around in Middleburg, like the imposing
dry stone walls that outline the perimeter of so many farms. Classic hand-
painted signs quietly display the names of the shops and farms in a refined and
understated mode. The hand-painted hood ornaments of foxes, horses, favorite
dogs or pigs and goats adorn station wagons, trucks and SUVs in the preferred
colors of navy and dark green, sometimes silver. The fine art that graces the
paneled or faux painted walls and the china on the table of the dining room
make a statement. The architecture of the houses AND the barns is the ultimate
manifestation.

Fashion, not fashionable. For when it comes to clothing in Middleburg there is a definite look. "That's what I like about it," says Patty Callahan, an artist and long time resident we will get to in a minute.

Over and over again, on the subject of clothes or fashion, someone will parrot what Patty points out. "Whenever you go in The Coach Stop you can always tell the out of town women, they're all dressed up. They're also easy to spot walking down the street. Not only do they stick out like a sore thumb, but they're also walking with their husbands."

Cathy Zimmerman undeniably defines and exemplifies Middleburg style. "Growing up here, I've gotten to where I don't notice what people wear," she says, sitting in my office one wickedly cold January morning. "If someone does wear something incredibly stylish or new, it jumps right out and stands out as strange." She's wearing jeans, a worn and soft turquoise cotton turtleneck, a white and beige boatneck cotton sweater, two thin gold bracelets, a large watch I cannot define without being too obvious and a pair of slightly old L.L. Bean boots.

The boots, she says, usually have "poop or paint on them." You see, she is an artist and a horse lover. Petite and blonde, her outfit isn't put together, it's old and the sweater is out of season. But that's what makes it. It's actually a spring or summer sweater. But this is what sets her apart from the ladies who come to lunch in Middleburg. Or, even those who have recently moved here. It's a sense of local style.

I have always loved to write about one woman who has been wearing the same long tartan skirt at Christmas for over twenty years. Some things are timeless and elude fashionable.

Cathy has an eye for detail that comes across in the watercolors she does of area landscapes. "I notice things. I appreciate everything around me and I have since I was little," she says. "An artist sees beauty where most people don't. Like the fog, someone else might say 'I wish the sun would come out.' I like the fog."

That is quite evident when you see her artwork of a foggy morning across a plowed cornfield with the mountains looming in the background. This is a scene she and husband, Tad, view often as they ride with the Piedmont Fox Hounds, a pastime she took up after a 15-year hiatus.

She also has rendered decorative painting in many homes in Middleburg. "It's in lieu of wallpaper. A way of putting some personality into decorating," she says. This could include a faux potted plant complete with worn terra cotta container painted on the wall of a hallway to add dimension. Or perhaps a pastel border of ribbons and vines added in a guestroom to coordinate colors and textures. Her compositions on the walls and in her watercolors are skillful and exude character.

"I do like to get dressed up," she adds. "I don't wear jeans outside of Middleburg. It's nice to feel attractive once in a while." (There was never one ounce of doubt about that.)

Karen Jackson at Tully Rector's Men's and Women's Wear walks a fine line between the local wants and the newer desires when it comes to sportswear. As buyer, she says, "I didn't want to go outside that look of basic country, tweed coats." So the shop carries the standby lines of cashmere and tweed from Barry Bricken, as well as the high-end jackets from Belvest made in Italy. "I cater to all types, which is not easy to do."

For the younger crowd and the weekend visitors, she offers the ever-so-trendy designs from Theory and Katyone Adeli. "They know what it is and it's very expensive," she explains. "They aren't afraid to wear it."

Another aspect of Middleburg style can be seen up and down the streets in the village and along the long country roads…the signs. They are an integral part of the character.

In town: The Upper Crust, The Finicky Filly, Black Coffee Bistro, The Coach Stop, The Piedmont Gourmet, the Middleburg Animal Hospital, The Powder Horn Gun Shop, Wisdom Gallery, Costin Updegrove and Combs Accountants or Waller Picture Framing.

Also, Salamander Farm, Foxcroft School, Hillmount, Dencrest, Marcrisda, The Cabbage Patch, Rabbit Hill Farm, Turkey Roost Farm, Pan D'or or the Welbourne Stickball League.

In 1980, Patty Callahan and husband Ben Jackson built a house and the end of Quail Run Road. "I was pregnant and did not want to go back to work in D.C. and commute," she says. "Although I had a degree in political science, my first love was in the fine arts. So here I was living in the country and I needed something to do."

There was a sign at the end of their lane that was rather large. It had a huge quail on it and was lettered "Quail Run." It was big and rough. Replacing the sign was Ben's idea. "With my background in art he thought I could come up with something more appropriate," she explains. So, she picked up a book on lettering, chose a font and sketched out something on paper. She found a bird book and used it to create a silhouette of quail and there was the design for the sign. Ben cut out the wood and framed it. She painted the sign and that was the beginning of Quail Run Signs.

Then, one thing lead to another. Soon after hanging the sign, a neighbor called and asked Patty to paint one for her place. Then she ran an ad in a local paper. Since that time she has educated herself on lettering technique and using materials like brushes, paints and wood. She also subscribes to trade publications and attends sign painter seminars across the country.

"I have challenged myself to learn other sign techniques like carving and gilding and designing signs that are dimensional," she explains.

Surprisingly, she has not done many "slow down for the dog" signs. "But," she adds, "I did do two tiny signs for Jackie Mars that say 'Please don't let the cat out.'"

Patty believes the signs came about for two reasons: tradition and as directional tools. "As you well know, it's a very English tradition to name your place, modest as it may be. Remember that the Kennedys named their place Wexford back in the '60s, so it's something that's been done for a long time."

Directions from one place to another in Middleburg often sound like this. "Go down Snake Hill Road, until you get to that little curve by the silo, turn left and go about one mile down by the coop and our place, Quail Run, is on the left. You'll see the sign out front."

"We forget that today people name their places for different reasons," Patty says. "If they are building new, they see it's been done before so they name their place in order to make the statement and to create a personal family identity. Often times they get the kids involved. If they purchase an existing house that does not have any historical significance, they may choose to change the name to make it personal. Sometimes they choose to adopt the existing identity thinking it means something."

And by the way, Patty says she would never recommend that a new owner change the name of an old place. "Remember when Salamander Farm was named Cotswold? Who did that and why did they do it? I don't know who it was but I suggest that it is ego. I believe in individuality but I also believe in respecting history. My personal opinion, but there you have it."

One part of the sign is extremely important--the color. "No doubt about it, dark green or Charleston green is the color of choice," Patty says. "I mix up my own colors because sign paints only come in red, yellow, blue, green, etc. I mix that dark green up by the gallon. For good reason though, it is a great color." Ivory is the next most popular color, followed by maroon. And she adds, "Some folks will use racing colors or farm colors for their signs. The two that come to mind are Faygate for racing colors--lavender and red--and Salamander Farm for show colors--blue, red and gray. All that I know is that the horse trailer is painted in those colors and the stationary is printed in those colors."

And the price for a custom designed sign from Quail Run Signs? It runs anywhere from $150 to $3,000, depending on size and details. "Essentially, I feel like this wonderful job just fell into my lap. I was able to stay at home with my children. I got to create something and see a design to its completion. And, I've met lots of wonderful people, and some are good friends now. It has also served to make me part of a very special community."

Whenever a neighbor asks about a stone mason, the name Harris comes to mind. This African-American family has been building and restoring the worn yet rugged dry stone walls for generations. There's Aubrey Harris, Gilbert Harris, Charles Harris, Cardozo Harris or Greg Harris.

Charles Harris assembles a fine looking fortress. And while he does this he will also tell you tales of his stone building family...all three generations. Back in the 1980s, he told a customer about his Hodgkin's disease and sadly he passed on, as had his brother Gilbert, as has his father, Aubrey who drowned while fishing. Now brothers Greg and Cardozo continue the tradition.

Many of their mortar free works of art enclose the priceless horses of well-known residents from Joe Albritton to actor Robert Duvall. The solid stone fences they build somehow make a subtle statement natives give credence to, but rarely utter: "We've been here a long time and intend to be here long after you." An occasional paneled chicken coop breaks the sequence of stone for mounted riders to jump. Driving down the winding dirt roads, gazing at the grazing horses and cattle, the stone walls are the first thing anyone notices. These sturdy boundaries once delineated the battle lines for what many still refer to as the War Between the States.

"I look at it, it's like a puzzle, " says Cardozo Harris, pausing for a moment as he works on a multi-year project on a local farm, restoring miles of fences he estimates are at least 100 years old. He steps back and examines the massive pile of rocks to study the shapes and sizes. Sometimes he has to roll a 35- or 50-pound foundation rock into place. He will reconstruct about 15 feet during a day, depending on whether he needs to haul rocks to the site. The cost will range from $12 to $18 per foot.

His grandfather, Teddy Harris, worked full time on a nearby estate as a stonemason. He, in turn, taught his son, Aubrey Harris, the trade. Cardozo started when he was 14. "My dad worked all over the place," he recalls, meaning the wide swath of Middleburg, including neighboring towns such as: Upperville, Delaplane and The Plains. He took his sons along for extra help. They learned to build everything from walkways, entrance posts, steps, patios and chimneys in dry stone, even a building or two.

"To lock each stone in the cross over from one side to the other, I try to find a long stone," Cardozo explains. The art comes in putting it all back together. They were taught to "try to put it back to where it went, but not so it looks too new."

There are other stone masons in the area, but the effect is not the same as when a Harris finishes a stone structure. Some try to use cement between the outside walls with rocks a tad dissimilar than the native sandstone, slate or granite, which they call iron stone. The result becomes too flawless...nouveau rock. The Harris masons labor all year, in the summer with the snakes and in the winter warmed only by a moving kerosene-heated tent.

Greg Harris owns his own stone business and adores the outdoors. "I love it outside. A lot of people would say, no matter what I'm not going to freeze." Both men try not to disturb the animals. "I put the grass back for the ground squirrels," Cardozo says. "They're getting a new home. But if there's some bees or something, I'm out of here."

"Of every 20 stone masons, only one is a master," according to British authority Richard Tufnell, International Coordinator of the Dry Stone Walling Association of Great Britain and director of the Dry Stone Masonry Institute in Lexington, Kentucky. Tufnell has overseen restoration projects in Scotland, Spain, Zimbabwe and Switzerland.

"Dry stone walls are durable, flexible in earthquake risk areas, the stones are free and it is environmentally friendly," he says during a National Building Museum lecture in Washington, D.C., expounding on his product not unlike all the other flacks on nearby Capitol Hill. "America can hold its head up on the quality but not so much on the number of craftsmen. We are trying to create a master mason certificate."

The Harris brothers certainly would qualify if such certification existed. Until then, their trade must rely on the somewhat mixed blessing of this small town life...word of mouth. In Middleburg, if your neighbor says these men are good stone masons, then it must be true. After all, didn't Robert Frost teach us... good fences make good neighbors?

"I am still amazed by the stone walls with the Blue Ridge Mountains beyond," says Nelson Hammell. In 1987, he started Devonshire, the exquisite English garden shop that now occupies the old bank building at the main intersection in town. With partner Pete Hawkins, it has since grown to 12 shops in such chic spots at Palm Beach, Carmel, Naples, Bridgehampton and East Hampton.

On the subject of Middleburg style he says, "My focus would come now from spending time away, yet I still have a home and business here." He's able to see it from a different perspective and relate it with the other areas where he does business. "It's restrained yet confident," he says.

And much of it comes from the Anglophile way of life, he adds. "Middleburg style is totally dedicated to English country lifestyle. It's totally out of favor elsewhere. It's not new and future oriented and people here have never sought to be cutting edge. There is not interest in being cutting edge. The similarities are apparent. The parallel is people from the townhouses in London going to Wiltshire or Lincolnshire or Sussex and the countryside with just family and friends, gardening and small parties."

"Middleburg is a retreat and not a resort," Nelson explains. "It's been that way since the financiers from upstate New York started bringing their horses down here. It's a love of the countryside and the horse. And it continues to be a retreat with the political figures that have lived here, like Lyndon Johnson and Lloyd Bentsen."

Nelson notes that for the most part the houses are tucked at the end of the lane or backed up to a tree line. "Drive down Zulla Road and you'll see," he instructs. "For the most part it's unassuming, most every house is obscured by nature and enveloped by landscape. It leaves a visitor wondering."

Contrast all of this in Middleburg to the Hamptons, for example, where Nelson says "the opulent wealth is displayed in the houses and the toys are

Photo by June Hughes

parked right out front."

The homes in Middleburg are built for "comfort," according to Nelson. "They are not announcing one's arrival." Many people have homes in other parts of the world and "that's where they can have the Impressionist paintings and furniture from Bond Street. In furnishing the homes here, he says "there's a blend of Jack Russells, a worn sofa, riding boots and a mud room. And no three-piece suits."

The equestrian community, of course, is the backbone. "There are only two or three places like it in the entire country," he says. As opposed to Wellington, the horsey enclave of show jumpers and polo ponies far west of Palm Beach. "It's a success," he notes. "But there's no sense of history. It's instant horse gratification. In Middleburg the origins are humble with layer upon layer."

"The barns are almost as important as the house," Nelson concludes. "People spend as much time with their horses and in the house, and this is as it should be in this community."

No one would know this better than architect John Blackburn, who has designed several impressive barns in the area. "In terms of horse barns and residential structures, my impression of the typical historic Middleburg style is primarily a Federal style of architecture," he says. "It's a simpler style, less adornment, using all the natural materials such as wood, brick and stone, slate roofs (metal roofs came later but are very common to the area.) Stone is pretty common because there was so much stone and they had to get rid of it in order to plow the fields."

At Robert Smith's Heronwood, which Blackburn's Washington, D.C. firm designed, they used stone in the barns. "There was a lot of the old stone fencing dividing the fields. However, the fields did not work with the layout of the new horse farm and they had to be removed," he explains. "Therefore, we decided to use the stone in the buildings for much the same reasons the early buildings were constructed of stone. The shape and forms of the barns and other buildings at Heronwood and Rutledge were derived from Federal shapes and forms. For example, the stone end of the Heronwood barn is the same proportion as a typical Federal style two story residence. Though the design of a modern day horse barn could not be made to fit into a typical 19th Century barn, the same materials, shapes and forms were used to create the Heronwood and Rutledge barns.

They also used stucco on the exterior as well as stone. "Stucco is a fairly common building material in the older Middleburg buildings and we used it partly for maintenance reasons." To come up with the final designs, a team from the Blackburn firm spends time photographing all the barns in the area to determine the final elements.

"My clients in Middleburg seem to all want traditional styles and that tradition is typically Federal," he says. "However, at Heronwood and Rutledge we were able to blend both contemporary and traditional." He also has designs in the works for Carol and Robert Foosaner's Rocana Farm and Hinton Nobles' Wood Hill Farm.

"I think Heronwood captures what I like to achieve in architecture in terms of style. I like design to have roots, to have a sense of tradition and the place it's located. If you study traditional architecture, the style in a particular area, especially in the 19th Century in this country often is a reflection or blend of the traditions of the people who settled the area and of the region context and available materials, topography and weather, etc.

"When I design a building, especially a barn, because of its closeness to nature and the context of the land, I try to find the essence of the style of the area and design a building that embodies the local tradition without replicating it. Modern day horse barns are not anything like an 18th or 19th Century barn, which was typically used to house a variety of animals and functions.

"Today's horse barn needs to be efficient. It needs to respond to the natural environment in a way different than was thought to be the case in the 18th and 19th centuries. Therefore, the challenge is how to combine modern thoughts and technologies with traditional elements and materials without creating a replication. I think we were successful at Heronwood with that philosophy."

Architect Tommy Beach works out of his studio at home. He also has designed a number of notable homes and barns in the area. Salamander and Rallywood are two that he names.

"One thing that sets the Middleburg area apart is a special sense of history and taste and the money that goes along with it to preserve it," he says. This allows him to "do new work that is compatible with and reinforces the indigenous historical character of the area."

"He makes it all come together," says client, Leffert Lefferts. However, Tommy cautions, that all is not perfect here. "Unfortunately we are coming to a headwaters. There's new money that lacks taste and sensitivity. That's why so many McMansions are springing up. People used to know better."

He considers himself fortunate. "I've had a dozen clients of new money that recognize this. They don't know, but are willing to ask and learn. I call my style a refined Virginia farmhouse with a flare for the Federal design," he continues. Like John Blackburn, he also uses materials that are "compatible with the area: stone, metal roof, stucco and wood siding."

"My pride and joy is the Sporting Library [The National Sporting Library, a collection of 12,000 volumes] and The Chronicle [The Chronicle of the Horse] buildings." Just on the west end of town, the complex reinforces his philosophy of incorporating details to make the structures appear old.

For example, the stone was deliberately set unevenly and the stucco has no perfect corners. The stone was then whitewashed, a component some questioned, according to Beach. "Ninety percent of the people around here think that even ugly stone is good," he explains. "There was such a dichotomy between the different elements that with time it will only improve."

Tommy Beach can also list one of the most impressive names among his clients, but he doesn't. He usually just says "a client in Upperville." But it's no secret that he has done work for Bunny Mellon, the absolute arbiter of style.

Mrs. Mellon is a landscape designer whose credits include the Rose Garden at The White House and an adjacent children's garden for Jacqueline Onassis. She also has done work for the American Horticultural Society and with the celebrated fashion designer, Hubert de Givenchy.

In 1976, she commissioned the architect Edward Larrabee Barnes to do a garden library to house her impressive horticultural and botanical collection of 3,500 rare books and 10,000 reference books. Distinguished by large windows and a combination of flat and angled roofs, it has a Mediterranean feel and was completed in 1981. Who else but Mrs. Mellon could have the confidence to deviate from the tried and true traditional? (Although it is a private library now, it is intended to be available to scholars and gardeners in the future.)

Local stone was used throughout, for she also adheres to the dictate of using indigenous materials. When the builders had to explode rock in the foundation area, nearby citrus trees were expertly replanted. Painted white throughout, there is an oversized sundial on one side.

Once inside, a visitor will spot a collection of garden tools on a table near the entrance. Her friend, the noted sculptor Diego Giacometti, designed a table for the space. And speaking of friends, the celebrated French jewelry designer Jean Schlumberger designed a flower urn, which adorns the top of the entrance pavilion of her greenhouse.

Tommy Beach has also been referred to as her friend. So when a new wing was needed for Mrs. Melon's grand garden library, he got the call. It matches the original structure flawlessly in composition, proportion and materials.

Bunny Mellon gives credence to integrating buildings and their surrounding gardens into the countryside. It's no wonder she chose Tommy Beach, because he believes that sighting a building correctly "will make it look more like it's been there and not look naked up there."

Penny and John Denegre (she is a joint master of the Middleburg Hunt) hired David Neumann of the Middleburg architectural firm Versaci Neumann and Partners to design their house at Foxstone Farm.

Penny, a champion side-saddle rider, inherited her love of horses and the countryside from her mother, Pat Rogers, and it looks as if it will be passed down another generation to her daughter Alden, too. Dozens of silver trophies line the shelves and walls at their home. She refers to the style of her house as "Tidewater Georgian," with some of the elements the settlers from England brought along. Yet, "it's been modified to the countryside," she says.

Joanne Swift, owner of The Shaggy Ram, defines style as "simple but sumptuous."

"I wanted a central hall front to back. And I wanted it to be symmetrical," she adds. "The challenge was to make it functional inside. But that's the challenge for most architects."

The firm has drawn a new fieldstone Virginia country house in Georgian style for Molly and Clarke Ohrstrom at Palmerstone. Senior partner Russell Versaci articulately sums up his interpretation of architectural style in this town in an e-mail note: "We Middleburg architects take great pains to make houses with a recognizable pedigree, where the prescription is to 'make it look like it has always been there.' Traditional American farmhouse and English country styles are the preferred forms of architecture. There are plenty of good models to be found around the Virginia Piedmont, so the job of creating a new house that fits seamlessly into the Middleburg style is never a daunting proposition. But if your taste leans toward cutting edge design, you best set up shop somewhere else."

Joanne Swift owns The Shaggy Ram, a home furnishings boutique, and also does interior design work. When referring to interiors she says the style is "simple but sumptuous." In the drapes for example, "the fabric does the speaking."

Her customers prefer such manufactures and designers as Pierre Frey, whose high-end French fabrics include silk from Lyon and the classic Toile de Jouy. From Brunschweig and Fils as well as Colefax and Fowler the infallible historic patterns of glazed chintz English florals are infinitely preferred. Names such as Chatsworth (after the famous English country home of the Duke and Duchess of Devonshire), Californie and Les Papillons are favored.

Swift lived and worked in a number of imposing high spots---Vale, LaJolla, Florida and Europe--before coming to Middleburg. "They all had style," she says. "A good decorator can make any abode warm and inviting and comfortable. Good style is timeless."

The English and French influence oozes in her main street shop with the antique pine furniture and small objects, often with a dog or horse motif. These things "can go into any home," she says. "Wherever you live, you can incorporate.

"I believe that someone's home is very important. Frequently someone will come in to my shop and say, 'It must be nice to have this lifestyle, not opening until 11.' But they don't know that at six in the morning, I was in the barn watering horses and wearing Wellies [army green Wellington boots from England]. I am constantly working and at the end of the day I'm mowing. It's constant work."

Joan Gardiner designs and makes tiles. She is best known for her hand-painted relief tiles. She has been doing this for over 20 years from the home she shares in Unison with husband John Gardiner, a fiction writer. (His short stories have appeared in the New Yorker and his most recent book, Somewhere In France, was published in 2000 by Knopf.) Her workshop is in a converted barn and his writing space is in a separate sparse structure.

She first came out to Middleburg as a potter. As a way to indulge her horse passion, she worked part time as a horse-shoer. When the Gardiners put an addition on their house, she made some tiles and the tile installer was impressed. He immediately sent her new business.

The timeless designs, such as a copy of a Canton china pot with flowers growing out of it, have been popular. It's almost like a puzzle. Each work of art—the china pot, bunny or a bird—comprises anywhere from a few tiles to 1,000 pieces.

"When you have Canton meaning the real thing, it means that you had family that came over on the first boat. It means you have old connections to your money," she says, noting that she has seen people in Middleburg put these priceless objects in the dishwasher. "It blows my mind. They enjoy the china, but I hate to tell them be careful. These pots are so chock a block full of symbolism and I love to copy the pattern. Most of the jobs in the area have been provincial and there is a reverence for old things. They don't want to add something that distracts.

"But there are new young families, more and more that are coming in and building from the ground up or renovating and they are completely new and educated and I call them more sophisticated than those who have been around. It's exciting and they see connections to a glaze called Celadon that nobody would look at before. Now all of a sudden they recognize the beauty."

Joan's tiles are used as back splashes in the kitchens, mantle surrounds and even in children's bathrooms. "People like to be playful with the children's rooms and I do animals here, usually animals that have been in their lives." She charges $34 per tile and up.

She describes Middleburg style. "I think that an awful lot of the possessions of the larger landholders have objects that are passed down. They don't acquire new art," she says. "The sofa needs to be recovered and the money often goes to other things like horses or trailers to pull the horses and even to travel. They have this thing, not wanting to buy new things, they have valuable pieces. It's almost like anything new wouldn't have value. The exception would be a portrait of a dog or horse. This has to unique to this area."

"Horses are the common denominator," says Greg Dubenitz, owner of The Sporting Gallery. "Somehow the sophistication of these people who have bought farms here defines what they have around them." His business in the circa 1820 Duffy House, a classic Federal building on the main street, specializes in fine art--both antique and contemporary--sculpture and objets d'art. All of it is inspired by the sporting life of all forms of hunting, fishing and the great outdoors.

Middleburg connoisseurs of British antique horse paintings favor the work of 20th Century artist Sir Alfred Munnings and 18th Century artist George Stubbs, whose works run into the hundreds of thousands of dollars.

Greg's cozy shop is laid out in a series of rooms. There are old pine mantles and lovely wooden floors. A bronze of "Polo Ponies and Players" by Phyllida Meacham about 18 inches high is $14,500. A watercolor by Peter Biegel called "The Limerick Fox" is $3,500.

The pattern of Royal Dalton porcelain called Coaching Days is a very popular item to collect. Here a pitcher and seven beakers, circa 1905-1929, sell for $795. Figurines of every kind of terrier imaginable, from a personal favorite Dandie Dinmont, Yorkshire and of course the Jack Russell, are captured in playful poses.

"Some have nothing but horse art in every room and that's all they want," he says. "And others have created their homes with more variety. They don't think of their house as decorated. It has just evolved."

CHAPTER 5

Judy and Lang Washburn

MAKING MIDDLEBURG TICK

I was walking through the Safeway parking lot late one frigid afternoon during the Christmas season and what should catch my eye? No, it wasn't eight tiny reindeer. And I promise I wasn't looking for this but, how about the vagrant who was sitting with his car door wide open wearing nothing but a Santa hat? He was trying to…shall we say…get up for the holiday season.

As we have already determined, we are not in Mayberry Aunt Bea. Which means that Middleburg is not immune to anything.

A quick call to the local police and he was ushered away quietly. It was just one of the many calls the town office may get on any given day. The staff of three full-time and one part-time policemen, does everything from getting babies out of locked cars to taking care of anyone caught celebrating Christmas in an inappropriate manner. (I was going to say, anyone getting caught with their pants down, but…in some cases that might not be an offense. Even though it could be offensive.)

The policemen in the village are the infrastructure of Middleburg: the essence, sum and substance and foundation. And there are others, like Bobby Bailey at the BP Station, who has been flirting with the women while pumping gas for years. If you have a flat tire or are out of gas he will come to your rescue in a heartbeat. And up at the other end of town, Billy Journell, owner of the Exxon, will do the same thing. In his off time he's an antique dealer, an expert In old silver and fine furniture.

Or there's the late Mrs. Everhart, who lived in a Lilliputian apartment on the backside of the main commercial block of shops. Those in the know used to take their riding clothes and other suits to be altered there. Her son, Smokey, also repairs saddles and boots.

And then there's Franklin Payne, the former postmaster up the road in Aldie. He's the man you call if you're planning a big party and need a crew to park the cars. These people make this town unique. They are among the people who make Middleburg tick.

Tim Dimos spent his entire childhood in Middleburg. He attended the local Hill School from kindergarten through eighth grade. His parents, fondly referred to as "The Greeks," owned a restaurant smack in the middle of town that is now called The Coach Stop.

He ventured off to Deerfield Academy in Massachusetts for prep school. He returned to the University of Virginia for a total of seven years. "I graduated from the College of Arts and Sciences in 1966 and the law school in 1969," he says. His law office is just up the street from the town office on West Marshall Street, which is convenient since he is the mayor. His practice is confined to tax, trusts and estates and exempt organizations. His law partners are Dickens and Oscar.One is black Labrador, the other a yellow Labrador.

He is often seen walking to the post office with one of his "partners." He started out on the town council and was elected mayor in 1996 and is now in his third two-year term. "I was prompted to run for mayor by the then incumbent mayor, Carol Bowersock [one of the well-known Bowersock twins], who assured me that the job required only about one hour per week," he says. "Looking back, I don't know what is funnier—that she said it or that I believed it."

Anne Lackman, who served as mayor from 1988 to 1992, recalls a shooting incident involving a town police officer. The only catch was, the officer was not shot at, he was the shooter. It caused quite a stir at the time. "It was like the Keystone cops," she recalls. Not to give the impression that everything exciting happens near the Safeway parking lot, but…the officer was attempting to arrest an alleged drunk driver on Pendleton Street. When the car headed in his direction, the officer fired his service weapon at it.

In a town where everyone knows everyone else, Lackman says "the cop knew where the other guy lived. He could have gone to his house to arrest him. He didn't have to have a shootout."

The officer was eventually fired and the dust settled. No word on the drunk driver.

Other than an occasional drunk and very rare shootout (that does not include the jealous lover shootings), the town is usually fairly quiet. At the monthly town council meetings, there are discussions on trash pick-up, recycling, snow removal and the never ending debate on traffic coming through at breakneck speed.

And what does the mayor of Middleburg earn in compensation for all of this? How about $1,000 per year? And worth every penny, no doubt.

Kay Colgan makes Middleburg tick, too. She creates a lot of heavy breathing in town and it's all legal. "Step touch, step touch, grapevine right, grapevine left." The group of women lined up in front of the mirrors at the diminutive Middleburg Fitness Center includes some who are thin and some who are well…not so thin. On any given day, participants could include Olympic equestriennes, a member of the duPont family, a bank teller or school teacher. The camaraderie is contagious.

It doesn't matter. The goal here is the same. Sweat.

Kay started teaching choreographed aerobics over twenty years ago. "This was not my chosen career," she says. "However, once I was involved, it became my happy spot."

In her role as a personal trainer, Kay's first client was Anne Lackman's 91-year-old father-in-law, William Lackman Sr. "Since then I have become the manager of Middleburg Fitness and train approximately 20-25 clients a week."

She is certified by the American Council on Exercise and the National Professional Trainers Association. She also has an undergraduate degree counseling from Old Dominion University. In between, she teaches just about every kind of fitness class--low impact, high impact, step, double step, slide, boxing, yoga, stretching, body sculpting, senior classes, children and the latest rage, Pilates.

"The only class I have not taught is spinning," she says. "Fitness is not about a certain size, it is about being healthy. Some of my clients have done the most amazing things or traveled to the most fascinating places. One of my clients in particular who is a fantastic athlete, but modest, showed the world what she could do in England in a very large and well-respected three-day event. I just think it's amazing the level of focus and perseverance that these athletes have."

Another client was headed for the Olympics.

"I would see her in the gym working out so focused and committed.I think the level of commitment that she had is staggering. She went to the Olympics, but it would not be her turn.I think she knows, even though she did not compete, she's a true success."

Kay's background in counseling comes in handy, she says, "You know there are so many clients who at times were met with the pressures of life and they needed to talk and I thank God that I was there to listen.Ninety percent of my position is listening. I have made a lot of friends with this business.We might not socialize or be a part of each other's life in that way, but we are connected."

Tucker Withers was living in suburban Maryland when he read an ad in the Sunday classified section of *The Washington Post* about a house for rent in Aldie for $800. "It was just after Halloween," he explains. "My girlfriend and I had gone out as a brick and a brick layer. I got drunk that night and she kicked me out. I thought I would move to the country."

Tucker's career to this point had been… shall we say… varied. He's been a census taker, a bartender in the Bahamas and worked as pizza maker in Alaska. He also worked on the Finance Committee to Re-Elect President Nixon in 1972 during the Watergate era. "I had to solicit money on the telephone," he says. "And the question people would ask me was, 'Don't you have enough money yet?' And my answer was always, 'We haven't met our goal yet.'"

Tucker ended up buying an old house in Aldie. "I put up $5,000 and my payments were $500." He started an antique shop on the ground floor and lived upstairs. Business boomed. He now owns ten buildings in Aldie and runs the Little River Inn as a bed and breakfast. He's known as "The Mayor of Aldie," even though there is no such official position. He entertains guests with stories and history of the area. For breakfast he whips up a batch of his famous Dutch Apple Babies—a popover with apples, pecans and raisins.

And he's had some interesting guests along the way. For example, he can now divulge that: one former Middleburg business owner, who left town in the dead of night to avoid paying a long list of creditors, had a standing Wednesday afternoon reservation with a man from Washington. No one has seen or heard from her since.

In June, 1991, Bill Clinton and Paul Tsongas were guests at the Inn. They both signed the register, which Tucker proudly displays. They were in Middleburg for a political pow-wow at Pamela Harriman's. "They sat at separate tables the next morning during breakfast," Tucker says.

"There were two other women with Clinton, they didn't sign the book," Tucker says, noting, "they stayed upstairs in one room with a shared bath down the hall and Clinton stayed on that floor too, with a private bath."

Then there was the time a well-known Washington television journalist and his wife came for a weekend getaway and the antique bed collapsed. "Thank God they didn't get hurt," Tucker says, always smiling. He fancies Hawaiian shirts and wears Bermuda shorts 90 percent of the time, no matter the weather, the occasion or the season.

In his off time, he performs for the Middleburg Players, putting a realistic touch to the role of Oscar Madison in "The Odd Couple." He plays poker in a weekly game with a couple of real estate types, a retired banker and a former policeman, just like Oscar. That's how he's made so many successful real estate deals in Aldie. And, on his poker game and his inn, Tucker likes to tell everyone, "I favor a full house."

Toby Merchant dispenses prescriptions, home remedies and sage medical advice. Add to that the latest jokes and up-to-date news and information from near and far, from behind the front counter of The Plains Pharmacy ever since he arrived in the late 1960s, fresh out of pharmacy school at The Medical College of Virginia.

A native of Manassas, about 15 miles east on Route 66, Merchant, now In his early 60s, settled in the tiny town mostly because he happened to be watching the nightly news one evening. In particular, he was riveted by story about a major fire in The Plains set off when a train hit a tanker truck carrying 15,000 gallons of diesel fuel. The resulting hellish blaze burned down most of the town.

A friend told him not long after the fire that the pharmacy had not been destroyed, and that the woman who owned the business was looking to sell. "I went up that weekend to visit my father in Manassas, and I went out to The Plains, which was still smoking," Merchant says. "I talked to the lady, and I bought it. It even had a lunch counter."

The previous owners also enforced a policy in those days of not serving blacks, but Merchant would have none of that. "I opened it to African-Americans the first day we opened the doors," he says. "It was the best decision I ever made. I wasn't going to wait for the law to tell me it was the right thing to do. I knew it was the right thing to do."

In those days, ice cream sandwiches, coffee and Cokes went for a nickel, low even for the late 1960s. A few weeks of shelling out more for his food products than he was taking in, "Doc" Merchant, as he is known far and wide, decided to raise the prices on all of the above to a dime.

"The second day I did it, a guy came in with his own cup of coffee and sat down at the counter," Merchant laughs. "He said 'you came down here from Manassas and all you did was double the price on everything.' We kept the counter open for a few more years, but it really wasn't worth it. We had a marble counter and everything, but I decided to put it out on the street. Pretty good piece of marble, but somebody took it, and that was that."

In 1971, Merchant took a telephone call from a woman living in nearby

Marshall, six miles up the road, who had congestive heart failure and needed oxygen right away. He arranged to buy the oxygen in Manassas and personally delivered the equipment to administer it. Soon word had spread that the pharmacy could provide similar services, and before long, Merchant was on to something big. "I was getting calls from everywhere," he recalls. "I hired a respiratory therapist, and we starting branching out."

Now, in addition to the pharmacy, Merchant has a thriving medical supply and therapy business known as Convaless. He will deliver and provide medical support people to handle oxygen, IVs and other therapies, including nutrition, in addition to selling or renting home hospital beds, wheelchairs or any other medical equipment for the home or office.

A few pre-Viagra years ago, one of the hottest selling items was a product known as "Erectaid." Feel free to fill in the blanks.

Merchant and his wife Barbara, a former school teacher and mother of three grown children and grandmother of one precious boy named Will, now run an operation that has 47 employees, including oldest son Fewell. The company services 17 Virginia counties, ranging from Green County near Charlottesville to Virginia's Northern Neck and 60 miles west to Woodstock. Still, Doc Merchant also remains committed to the pharmacy. In an age of burgeoning drug store conglomerates and supermarkets that peddle pills right next to the Pepsi display, he spends more than his fair share of time filling prescriptions that always include detailed written instructions on how to take the medicine and possible side effects.

But Doc Merchant does his best work with his mouth, and his head. Never mind serious brain surgery in the mid-1990s to remove what turned out to be a benign tumor. He has fully recovered and remains a valuable source of medical information, including homeopathic and home remedies—as well as a modern day town crier, with news bulletins available on a daily basis.

His customers range from farm workers to horse grooms to the titans of commerce, government, media and industry who often come in for a chat. Willard Scott, Robert Duvall and a cast of thousands are regulars, and they can still get a reasonably priced Coke out of the fridge. It's not a nickel, or even a dime, but, it's well worth the ensuing priceless inevitable chat with Doctor Merchant.

For most of the last four decades, Morgan Dennis—it does of course, rhyme with tennis—has been teaching, playing or setting up matches for members of the Middleburg Tennis Club, a mile from the Post Office but not quite so public. The club used to be located only a few blocks away from the middle of town, essentially in the backyard of Middleburg builder Bud Morency.

Dennis grew up in nearby Warrenton and showed up as a college student (North Carolina) to give lessons in 1965. There were only two hard courts, a tiny changing room and one unisex toilet for the then 30 members.

With a few brief interludes, including one to work as a pari-mutuel clerk at Gulfstream and Delaware Park, Dennis has been involved either as a club builder and contractor, teaching pro, waiter, bartender or general manager of a club that now boasts 300 members and a waiting list to join. He's a fabulous player himself, learning the game while spending summers in Cape Cod where his father Wesley Dennis, the great illustrator and artist (*Misty of Chincoteague*), often got his inspiration.

Middleburg has no full service country club per se complete with 18-hole golf course, lunch and dinner dining, workout area and plush locker room. The original founders of the club at its current site did think about including golf at the time. Instead, they simply decided to focus on tennis, and there are now six outdoor clay courts and three more inside the barn-like gray building that also houses a rather sparse and eclectically furnished dining area, pro shop, locker rooms and clubhouse.

At the epicenter of it all is Morgan Tennis, err Dennis—the patient soul (save for rowdy toddlers) who makes it all somehow work. Sweet 16 party, rehearsal dinner or wedding reception (including his own)? Call Morgan. Need a certain special brand of champagne and 100 flutes for your Christmas or New Year's Eve party? Call Morgan. Size 12 1/2 Triple E tennis shoes? Call Morgan.

To most of the hard-core tennis-playing members, his very best work comes when they call him at noon to wonder if there's a game open at 4:30 or 6. Dennis almost always manages to find a spot on such short notice, and more important, in a game compatible with that player's skill level. He has a remarkable knack for seeing a player hit three strokes and knowing immediately whether he or she belongs in an A game, or back with the Bs and Cs.

Morgan's most frenetic time of the year comes between January and early spring, with the club's much anticipated major championship doubles tournament for men and women. Virtually every tennis playing member is involved in an event that pairs players of vastly different skills and drives Dennis crazy trying to schedule matches around members' busy work and winter vacation schedules.

Jeff Austin, a Washington sports agent and former touring professional whose sister, Tracy, was a mega-star in the 1980s, is always partnered with a mostly rank beginner or someone who almost never plays. He's allowed only one serve, and has to play with an old-style wooden racket.

Morgan's teams, whether it's an A plus C partnership, or a B-minus with a B, invariably produce tight, tense matches, often witnessed by rowdy spectators watching the main court behind the dining area windows overlooking the action. Great shots are accompanied by spirited raps on the glass viewing area from wives, children and friends.

The tournament is always the talk of Middleburg while it's going on, with the inevitable "how did you do?" or "who's your next opponent?" dominating cocktail party conversation—often even ahead of horse talk—for months.

In February, 2000, members of the club, if they already didn't know it, learned just how valuable Morgan was to enriching their lives. He was diagnosed with a brain tumor, as well as lung cancer, and underwent major life-threatening surgery followed by radiation and chemotherapy that cost him his hair, but not his fighting spirit.

Friends arranged for him to be treated at the famed M.D. Anderson hospital in Houston, and Morgan took an extended leave of absence from the club, but not from his countless pals. Many members visited, called, wrote, sent food, flowers, cards and goodie baskets to he and his effervescent wife Sue, even when they lived in a Houston apartment following the surgery.

When he was released from M.D. Anderson, he was still using oxygen after an operation on his lung and was told he could not fly back on a commercial airline. Instead, member and Middleburg resident Bob Rosenthal, founder of one of Washington's largest car dealerships, dispatched his private plane—a Gulfstream 2—to Houston to pick up Sue and Morgan and fly them back to Virginia. Several friends were on board when it landed in Texas and accompanied them back home.

Several months later, Dennis was able to go back to work part-time. It's always been a labor of love anyway, and his mere presence behind the bar or—as always, on the telephone—provided great joy to one and all. He's now back to full health and cancer free and can't say enough about the support he received not only from club members, but from all around the community. "People have been so good to us," he says, his voice cracking with emotion. "I can't begin to thank everyone who wrote or called. I've got a bucket of cards at home that'll take years to answer. I just have to get my full health back, and I'm just so happy to be alive."

WHY DID WE LOSE
SO MUCH IN 44 YEARS?

JOHNNIE T. SMITH

In 1938, I became a citizen in the town of Middleburg. I found that it was an "open town" for Negroes. The blacks had a barber shop, restaurants, pool room, and later on two licensed beauty shop operators, Jessie Cook and Mollie Smith, owner. Also in town were a blacksmith shop, owned and operated by John Wanzer. Willy N. Hall, a third-generation general contractor was the only eligi¬ble contractor who could bid on the remodeling of the Leesburg hospital (Loudoun Memorial Hospital), which involved one million dollars of federal funds.

There were three private cabs in Middleburg, John Moten, of 45 years service, Albert Bushrod, and James "Jimmy" Robert; two roofers or tinners, C.P. Cook and Son, partners (C.P. Cook, Sr., deceased and C.P. Cook, Jr., retired) and Theodore "Bully" Bolden; one shoe repair shop, Clardon Fisher, owner; two cleaning and pressing shops, Carl and Pauline Dawson, partners and George Turner. Later on, there were two general contractors, partners Charles Turner and Edward "Sonny" Date, and William Jackson; one painting contractor, Moses Grayson; one tailor, Madison "Mack" Taylor, who specialized in riding clothes; one chair mender (cane), Armisted Smith; and two baseball teams (male and female). On the male team presently from Shiloh, were Charles "Jack" Turner and on the female team, Dorothy Turner and Sybil Hall.

On the 30th of May and the 4th of July holidays, the blacks had a parade, which involved mostly the Odd Fellows, Elks, and Household Ruths, marched through the town of Middleburg; horse racing and baseball games at Hall's Park, land was owned by W. N. Hall. Joe Louis, the World's heavyweight champ, showed up at one of the events, which was a pleasant surprise for all.

The Marshall Street Community Center was built (by Mrs. Howell Jackson) and turned over to the blacks to operate as they saw fit for $1 a year. After $1,500 was raised by the blacks, it was fun for all. I know because I was among the few. Charles "Jack" Turner is the only charter member now on the Board and he has a hard time getting a forum to hold a meeting.

The county built Banneker School, then the elementary school for blacks. One principal and six teachers were placed there. I raised the money to buy the refrigerator, stove and etc. for the kitchen. It was quite

Why Did We Lose
So Much in 44 Years? *(cont'd.)*

a bit of fun at election time for the PTA (Parents Teachers Association) President, like politics today, we loved it.

A few years ago, the Middleburg Bank opened its doors for the first time to allow the blacks to buy stock. Only a few bought them then. Of course, that gave us a chance to sit in the Stock Meeting and find out what was going on.

There was one doctor, general practitioner Dr. Maurice Edmead. He lived in Middleburg for many years. He then moved to Washington and practiced there until he died a few years ago. Many people from Middleburg continued to be a patient of his in D.C.

Shiloh had a very good men's singing group, under the leadership of Rev. Chambers. Charles "Jack" Turner was a product of that group.

The blacks still have their two churches and cemetery. The cemetery is nearly full, only single graves for sale. The Cemetery Committee has money but cannot buy any more land becausee the property adjoining the present plot is not for sale or cannot be bought. Members of the Cemetery Committee are Richard Washington, Philip Cook, Glanwood Moore, Charles Turner, David Fisher, and Johnnie Smith, Sr.

There are about 12 black people employed in the town of Middleburg. The blacks are no longer moving into town. The houses that are being built range from $90,000 or more and that is out of reach. Our sons and daughters move out of town after their education and that seems to hurt our two churches. But what can you say?

Today we can only look to Shiloh and Ashbury for some kind of leader¬ship, if that is possible.

We have Charles "Jack" Turner as Town Councilman, election comes up in two months. If you are not registered to vote and if you don't vote we may lose him. Philip Cook represents the School Board for Mercer District. He is appointed by the County Supervisor. Today, we have one teacher, no cabs, no restaurants, no beauty shops, no contractors, no pool room, no cleaning and pressing shops, no strong worker in the NAACP, no vacant land, no Elks Lodge, and if Charles "Jack" Turner retires, I am afraid the Marshall Street Community Center will close.

Our future looks bleak. Let's help our fellow man so that we may be as strong as we were 44 years ago. Thank you.

CHAPTER 6

HORSE TALES

Nina Fout won a bronze medal in the three-day event team competition at the 2000 Olympic games in Sydney.

*T*his is how it all starts…

With a pony. But you also need a little girl to go with the pony.

Meet Katie Aldrich, age nine. She loves ponies. She eats, sleeps and breathes ponies. The night before a horse show, she lays out all her clothes on the bed: jodhpurs, boots and navy blue jacket. She can't sleep. She won the Walk-Trot class at the big Upperville Colt and Horse Show; there were a gazillion other little girls in there, too. But this one is a standout.

In the fall, she gets up on most Saturdays and Sundays at five in the morning to go fox hunting. She usually rides a little gray pony called Moonraker, her favorite at Mrs. Dillon's stable where she takes lessons several times a week.

When asked how the hunt went one day, her response was short, matter of fact and to the point. "Went fast, fell off twice."

She recalls losing a stirrup going over a coop. (That's also called a chicken coop). The coop was part of a double jump, called an in-and-out, which refers to going in and out of the various fields around here. By the time the hunt was over that day, she went over those two jumps three more times.

Katie and her mother, Jennifer Aldridge, took up riding back in Princeton, N.J. just before moving to Middleburg in 1997. "We knew we would be riding here," Katie says one early morning. It is still dark outside and I am driving her to the barn. She is going out with the Middleburg Orange County Beagles on this Sunday. Her mother also will be riding, but will meet her there. "I hope the jumps aren't too high today," she says, concerned about the height on behalf of her mother. "She's a bit scared," she whispers to a friend.

But not Katie. At four and a half feet and 60 pounds, she is the quintessential little pony girl. She is blond with a smile from here to eternity. She cleans her tack and washes the pony, brushes the pony and then goes home and begs her mother to buy her another pony.

And what does her mother say about this?

"She says no," Katie reports. "And then I say, Pleazzzzzzzzze."

Katie takes lessons at "Mrs. Dillon's." This is the riding stable in nearby Philomont where a good portion (hundreds) of the young equestrian population around Middleburg has learned to ride over the last 35 years.

Mrs. Dillon is Nancy Dillon. Her father, Sam Graham, was a leading horse breeder. He had as many as 100 horses on his Tranquility Farm near Purcellville. She and her sister Barbara broke all the horses and he sold about 30 or 40 a year. They also went fox hunting and through their horse pursuits became friendly with the late entertainer Arthur Godfrey and his family. Godfrey also had a farm in Virginia and would travel to Florida in the winter. Nancy went along on several occasions with his daughter, Patty Godfrey. She has old photos of herself next to a sailfish she once caught in the ocean near Miami.

During the same era, she first met "Jackie [Kennedy], before she was married," Nancy says. It's a relationship that lasted many years. For now, when Caroline Kennedy Schlossberg brings her daughters to Virginia to ride, they hook up with Mrs. Dillon.

Nancy graduated from Mary Washington College in 1958 and started out teaching high school math. The very next year, she married William Dillon, a teaching golf professional also known as Bill or Billy. "Daddy said if we had a small wedding he would give us the land," she says during a rare mid-morning break. He gave them 50 acres. At the time, there were only two old stone chimneys on the property. They named it Chimney Hill Farm, used the old stones to build the house and through the years have expanded to 120 acres, chock full of horses, ponies and about 40 miniature aspiring Olympic equestrians.

"My kids were hunting, they were about five or six," she recalls. "And others begged me to teach their kids to ride. I had to buy ponies and make [finish] them and start giving lessons. We put the mileage on the ponies and then we could blame ourselves if it didn't work."

But it did work and Mrs. Dillon has been teaching ever since. Lessons are $25 with extra costs for hunting, showing and transportation. If you own your own pony, there are board bills, vet bills and shoeing costs. She has a good philosophy about instruction. The children learn to do it all, foxhunting, a bit of showing and cross-country riding. They have to go in the field and catch the pony, brush the pony, tack them up, pick out their feet, ride them and then wash them. They even learn the somewhat unpleasant task of cleaning the sheath (rhymes with Venus). They bring their lunch and eat in the hayloft or under a tree. In the summer, the kids are rewarded with a daily dip in her pool.

"I want them to really learn to ride," she explains. "We don't tell them how many strides between jumps like some of these automatic-type computer show ponies."

And she encourages neatness in their dress in the hunting field, too. When she arrives at the hunt or a horse show with two trailer loads of ponies, there are children hanging out of the windows of the trucks. Each one goes about the task of getting ready. There are no grooms waiting on these children. "One judge told me out of 30 kids in the class, he could tell which ones were mine, by their legs and their back and they way they sit."

They are known as Dillon riders.

She is a hard worker. Her weathered face reflects hours in the sun and her hands ache with arthritis. Her daughter, Daphne Alcock, helps, and granddaughters Tiffany and Kristen ride, too. In this family there is no choice but horses. All day long, Mrs. Dillon is teaching, riding, fetching, washing saddle pads, helping with the saddle soap. She also is very devoted to attending church every Sunday. She is strict about manners, vocabulary and attitude. For example, if children misbehave, they might not be allowed to go on that long-anticipated trail ride.

"I don't care how good a rider someone is. I want a good attitude and I want them to learn responsibility. It's not about who wins."

""Mrs. Dillon's" son-in-law, Graham Alcock, is the local dentist.

A horse dentist.

He's an excellent example of how everyone who loves horses finds their niche. A native of England, Graham came to the States twenty years ago. "I came for three months and stayed," he says in a still strong British accent. He started riding on the steeplechase circuit, first in Kentucky and then in Virginia.

"I thought I wanted to train race horses," he says. "I went to Florida and New York and it didn't work." Then he tried work as a blacksmith. And one day someone asked him, "Have you ever thought about being a dentist?"

Following a one-year apprenticeship, he was in business. Now he removes the sharp edges of molars, pulls baby teeth and checks overbites of equines from Virginia to Maryland to Georgia. In the trade it's referred to as "floating the teeth." He does about ten to twelve horses a day at $50 to $100 each.

He floated the teeth of the horses for Karen and David O'Connor of The Plains, the Three Day Event Olympic medal winners in the 2000 Games In Sydney, Australia. And just like the regular dentist, he sees his clients at least twice a year.

He's so busy that his answering machine informs he only returns calls on Monday and Thursday evenings. It's a physically exhausting job, but he says "it's neat being in a perfect world. I love the horse people and I love horses. What more could you want than to get out of your car and go into a barn and be with horse people?"

"Mrs. Dillon's" sister, Barbara Graham expanded *her* horsey upbringing by training racehorses. She's worked out of Barn One at the Middleburg Training Track for over thirty years.

She broke Kentucky Derby and Preakness winner Spectacular Bid. Her own horse, Vodka Talking, was a stakes winner and in turn was the dam of Rollodka, a winner of over $500,000.

The Training Track is almost a little town by itself. It hums with routine. There are eleven barns, over 200 stalls and a 7/8-mile track. Veterinarians Calvin Rofe, Ron Bowman, Paul Diehl and Tim Weed have their offices here. Every day before dawn, trainers, exercise riders and grooms invest hours in hopes of making millions, or at least a bit of future glory.

Maybe.

For more than 50 years, horses have dominated life for 70-something Fred Fox. He's a rare commodity here at the track--a black horse trainer. For many years the only jobs available to blacks in this area have been shoveling up after the horses, grooming, walking hots or occasionally going for a gallop.

On one early morning visit, a black co-worker calls into the tack room. "Tell her how life has changed for us Fred." Most of the employees at the track are either black or Mexican. There is an unwritten "pecking order" at the Training Track, according to one source. "The old black grooms have seniority. The Mexicans and the blacks don't work well together." Hence, most trainers employ one or the other. "At least one trainer has only recently been mixing it up," says one. "But one thing is for sure. You can hire a few Mexicans on to your [all black] team, but you can't bring in one black groom when everyone else already there is Mexican."

Fox does recall when things were different around Middleburg. "I remember going places to eat in town where you couldn't. You had to go to the back door at the Greek's place if you wanted to eat," he says, referring to what was called The New York Cafe owned by Vicky and Louis Dimos. Their son, Tim Dimos, now the mayor of Middleburg, owns the building currently occupied by The Coach Stop restaurant. Mark Tate and his brother Mike own the business, which claims "Where You Will Always Meet Someone You Know."

That phrase is more than true. The restaurant has been a local favorite forever. (Try the onion rings.) But look carefully around the room when you dine here. Everyone from Linda Tripp to Tab Hunter to Liz Taylor has been spotted in the cozy booths lining one wall, or taking a quick Horseman's Special (eggs, bacon, potatoes juice and coffee for $5.50).

But back to Fred. He went to school through the seventh grade at a little crossroads called Willisville. He started work at age 18 in Upperville at Paul Mellon's farm. Then he moved on to "Mr. C.V. B. Cushman's, taking care of field hunters." After that he went to work for James L. Wiley, a well-known and respected local horseman, then for his son Lewis S. Wiley. "I broke horses and galloped them," he says.

In 1955, he got his trainer's license. He saddled many winners for the Wileys in West Virginia, Maryland and Delaware. "I won a lot of races," he says, sitting in the tack room at the Training Track. There's a syringe with some sort of medication (not an unusual thing) and a training chart on the desk. The walls are lined with bridles and breastplates with the familiar scent of clean tack. "These are the best people I ever worked for. They treat us, my wife and I, like one of the family." He does not want to confirm that the Wiley family recently gave him a brand new truck. "They are just that kind of way," he says. "They like to keep things low key."

Now that Fred has retired from the Wileys, he has one horse of his own to train. He walks to the stall door at barn number eight. Dawn That Buck pins his ears back a bit. "He bites," Fred warns. "He's a really pretty gray horse," he continues, explaining that he claimed him for $5,000 at Charles Town, just over the West Virginia border 45 minutes from the Training Track. "I ran him back Sunday past in an allowance race. He ran a big race and finished third. When I run him back, I think he'll win." (Remember…Future Glory)

But Fred Fox has another career around Middleburg.

He leads the gospel-singing Middleburg Harmonizers.On the second Sunday in October and on Mother's Day, he and seven others perform at the Middleburg Community Center to a sellout crowd. They sing songs such as "What A Friend We Have in Jesus" and "I Got Jesus and That's Enough." In 1981, they made an album, "Going With Jesus."

He leads the big gray horse back to the barn and pauses before entering the shed row to stomp out his cigarette. "Doesn't that smoking affect your singing?"

"Oh, no," he says. "I learned to sing from my stomach."

Forty-something Helen Richards is an exercise rider at the Training Track. She is carrying her tack back to the tack room one early autumn morning.She could be the pony girl all grown up. Her long, blond ponytail hangs down from under her hard helmet. She wears chaps and black knit gloves with the tips of the fingers cut off.

"I started galloping when I was 18 and rode races for 15years," she explains. She won a few races as a jockey and mentions an allowance race at Delaware Park. She eventually knew it was time to quit race riding and came to Middleburg.

Each morning she gets on three to eight horses, maybe more. She gets paid $10 a head. "Some riders here make $250 a day, but I can't say who," she explains, adding that they get paid in cash.

She sees Carlos Canino, another exercise rider, across the way. They call out and greet one another. His horse is jogging sideways back to the barn. The steam is coming off the horse this crisp dawn. It's somewhat romantic, especially early in the morning, a photographer's paradise.

On any given day, Helen might be asked to school a young horse in the starting gate. "They need to get used to it," she says. Or she might gallop another for "one or two miles." And then there's the breeze, the full-throttle all-out zoom. In the afternoons, she's involved in buying and selling show horses. And she also points out that she no longer works in the winter.

Through the years she has broken her collarbone twice, ankle once, back twice and nose once. But, she says, "the thing that hurt the most was when I broke my little finger. Everyone is going to break something. You know it's going to happen, it goes with the territory."

Down Millville Road, a dirt road along the back of the Training Track, Irishman John McCormack is leading Lassie's Key, a four-year-old, for her early morning workout. The big brown mare looks around a bit. She puts her head down to have a closer look.And then she slowly walks down a ramp into the indoor swimming pool.

She slides into the 75-degree water with ease. As he walks around the side of the 30 by 50-foot pool, she snorts. There's a steady rhythm to her snorts. After about four laps, she comes out for a rest. A typical program will be 10 to 30 laps, with 10 laps equal to about a one-mile gallop.

Roger Collins owns the Middleburg Equine Swim Center. He came to Middleburg in 1989, like so many others looking for a little farm with a place for a couple of horses. He couldn't find what he wanted. "It was impossible in our price range," he explains, sitting in his kitchen. There are three black Labradors in the room, and one is snoring loudly. There's a cat sleeping nearby, too. There are left-over breakfast dishes filling the sink. All this is a very common sight with working horse people. The house is the least priority.

Roger commutes to work in Maryland at the American Red Cross in diagnostic manufacturing. The idea of a swimming pool for horses appealed to him. It was a way to supplement income and the rehabilitation aspect was in keeping with his profession in diagnostic manufacturing.

Not really knowing anything about swimming horses, he dove right in. The pool had been built in the late 1970s by Randy Waterman (now one of the Masters of the Piedmont Hunt, with much more on him later) and needed work. "When I tried to call him to find out where the pipes were buried, he never returned my calls," Roger says, adding that he replaced filters and did some refurbishing.

"It wasn't open to the general public. I wanted to make it a paying operation." So now, for $12 a dip or a book of ten swims for $100, many of the trainers take advantage of the facilities with about 20 horses a day wading in.

"It's an alternative exercise," says trainer Don Yovonovich. "It's good for the lungs and heart and better than being on hard ground. It's useful if you know how to use it."

The majority of the horses swim for conditioning, as a supplement to the groundwork, to keep them fit. "We are determined that we can replace 60 percent of the ground work," Yovonovich says. "There is a significant impact on the ground and on a sound disposition. The less ground work, the less chance of injury from galloping." About 30 to 40 percent of the horses come in for rehab after an injury. He has seen "miraculous recovery."

John McCormack leads the mare up the ramp and out of the pool. She shakes off and yawns. He hoses her off and says "she's bred to the hilt, you know."

Perhaps for... future glory.

The first thing anyone would say about Snowden Clarke is that he is sooooo gorgeous. He's eye candy--over six feet tall, a svelte 170 pounds, with twinkling turquoise blue eyes. Whether he's dressed in riding attire, blue jeans or for a dinner party he looks as if he just walked off the pages of *Women's Wear Daily*. And that's not so farfetched either. He'sappeared in several major magazines.

All this and he has a devilish sense of humor, too.He is also a fine horseman. And he's gay.

It's hard to write about horses and especially horse showing without mentioning the gay population. "I think it has to do with the pageantry," he says one early warm fall afternoon over coffee on the deck at Magpie Café. "Someone once said, it takes a pretty person to make a beautiful thing. I do think that birds of a feather flock together."

All that aside, he also runs a successful show horse stable. Though he insists his success is erratic, he's also expanding his horizons, which we will get to in a minute.

"My grandfather had horses and ponies," he says, explaining how he learned to ride. "He bought me a Dartmoor pony.He was wild right off the moors. All he did was kick, bite and shit."Despite all that, Snowden liked riding.

Eventually, his mother built a stall for his pony, Skuttle, in her garage in suburban Washington. "We had to keep him tethered on a rope," he recalls. By the time he got to high school, Snowden was knee deep in horses. "On the weekends I would go to Warrenton and ride." He also was often skipping school. In his senior year, he departed before finishing and went off to England to ride.

He stayed nine years and had several jobs, including one that took him to the Royal Mews in Ascot with Alison Oliver, who trained for Princess Anne. "I made 12 pounds a week and got to muck as many stalls as I wanted. I cleaned tack and rode three days week.

"Eventually, it was time to come home," says the 40-ish Snowden. There was never any question it would be Middleburg. He returned to breaking and training horses. "I like getting something unproven and finding out what makes it tick."

He sells his horses for $45,000 to $200,000, but says the income fluctuates and the expenses are high: rent, help, hay, insurance etc. "It's like Monopoly money. First you have a lot of it and then you don't." He recently had knee surgery and wears two copper bracelets and a third one in multi-colors "for stress."

In his off time, he rides in the gay rodeos, which led to his recent venture into television. He formed Out of the Box Productions and is producing a cable television series on worldwide travels for gay adventures.

"I preview events. If there is going to be a rock climbing expedition, then I go to the place, take a lesson and shimmy up the pole and talk about it."

He sits back. He is wearing sexy sunglasses. "The idea just came to me. It's all sort of a la George Plimpton."

Better yet—a la Snowden Clark.

Mairead Carr came to Middleburg from her native Ireland "by boat" after answering an ad in the British equestrian publication, *Horse and Hound*. Someone was looking for a rider to school hunters and jumpers.

"I didn't even know where Virginia was," she says. She was 18 at the time. "When I found out it was near Washington, D.C. I was thrilled. My whole country is the size of this county."

That was more than 20 years ago. Now she's a steeplechase trainer, but her career path has been arduous and difficult.

But, she persevered.

Mairead started out riding hunters and after several years turned to galloping thoroughbreds at the Training Track. The facility is a starting point for very young horsewomen, in case you haven't noticed.She's a strong, tough woman and can handle difficult horses to boot.She made$200 to$250 a week and she says she did that "for ages." All the while she lived in a cottage with no heat.She had a wood stove and paid $150 a month rent. "It was the most rent I ever paid," she says. "I've always been very lucky here, especially if I didn't want anything like heat." Sometimes that $150 was hard to come by, but, she persevered.

She slowly struck out on her own. First she rented a small barn at Beaver Dam Farm, then owned by the late Aileen duPont. She had a few steeplechase horses and some hunters. She moved to a cottage at Needmore Farm owned by Sheila and Dick Riemenschneider (for the record, since then divorced). Again, no heat, just a small stove.

"They were very kind to me," Mairead says. "They treated me like family." Once or twice a month she would go up to their house for dinner and was an invited guest at Thanksgiving and Christmas, as well.

One fall day in 1989, Mairead was out riding with Kevin Dougherty on his farm off the Atoka Road. They passed a little tenant house. "He told me 'if one more person asks me to rent this piece of shit, I'm going to tear it down'" she says. "And I told him 'don't do that, sell it to me.' It looked like a trailer without wheels." She took out a wall and added a bedroom, painted the interior walls and, of course, she added heat, "a major step up" she says.

Not long after that, a client had the idea of asking all her friends on the Atoka Road to buy a steeplechase horse in a syndicate for Mairead to train. Everyone up and down the five-mile road was approached and soon they were in business. "It's a funny thing but when someone relocated, they came in, too," she says.

The original group of 14 invested $650 each and everyone pays $145 maintenance a month. "That has never changed," she adds.They all show up at the point-to-point races and steeplechases and have a ball. They come to the paddock and cheer and always have a big tailgate. When their horse wins, they put the proceeds in the bank to buy a new horse.

"It does limit their spending on a new horse," she explains. "It was never meant to work that way. A $7,500 horse should run against one that is of the same value. But sometimes we end up running against a $50,000 horse that has won stakes races. But they have fun."

The "Hunt Country Stable Syndicate" has won many times, including victories at the Fairfax Races and the Blue Ridge Point-to-Point. They have owned four horses through the years. When the horses retire from racing, they donate them to the U.S. Park Police. "They are all walking around the national monuments downtown," she says. They currently own an eight-year-old brown gelding called Honest Ricky.

There has only been one glitch. One member of the group is elected annually to handle the money. One year, the "treasurer" held up the transfer of funds for the purchase of a new horse, for no apparent reason. "He kept asking for a bill of sale," Mairead says. "But we couldn't produce one until we paid for the horse. Eventually another member of the group had to quickly buy the horse [and get reimbursed] or we would have lost him."

Needless to say that member was quickly excommunicated. "He kept showing up at the picnics and they finally had to ask him not to come anymore," she says.

Many horsewomen have similar stories....

Leah Palmer is long (5-9) and lanky (123 pounds, with her riding boots on) and 30-something and single. She started riding at age 12 back in New Jersey. She lives, eats and breathes horses. Ditto for Betty Douglas, who has a stable full of ladies who ride. They're all living out the dreams of our little girl, Katie Aldrich.

Born and raised in Virginia, with parents who were deeply involved in the horse world, there was just no way Nina Fout wasn't going to turn out to be an equestrienne. The big question was how far could she rise?

Try Olympic equestrienne.

As in bronze medal in the Three-Day Event team competition at the 2000 Sydney Olympics. Teammates Karen and David O'Connor claimed The Plains as their official base, but they didn't grow up here. Their sponsor, Jackie Mars (as in Mars Bars), maintains a farm in the area.

Nina's father, Paul, has trained racehorses in Middleburg for over 40 years. A former publisher of Spur Magazine, he is responsible for Alfred Hunt's hurdle winner, Prince's Image, and Peggy Steinman's Col Star, the winner of the Flower Bowl Handicap at Belmont, and Don Panta. He's also well-known in the steeplechase world as the trainer of Virginia Guest Valentine's famous hurdler, Life's Illusion, the only filly ever to win the coveted Eclipse Award. He also was instrumental in putting together the 1977 purchase of the Middleburg Training Track, then owned by Paul Mellon.

Nina's mother, Eve, is a lifelong equestrian and the major force behind the Middleburg Orange County Beagles. Nina's brother, Doug, also trains racehorses, and his wife, Beth, runs a hunter barn and watches their twins, Dun and Caroline. A sister, Virginia, lives and works in the technology field in California. A friend describes the family as "highly competitive."

We are on the deck at Magpie Café. Nina is just back from the Olympics and several people stop to offer congratulations. She went to New Zealand alone for a week's vacation after the Games, visiting friends and fly-fishing. Extremely independent, she immediately offers that she is "disheartened" that organizers of a victory parade in her hometown of The Plains couldn't wait a week for her to return. They went ahead with the festivities without her, with the O'Connors the focal point of the parade and all the pictures in the local papers.

She orders a Diet Coke with no ice and a slice of lemon. In her 40s, she knows what she wants. Her Jack Russell Terrier, Pip, has joined us. He puts his head on the table. Pip bears a striking resemblance to the famous television canine, Eddie, on Frazier. "He missed me," she says, adding that "he's also "F-A-T."

Three-Day event competition could very well be among the most demanding of Olympic sports. The first phase is dressage--a ballet on horseback with intricate, subtle movements-- followed by a grueling gallop over solid and deceptive fences, ditches and water. The final day of stadium show jumping seems tame compared with the other parts. It's not for the faint of heart.

"Growing up in the area in a family that's horsey and involved in many facets--pony club, fox hunting and racing--it was my personal pursuit to get into eventing," she says. "It was a natural extension of pony club." She also rode sidesaddle, a handful of timber races and did some lower level show jumping. "It made me a well rounded horse person."

She was always "aware of the peaks and valleys" of the horse business. "I never wanted to do horses 24/7. I wanted a career. I spent most of my life juggling the two." In her non-horsey life, she owned The Sporting Gallery of Art, a retail shop and framing service in Middleburg. As her business grew over 16 years, "so did the workload." Eventually something had to give and just four months before the Olympics, she closed the shop. Her Olympic aspirations were getting closer.

"It all has required an enormous amount of discipline," said a friend. "She did it as an amateur and without a financial angel."

She calls her horse "Beans"; his real name is Three Magic Beans. "The first time I sat on him I knew he was world class," she says. He came to her via her father and brother. Both had tried the horse at the track and over hurdles with mediocre results. She says he's talented, bold and fearless. "There isn't anything he can't do, but he can be "a bit of a juvenile delinquent." He gets agitated by applause and when caught in close quarters. "He jumps around a bit and some would consider him dangerous when he double fires with his two hind legs," she says. Whenever possible she travels with him on the airplane because "I'm a bit of a nervous ninny and want to be with him."

Like all riders, Nina has taken some tumbles, and is very matter of fact about it. "I've had a lot of broken bones, I'm a quick healer." One friend also said she doesn't know the word fear. She once broke seven ribs, had a punctured lung and a neck injury that left her with permanent damage. The slight scar in her forehead is from field hockey. "I've always loved team sports," she says. "I had always hoped to ride in the team competition." It was her final score that clinched the bronze medal in the team competition. The coach for the U.S. team was Mark Phillips, better known as the first husband of Britain's Princess Anne.

Her hair is blond and pulled back and her look includes gold hoop earrings, cell phone on the belt and a bold and bright blue and white striped shirt completing the equestrienne's clean, collegiate look.

It all hides one thing.

While at the games in Sydney she received countless corporate gifts: luggage, caps, clothing and so on. She also gave herself a present. She had a kangaroo jumping over the Olympic rings tattooed on her body, but won't even tell her family the exact location.

Another well-wisher stops. He later adds that she is "one fierce competitor." Which prompts a final question. When she was a little girl did she dream of riding in the Olympics and winning a medal?

"You can dream about that but that's only part of the equation and you have to work hard and be dedicated to meeting all the challenges ahead," she says. And you need the support of your family and friends so you have someone to share all that with."

No problem in the Fout Family.

Okay ladies, you can swoon over this one. A dashing young polo player who owns a successful vineyard.

Tareq Salahi, early 30s, is one of the most eligible bachelors in the countryside. And he's a gentleman to boot. He started riding when he was five on his parent's farm in Hume, which is about a half-hour drive west of Middleburg and deeper into the countryside. But you can spot him during the polo season at Great Meadow over in The Plains.

From ponies, he graduated to jumping and then to show jumping. He went on to ride in several Grand Prix events in Belgium, France and Germany. But at age 16, he discovered polo.

"I was introduced to it by Col. Billy West, one of the last true members of the Army Calvary," he says one late summer afternoon. He is sitting on the deck at his Oasis Vineyard, the family farm. The sun is slowly sinking in the west over the Blue Ridge Mountains. There is a gentle breeze and it's the middle of the grape harvest. It's been a good year. His cell phone goes off seven times during a 90-minute conversation.

"When I made the transition to polo I met people that I clicked with," he says. He loves competitive sports and played ice hockey in school. "Polo was my escape. I discovered friends, and the winery and polo go hand in hand."

The polo also came in handy in college. It was almost as if it was a required sport when he enrolled at the University of California-Davis to study enology and viticulture. In 1997, his father, Dirgham Salahi had already planted their first one-acre crop of grapes. "We were told we would never make it and the vines would die," he recalls of that first crop of Chardonnay, Cabernet Sauvignon and Merlot. "We were the fifth vineyard in The Dominion [local lingo for Virginia]," he says. By 2001 there were 70 such businesses.

From one acre of vines, they went to five, then 10 and then 20 and now there are 100 acres planted with all types of grapes, from Chardonnay to Riesling, Gewürztraminer and more.

An employee politely interrupts about time sheets. The cell phone rings again.

In his college class of 30 students, he met others in the family wine business--Bobbi Mondavi, Mike Sebastinai and Nina Gallo. He studied microbiology, sensory evaluation of wines, trellis systems, vineyard design and root stock selection.

And wouldn't you know it, as fate would have it, the school also had a polo team. "I joined as a freshman and we won the Intercollegiate national title three years out of five."He stayed five years to add the additional bachelors degree in business management.

Now he's moving the vineyard into the 21st Century with new technology. "In the past we didn't even have an automatic labeling machine," he says. Or designing the website, Oasiswine.com. He organizes special events and dinners--A Summer Solstice Wine and Opera, Valentine's Day Guest Chef Dinner, Murder Mystery Wine Dinner or a Mother's Day Champagne Brunch.

It's always served up with Oasis Wine, like the Chardonnay-Barrel Select fermented in new French oak and the winner (over 2,800 other entries) of a Gold Medal at the 2000 San Francisco International Wine Competition sponsored by *Bon Appétit* Magazine.

In between the vineyard, the cell phone and the special events, he often hops in his black BMW convertible and goes for a little "stick and ball" as the polo crowd says. He has played on the U.S. team against Great Britain on several occasions and has met Prince Charles. His own Oasis Polo Team has won two United States Polo Association National Arena Titles, in 1997 and 1998.

"I believe in fate and how everyone influences other lives and day to day in small things, like having a glass of wine, putting a smile on someone's face or falling in love."

Cheers.

CHAPTER 7

VULPES CINEREOARGENTEUS

Hank Woolman has been the Honorary Huntsman of the Middleburg Orange County Beagles for more than twenty years.

*T*he sport of fox hunting includes the age old ritual of blooding. Once killed, the fox is broken up and cut into fragments with a knife. "From as close to the heart as possible, the huntsman takes blood with two fingers and swipes the cheek or forehead of uninitiated riders," according to one intimately familiar with the rite.

The fox is dispatched by the hounds and efficiently killed. Sometimes he's denned or put to ground (run into a den) or treed or caught on the open ground.

"The fox weighs 12 to 15 pounds and a hound weighs 60 to 80 pounds," says one staff member. "And they usually break his neck or back in one bite. One bite would crush him. They go pretty quick. There's no fear in the fox, it's a surprise he's actually been caught. His heart pops."

The staff member also notes that kills are infrequent, if not rare. "He's gone in no time."

The master then gives the word to the huntsman as to who will have the distinction and honor of participating in the ritual "blooding."

"You can't wash it off until sundown. It's your badge you have to wear it for the day. If you do that you will always have good hunting. It's a solemn event because you know that fox will never show you sport again. It's a bittersweet moment," says one participant.

The distribution of the pads (feet), mask (face) and brush (tail) is also determined. Frequently the pads are awarded at the first kill. The mask is usually awarded to the first rider (other than the staff) to arrive at the kill.

In his autobiography, "Reflections in A Silver Spoon," Paul Mellon recounted a story about the day his wife Bunny was sitting in her car watching the hunt and a man came by and asked what was going on. "It's a fox hunt," she said. "The hounds are looking for a fox."

"Oh," the man said, apparently satisfied. Then he added, "I thought that only happened on lampshades."

Fox hunting is the inner core of life in Middleburg. It's the original glue that held this community together. Some may say that the glue is in jeopardy with the threat of development, which could endanger the necessary open space.

For now, the sport of fox hunting continues. There are five hunts in the area: Middleburg Hunt, Piedmont Fox Hounds, Orange County Hunt, Snickersville and the M.O.C. Beagles (stands for Middleburg Orange County). A fanatic— and there are a few—could go out seven days a week.

Someone once said that it's the rider's attire that gave the sport its elitist image. What the uninformed might not know is that many parts of the wardrobe are utilitarian. The white tie (which a novice might call an ascot) is known as a stock tie. It is to be used as a sling or (God forbid) a tourniquet, if necessary. It is to be held together with a simple gold pin. (No diamonds please.) Ladies are to wear simple gold stud earrings, too. If you wear hoop earrings and rush through the woods, you may end up leaving an earlobe behind. A member of the staff carries wire cutters. And some may carry a flask--to fend off the chill, of course--but a little liquid courage may also be needed. They're referred to as hounds, never dogs. The bright red jackets are called Pink coats after the man who designed them. They are also called scarlet.

For the record, there is no debate on the ethics of the hunt, as there has been in Great Britain. If there is any question about the fox being a nuisance, you should have been around when a pet duck or chicken is ripped to shreds. It's difficult to explain to a child. The only controversy around these parts through the years has come not from boundary disputes but from the personalities involved. And there have been some doozies.

Roger Collins, owner of the swim center, put it perfectly. "Fox hunting is ingrained in the society around here. But there are too many egos involved. They aren't basing it on sound policy."

One of the biggest disputes in recent memory involved the Middleburg Hunt, established in 1906 and recognized in 1908 by the official governing body of the Masters of Foxhounds Association of America. The area is about 10 by 15 miles and through the years has included land belonging to Pamela and Averill Harriman.

In 1992, a dispute erupted involving joint masters Meg Gardner and Jim Gable. Meg is the whimsical gardener featured in our chapter on the garden club ladies. Jim Gable is a highly successful orthopedic surgeon in Leesburg and an avid foxhunter. One clear, cold spring day, the members were out having a grand old run near Foxcroft School, the smart boarding school for young ladies just north of town.

"I was leading the field and my horse was going flat out at a full gallop and he collapsed in a heap," Meg says. He had a heart attack and was dead before he hit the ground. Meg fell and was knocked unconscious. Dr. Gable jumped off his horse and came to attend her. "He asked me to follow his finger, which I did from about twelve to three o'clock." She doesn't recall much, but knows she fell in and out of consciousness.

"Gable told someone to call 911," she says. And then things went from bad to worse. Gable sent Peter Hapworth for help. "Hapworth mounts up on his horse to summon help. He jumps out of the field at Foxcroft and flips off," she says. He broke a collarbone. "When the ambulance came they took Hapworth off," Meg recounts. "Then my husband drove me in the car to the hospital. We both ended up in the emergency room at Loudoun Hospital. We passed in the hall as they were wheeling us on those meat slabs." As a result of the injury, Meg decided to hang up her tack, as horse people refer to retirement. "I'd had four bad falls, stepped in a hole once, flipped over wire, fell backwards into a creek and that was enough."

She resigned as joint master. A meeting of the board of governors was called and Jeff Blue was elected as the new joint master. All of which would have been fine, except according to some, "Gable didn't like the way things were unfolding." He resigned.

Before long, Jim Gable had formed a splinter group, "Dr. Gable's Middleburg Hounds." They began to hunt the same countryside as the Middleburg Hunt. The fox fur was flying. Letters went back and forth.

On August 15, 1992 the Middleburg Hunt informed subscribers, landowners and friends that "an unauthorized or outlaw foxhunting pack" was forming. "In view of our responsibility to landowners and the preservation of the sport, the Board of Governors of the Middleburg Hunt is opposed to this encroachment."

On August 18, Robert P. Forman, first vice president of the National Beagle

Club in Aldie, wrote to Dr. Gable.

"This letter cancels my note to you of 29 July concerning your hunting foxhounds at the National Beagle Club (Institute Farm In Aldie). At the time I signed the note I was led to believe that you were still Master of the Middleburg Hunt. Regrettably, I find this assumption was incorrect. The National Beagle Club conforms to the customs, policies, and procedures of the Master of Foxhounds Association. Since Institute Farm is in the country registered to the Middleburg Hunt by the Masters Association for many, many years, it is not appropriate for us to allow any other foxhounds to hunt there without the concurrence of the Master of the Middleburg Hunt."

Wilma Warburg, a large landowner, wrote a letter to Gable dated August 26:

"I have been both amazed and shocked by the lengths you have gone to in your recent attempts to sabotage the Middleburg Hunt. I am quite unwilling to allow any other than a recognized hunt to hunt on Snake Hill land. Since the group you have chosen to label "Dr. Gable's Middleburg Hounds" is an "outlaw" or "renegade" (unrecognized) hunt, I therefore join with Duncan Read in urging you to strongly to abandon any plans you may have for operating your own hunt anywhere on the land allotted to the Middleburg Hunt."

At an October 22 meeting, The Masters of Foxhounds Association didn't even allow Gable to resign. They rejected his resignation. He was expelled. His organization was labeled as an "outlaw" pack, a powerful stigma in a sport swathed in tradition and properness.

The *Blue Ridge Leader,* a small area newspaper, printed an unsigned letter in January, 1993, that countered "The Middleburg Hunt is governed by an archaic and anachronistic constitution that makes the Board of Governors a self-perpetuating and self-approving entity, whose only criteria for membership is an invitation from the existing board to join and the payment of a large sum of money."

The letter concluded: "Dr. Gable is a valuable, responsible, highly respected and public spirited member of the community, and members of nearby hunts, knowing the facts, have chosen to ignore the prohibitions of the Masters of Foxhounds Association by continuing to hunt with the new hunt and to attend its functions."

The dust eventually settled. The Middleburg Hunt now meets on Monday, Thursday and Saturday. Jeff Blue continues as joint master with Penny Denegre.

Jim Gable is now a joint master with the Loudoun West Hunt, which ironically enough splintered off from the Loudoun Hunt in 1994. And one other non-recognized group called the Snickersville Hunt.

———

The Piedmont Fox Hounds, established in 1840 and recognized in 1899, covers about 12 by 20 miles. It boasts of deep Virginia roots, founded by Col. Richard H. Dulany of Welbourne not far from his home base near Upperville. Around here, the name Dulany is cherished.

A well known (some would say legendary) fox hunting gentleman, Harry Worcester Smith, who founded the Masters of Foxhounds Association in 1907, rode with Piedmont. His grandson, Tommy Smith, was the first American to win the British Grand National steeplechase in 1965, riding a horse named Jay Trump. Later, Joseph Thomas was a patron of Piedmont. He renovated a farm called Huntland with elaborate kennels, lodging rooms and a mansion that remains an architectural showpiece to this day.

The territory includes the land owned by the Mellon family. And it's understood that on Thursdays they often hunt in these parts. Annual subscriptions run between $1,850 for landowners to $3,500 for non-landowners. Capping fees are $150.

Randy Waterman has served as master since 1987. A devoted sportsman, one member of the community described his riding style as "roughish."

"Oh yes," says this person, "He kills the foxes, he even kills them when it's not in season."

In the late 1990s, Waterman began to share this "title" with Turner Reuter, Jr., whose business interests in Middleburg include The Red Fox Inn, Mosby's Tavern and Red Fox Fine Art. Mildred "Bucky" Fletcher Slater, an attorney in Upperville, and T. Garrick Steele, a businessman in Reston, are also listed as joint masters. These names will come into play as the latest manure-to-hit-the-fan saga unfolds. Around Middleburg, it's easy to see how everyone's path begins to cross if you stick around long enough....

One Sunday evening in April, 1999, William Katz, his wife Susie and teenage daughter, Liz, came into town for a quick dinner at The Coach Stop. Bill Katz is a vascular surgeon with a large practice in Ohio. They divide their time between Ohio and Oakfield, an 88-acre farm in Upperville, which is part of the Piedmont hunt.

They ran into several friends, as one is always apt to do at The Coach Stop. Nat Morison was there. He's an Upperville neighbor who owns the legendary Welbourne and is a great, great grandson of Piedmont hunt founder Richard Henry Dulany.Another friend, Susan Scully and her daughter, Elizabeth, joined them and later Charles Scully sat down at the booth.

Meanwhile, across the street at The Red Fox, Randy Waterman was having dinner with his mother, who was visiting. After dinner he took her up to her room at the Inn.

After dinner at about 10 p.m., the Katz family was heading west in their 1999 green Land Rover Discovery, about the same time as Waterman. Waterman was driving a 1994 green Chevrolet pickup truck. But they did not recognize him.

According to reports from Virginia state trooper Franz Mahler, when Susie Katz went to pass Waterman, his truck swerved and struck her vehicle. The Land Rover rolled over and Dr. Katz was catapulted 30 feet through the closed glass sunroof. He was flown by helicopter to the Fairfax Hospital where he spent five days in intensive care.

He had ribs broken in sixteen places, a broken shoulder bone and a rotator cuff injury.His kidneys were contused and he had difficulty breathing, not to mention 100 stitches in and about his head and face.

Mrs. Katz had a separated shoulder and abrasions on her head and neck and a concussion. Liz had a ruptured lumbar disk and glass shards in her skin.

At the time of the accident there was no way to know if Waterman was injured. He left the scene and did not call the authorities for three hours. Three months later he was indicted on felony charges of hit and run, which are still pending and could result in a five year prison sentence and a maximum $2,500 fine.

One of his attorneys in the case?

Mildred Fletcher Slater, a joint master in the hunt.

The Katz family was officially represented by the Commonwealth attorney, but also hired local legend Blair Howard to consult.

Waterman posted a $10,000 bond and the trial was set for the following January.Folks from Upperville to Aldie to Warrenton were anxiously awaiting the proceedings.Tongues were wagging at the post office and anywhere else groups gathered.People were marking it on their social calendars, planning an outing to the courthouse in Warrenton. But when the day came, a mistrial was declared when it became evident that the prosecuting attorney might be called to testify.

A new trial was set. Waterman's legal team had expanded to include Rodney Leffer. He claimed in circuit court the mistrial was flawed and another trial would constitute double jeopardy. The trial judge upheld the mistrial and the case was set to go.

Well over a year after the accident, Waterman's team appealed that decision, which was then sent to the state Court of Appeals.That body denied Waterman's appeal and that decision was appealed to the Virginia Supreme Court. Need we say more?

The case was moved to the next county where the prosecuting attorney there excused himself. And so on and so on. Meanwhile the natives were getting restless and some of the landowners were furious that Waterman was still serving in the prestigious and coveted position as master.

The Washington Post reported that "one longtime landowner in the territory, who also asked not to be identified, said that if Waterman is not removed, landowners might step in and resolve it themselves by taking down their land--withdrawing permission to hunt."

Waterman built a six-foot high chain link fence around part of his property. One prominent member of the hunt referred to it as "Jurassic Park." The Katz's closed their land and also were planning to file civil charges that could reach up to $10 million.

Then Waterman surprised everyone and announced he was pulling up stakes and moving to Alabama and taking some of the hounds with him. Friends said he was seeking larger fields to hunt. Others speculated that the move came too closely on the heels of the accident.

Still the show went on and members of the Piedmont Fox Hounds continued to go Tally Ho.

The Orange County Hunt was established in 1900 and recognized in 1902. The territory is about 16 miles by 12 miles. It's often been referred to as the tooth brush hunt, since visitors are encouraged to spend the night in the area and not just ship in for the day. The word "exclusive" also pops up quite often. Capping fees are $100 per week, $150 on weekends and holidays and annual subscription dues run $3,350 for regular members and $1,900 for grooms.

The name Orange County actually comes from the area of upstate New York near Goshen from a group that included financier Edward H. Harriman, John R. Townsend, F. Gray Griswold and J.O. Green.It's always been known as the group from "up north," as opposed to The Piedmont Hunt, which prides itself on its Virginia roots. The cold, icy winters brought them to The Plains, where they built a boarding house, kennels and stables.

Harriman would bring his private rail Pullman cars and park on the tracks. Friends and horses would make the trek. And according to reports, the train included facilities for the New York types to keep in touch with business back home. The train was parked just around the corner from what is now a restaurant called The Rail Stop, which once was owned by actor Robert Duvall, a non-fox hunter.

Many well known names have been associated with or hunted with Orange: Marshall Field, Hubert Phipps, General Billy Mitchell and a smattering of duPonts.

Ambassador Charles Sheldon Whitehouse shares the honors as master with James L. "Jimmy" Young and Joel McCleary. Young has served in this position the longest of the three.His father, Robert B. Young, was also a master and lived at Denton where Jimmy and wife Sally reside.

Jimmy revels in his role, so much so that his vanity license plate reads MFH OHC (Master of Fox Hounds Orange County Hunt). A part time writer, he has produced "Field of Horses," a compilation of equestrian photos by the late photographer Marshall Hawkins. Jackie Onassis, who often rode with Orange when she visited Virginia, wrote the forward.

McCleary came to the area when he married Lavinia Currier, a member of the Mellon family.

But back to Mr. Whitehouse. It's difficult to call him anything else. He's a dapper, distinguished, very proper gentleman. His friends call him Charlie. A reporter once called him by his first name, but it wasn't the thing to do.

Mr. Whitehouse first came to the area as a young man to visit friends of his parents.

"Back then, it was basically New Yorkers who came down here to hunt," he recalls. "They didn't live here full time, only part time. The entire Zulla Road was lined with New Yorkers, of course, you know that's how the Orange County Hunt was started. The Harrimans came down. But after World War II people started to live here full time."

At the time of our interview and several others, he sits on a floral chintz chair. Several dogs plop down--black Labs, a couple of Corgis. He doesn't wear socks and looks as if he should be walking down Worth Avenue.His wife, Janet, is an attractive, warm and gregarious woman with a perpetual twinkle in her eye.They live on a 70-acre farm with a breathtaking view of the countryside.

Leather photo albums and books line the shelves. The magazines on the coffee table include *Foreign Affairs, Harpers, The Chronicle of the Horse* and *Yachting*. His interests are wide and varied.

A graduate of Yale University, he found time each year to come to Virginia and ride and hunt. His education was interrupted by the World War II. He served in the U.S. Marie Corps from 1942 to 1946 and learned to fly. After graduating from Yale in 1947, he joined the State Department as a research analyst and made his way to Middleburg on weekends.

His Foreign Service career began in September, 1948 and until 1952 he worked as a political officer in Belgium, Turkey and Cambodia. "The general pattern of my posts was in French-speaking countries. Even though this included some of the rough corners of the former French Empire," he says.

The work also included some perils. While assigned as the Deputy Chief of Mission in Guinea, the entire mission was placed under house arrest for six weeks. "The 60 families were allowed to go to and from but things were very guarded," he says. "At one point I had to smuggle walkie-talkie radios in the groceries."

In every post, he tells of problems. In Belgium, the return of King Leopold brought riots. In Turkey, mobs ransacked Greek and Armenian-owned shops. And in South Africa in 1960, there were massacres because of apartheid laws.

Ambassador Whitehouse bought his Virginia home in 1966 as a weekend and vacation retreat before going off to Guinea.He also has served as ambassador to Laos and Thailand.

Since retiring, he rides twice a week and joins the hunt about two or three times a week. Now in his late 70s, he had heart bypass surgery several years ago. He continues to ride and recently took the entire family to Ireland to ride. He is up bright and early each morning and can be spotted exercising his horses down a lovely dirt lane.

In addition to the horses, Mr. and Mrs. Whitehouse have worked tirelessly on preserving the countryside and its way of life. "I don't want to have the farms taken over and made into Levittown," he says. "It's a question of sticking to the plans and not being nibbled to death. No special exceptions." He has a map of the area charting the status of growth, or better yet, lack of development.

A portrait of his grandfather, William Whitehouse, hangs above the living room fireplace. He is dressed in hunting attire. His father, Sheldon Whitehouse, also was a diplomat.

A beautiful portrait by the society painter, Laszlo, of his mother, Mary Alexander Whitehouse, also graces the walls. In a nearby hall, two small paintings of his grandmother, Harriet Crocker Alexander, are hanging. Tradition oozes everywhere.

As we stand in the entrance hall, Ambassador Whitehouse casually puts his hand on one of a pair of massive, four-foot ivory tusks near the front doors. Some people would have put these out of sight years ago. He's not calling attention to these objects, because that's just not his style.

But I had to ask. Where did they come from?

"I shot him in Northern Rhodesia on the Luangwa River. That was before they were endangered."

Yes, and gentlemen like this are endangered too.

———————

Hank Woolman has been the Honorary Huntsman of the M.O.C. Beagles for more than 20 years. It should be noted that the position is truly "honorary", which means that he does not get paid to do his job. His "job" is to hunt the beagles. Not to be confused with the Master of the Hunt, who leads the field.

For seven years, he was a Joint Master of the Orange County Hunt, but he says in a refrain that is all too familiar in this sport, "the politics got to be so bad that I quit."

Hank is in his early 70s and a sportsman of the highest order--fly fishing, skiing, riding. If the truth were known, serving in this position is like getting paid to eat. The M.O.C. Beagles were organized in 1961. The patron saint and Master of Beagles is Eve Fout, whose daughter Nina won the Three-Day Event team bronze medal in the 2000 Sydney Olympics.

The pack was formed in connection with the pony club and they hunt the same country as Middleburg and Orange. But the main objective is to "teach young people to enjoy hunting."Children far outnumber adults, who are

Adults are strongly urged to be accompanied by a young rider, rather than vice versa when the MOC Beagles go out. Here Charles Matheson (far right) is accompanied by his granddaughter (left) Delilah Ohrstrom and daughter Lilla Ohrstrom.

strongly urged to be accompanied by a young rider, rather than vice versa. There are usually anywhere from 20 to 60 riders out on Thursdays and Sundays. The capping fee is $20 and a full year's subscription is $150 for a family.

It's difficult to write about Hank without first noting that the fingers on his right hand are gone. A lifelong farmer, in 1970 he got his hand stuck in a corn picker. It happened very quickly. And it never occurred to him that it would hamper his sporting activities. "I was going to find a way to do both," he says. "All I need is one good hand."

It hasn't slowed him down a bit. He loops the reins over his arm if he needs to use his other hand. As for fishing, he has a business teaching fly fishing summers in Montana and making cane rods for $1,000 plus each.

His second wife, Marsha, shares his interest in all sports. After his first wife, Barbara, died in 1990, a friend called to say he wanted to introduce Hank to a nice woman. "He told me she liked to fish and loves the outdoors," he says, "Yeah sure, I thought, she's probably six-foot- eight and 287 pounds." Not at all. She's petite and pleasant and serves as an Honorary Whipper-In for the M.O.C.

As huntsman, Hank knows the territory intimately. There are names for places like Lee's Ring and Fishback Ridge. He also identifies each beagle by name. There's Mystic, Mettle, Corkscrew and Pirate. Each one is named with the first letter of the dam or sire's name. They start hunting at age one and can go for five or six, sometimes as many as ten years. They are much smaller than foxhounds, fifteen inches and under, which makes them slower.

"A visitor came one day thinking it would be rather slow and said to me,

'My goodness these things get out from under you in a hurry,'" he says over coffee one morning on the patio behind The Upper Crust.

"We had just scattered kids from hell to breakfast." So he did what any good huntsman would do, thinking of all those children. He tried to slow it down. "All I did was cut out the checks (hunting lingo for resting points).

Later that fall, Hank had another accident. It was close to dusk at the end of a day out hunting. His wife Marsha sent email updates:

"We are not entirely sure, but it is my belief that he and the horse ran right into a six-strand high tensile fence that runs through the woods on the flat above the cabin on Goose Creek. The fence is very hard to see as it is nailed to trees, not posts, and at four in the afternoon it was getting dark. I think the horse, not seeing it, hit the fence and Hank probably hit the tree and top wire. The fence should have had flags on it as it paralleled an old stone wall and the wall had a big open dip in it right there so it looked like you could ride through the opening. I almost did the same thing earlier in the day from the opposite side but the sunlight hit the wire and sparkled so I saw it when I was ONLY A FEW YARDS AWAY. This kind of accident is not the fault of either horse or rider but rather just unfortunate circumstances."

About two weeks later she wrote again…

"Well, I said no news was good news, but the news is so good I feel I must share with you the progress that Hank is making. Each day is like a huge leap forward from the day before. It seems impossible that two weeks ago tonight we feared for his life and now we are fearing for ours. Today he asked for his guitar, and he actually managed to play it. Not quite up to snuff, but a left brain, right brain integration exercise he actually enjoyed.

Hank will probably be leaving Washington Hospital Center to go to a rehab hospital. His stay in acute rehab should be one week and maybe a second week in sub acute rehab. We are hoping he will be home for Christmas. I sure hope so. He still has a feeding tube as the nerves on the left side of the throat and the left eye are still under pressure from the brain bruise. The doctors feel time alone will heal these things so we continue to pray. Thank you all."

Then just before Christmas, yet another email. For even horse people have moved into cyberspace…

"Christmas Greetings and more good news about Hank's recovery. His progress continues every day. He is very alert and his cognitive skills are near normal. His sense of humor is in full swing. And his memory skills are nearly up to where they were before the fall. (Of course neither of us was scoring very high even then.) There are gaps in his memory especially back about 20 to 25 years ago. I can't help him with these so those of you who can will have to help out with that part. The two major things holding things up are the very slow recovery of the nerves in the left eye and eye lid and his throat. He failed another swallowing test yesterday which means the tube feeding will continue for probably another month.

We are counting our blessings and wishing all of you a wonderful holiday season. Thanks for your concern and support. You are a great group of friends."

Unlike other members of the hunt staff who use a proper brass horn, Hank always uses a cow horn to call his beagles. After his accident he taught his wife how to blow the horn. She took over the field while he recovered. Hank speaks to the beagles with commands like "Eehhhh" which translates to come along. "If one speaks and I'm confident that he is on to something I tell the others 'Up,'" he says.

What this is really all about are the beagles. "I know people who have fox hunted for 40 years and still don't get it," he said.

———————

Things did not turn out quite so well for John Heckler when his horse stepped in a hole on November 9, 1990 while out with the Piedmont Fox Hounds.

"It was a good morning," he recalls over 11 years later. "We got on a fox early and he dragged us to the north of the polo field. I went towards a red barn because I figured there would be a fox and sure enough here comes Reynard out of the barn. I couldn't get anyone's attention."

He tells of a very narrow jump that was covered in vines and that in he went, up a hill. "We were flying," he says. "I always stay three or four feet away from the one in front in case they fall so you don't step on them."

The grass was high. "All of a sudden there was a huge hole and I was on top of it," he says, adding that he was galloping about 25 or 30 miles per hour. "I tried to fall off and flip to my back, which is the way to fall. I ride back [an old British style of hunting seat] and the reason is, if you hit the fence you have a split second to flip."

His trusted gray hunter, Royal Blue, twisted to the right when he fell into the hole. "And I went left," John says, adding that it was only three feet to the ground since he was going uphill. "I hit on my left bicep and it went all the way through my body. When I hit the ground, I said to myself, 'that's it, you're gone.'"

The horse was fine and enjoys a quiet retirement.

John was not. His T-3 vertebrae was "broken into pieces, I felt pins and needles" and then nothing. Three women riders came to his aid and waited. It took an hour and a half for the ambulance to find them in the field. To make matters worse, the axle broke and they had to call another. "Why didn't they call a chopper?" he begs now, while sitting in his wheelchair in his study at Foxleigh, the home he shares with wife, Sheryl, a writer and interior designer.

He spent three weeks in intensive care. "Nobody thought I would make it," he says. He lost everything from mid-chest down. "I used to push and push and work and work and people would tell me 'you can't do that.' This is the moment of truth. One thing after another goes wrong. It has made me a more patient person."

John, in his early 70s, started riding at the age of three. "I rode horses, not ponies," he begins. "My Grandfather Maguire came to this country from Ireland. He supplied horses to the New York City public transportation system and later had the same business in Connecticut."

Between the ages of six and nine, John would go fox hunting with his grandfather. "He was over 80 years old by then," he explains, "and my grandmother, who was a first grade teacher, let me play hookey to look after him."

His grandfather also ran a livery stable, but died when John was just 12. All the horses had to be sold. "That included my own, Old Joe," he says. "Boys don't cry but it broke my heart and I went down to the lake and cried."

While married to his first wife, Margaret, a politician, John took up riding again seriously. They were living in suburban Virginia, while she served as a congresswoman from Massachusetts. An institutional investment banker, he also rode with many local hunts--Fairfax, Blue Ridge and Rappahannock. He even started to go to Ireland to hunt. He loves to tell stories about those memorable trips. His blood is green. "Three quarters of my family were Irish," he says proudly, and then points out the family coat of arms on the wall. He can intimately describe the big ditches and banks he negotiated in Limerick and Galway. And he does it with great enthusiasm.

He earned his pilot's license at 14 and at one time owned a J# Piper Cub and later a Piper Saratoga. He raced in sailboats from Newport to Bermuda, the photos of such outings hang on the walls along with the riding photos. Before the accident he drove a Turbo Porches, but that was six gears and hard to handle as a paraplegic. So now he sails down the country roads in a 850I BMW.

He has met actor Christopher Reeve and together they work on the Christopher Reeve Paralysis Foundation. "We're going to get fixed up and we're going to do it in three to five years," he says.

And any regrets?

"I'd do it all again," he says emphatically, which is his way.

HUNTING TERMS

Fox hunting has a language all its own. Here is a selection of terms.

AUTUMN HUNTING. . . . . Cub hunting

BOO HOO. . . . . When a hound is lost or frustrated and sings out

COFFEE HOUSING. . . . . Distracting field chitchat while others are listening for hounds

DOG. . . . . Male hound, male fox; any non-hound canine

EYE TO HOUNDS. . . . . By watching hounds and listening, to be able to tell what the fox has done and about what they are going to do

FIRST FLIGHT. . . . . Riders who plan to jump everything necessary and to stay close to the action

HOUND MUSIC. . . . . The sound made when hounds are in full cry

LARKING. . . . . Jumping fences unnecessarily when hounds are not running

MOB. . . . . To surround and kill a fox before it has a chance to run, also called Chop

MOUTHY. . . . . A babbler, a noisy hound

OVERIDE. . . . . To press hounds too closely, especially at a check; also, to get in front of a Field Master during run; both are bad manners

POINT-TO-POINT. . . . . Annual fund-raising horse races sponsored by the hunt, not sanctioned by the National Steeplechase Association and not to be confused with the Steeplechase Races

PUER. . . . . Hound dung

RIOT. . . . . When hounds chase anything they shouldn't

SCARLET. . . . . Proper term for the color of a red coat

SPEAK. . . . . To give tongue when on the scent

STERN. . . . . Hound's tail

TAILGATE. . . . . Informal snacks after a hunt

TALLY HO. . . . . A fox has been viewed

VIXEN. . . . . Female fox

Terms are reprinted courtesy of *The Bull Run Hunt, Newcomers' Handbook*

The Middleburg Hunt
Middleburg, Virginia 20118

Fixtures
November & December 2000

Saturday	Nov. 4	Opening Meet at Groveton Farm
		Governor's Breakfast 6:00 p.m. at
		Spur & Spoon at Foxcroft School
Monday	6	Chilton
Thursday	9	Dresden Farm
Saturday	11	Bolinvar
Monday	13	The Kennels
Thursday	16	Egypt Farm
Saturday	18	Foxcroft School's Fox Hound Day **9 a.m.**
		Meet at Covert (park at stables)
		Hunt Breakfast at noon
Monday	20	Opening Day of Deer Season
		Hounds will not meet
Thursday	23	Spring Glade
Saturday	25	Goodstone Inn
		Hunt Breakfast 6:00 p.m. by the kind
		invitation of Mr. Afshin Ghafouri
		at Rock Cliff Farm
Monday	27	Shelburne Glebe
Thursday	30	Big Branch
Saturday	Dec. 2	Middleburg **10:30 a.m.**
		Stirrup Cup hosted by
		The Red Fox Inn

The above meets will be at 10:00 a.m.
unless otherwise...

Please give every consideration to landowners through whose courtesy and kindness fox hunting is made possible. Avoid livestock. Do not ride over newly seeded or soft fields. When not hunting, specific permission must be obtained from landowners for cross-country riding privileges.

The field must stay together at all times.

Please make temporary repairs to any damage of jumps, gates or turf, and report such damage to the Masters.

Capping Fee

Adult - 4 Hunt Limit	Weekends & Holidays	100.00
	Weekdays	75.00
Juniors -14-21		40.00
Children under 14 with adult		Free

Capping fees should be made payable to Middleburg Hunt and are payable at the meet.

Hunting license and coggins test required by law.

Kennels (540) 687-8411

Hunting by permission of the Masters.

Jeffrey M. Blue, M.F.H. (540) 687-5446
Mrs. John B. Denegre, M.F.H. (540) 687-6069

Ms. Carey Shefte, Field Secretary

CHAPTER 8

CRIME AND PUNISHMENT

At the funeral of Argentinian polo player Roberto Villegas, a reading from a short shotry "The Maltese Cat" written by Rudyard Kipling through the eyes of a polo pony, refers to "Men riding with thier necks for sale."

*B*lair D. Howard is Virginia's answer to F. Lee Bailey, having successfully defended the likes of Lorena Bobbitt and arms heiress Susan Cummings. He's what is known as a "Good Old Boy" in these parts. He's a humble, southern sportsman. When he walks into the local greasy spoon in nearby Marshall, he meets and greets every redneck in the place. Why, he has even defended some of their sons on charges of breaking and entering, grand larceny and assault and battery.

When he walks into a black tie hunt ball, or dinner dance, it's the same story. He knows every other person at the party, and has probably defended a few of those elite guests, too.

He grew up in Alexandria, graduated from The University of Virginia and went on to law school at American University. His father, T. Brooke Howard, was a prominent criminal lawyer who tried over 100 murder cases during the course of an equally distinguished career.

"I always admired my father," he says "And in my mind I always assumed I would be a lawyer. There was no pushing on my father's part." However, he adds, "He did make it very clear to me about half way through UVA (pronounced you-vee-aay around here) that it was time to drop the fresh air courses or I wouldn't get accepted to law school."

During law school, Howard lived at home and after classes would work in his father's offices in Old Town, Alexandria. His first big Middleburg case came in 1980.

"We heard there was a murder case and all I knew about Middleburg was that the inhabitants lived comfortably and liked horses," Howard says.

Twenty years after that case, he sits in his office, decorated with fox hunting prints and photos of Howard on his horses. He has joined the horsey set. At the end of the day he says "I just want to grab the last few hours of daylight and get on my horse and ride." He's a regular member of the Loudoun Hunt and Thornton Hill Hounds.

His office is on Culpeper Street in Old Town Warrenton, the Fauquier County seat and the next stop over from Middleburg. He moved here full time from Alexandria in the late 1990s because so many of his cases originated here. He still travels throughout Northern Virginia.

In August, 1980 Theodore "Ted" Gregory, a Middleburg horse trainer, shot and killed his wife's lover, Howard LaBove, a local horse dealer, when he found the two of them in bed. LaBove died from three gunshot wounds to the chest from a .45-caliber pistol.

Gregory's estranged wife, Monique, a riding instructor, escaped death when she ran naked across a field fleeing LaBove's cottage and her crazed husband. She did not, however, escape injury. Seeking safety at the main house on the Middleburg estate owned by Oliver Iselin III, she put both her arms through a window to get inside and hide, and needed over 300 stitches to close her wounds.

Gregory was charged with four offenses--the murder of LaBove, the attempted murder of Dana and the use of a firearm in committing a felony in both cases. Gregory's father, Joseph, first came to Howard.

"The story we were told was that he had no prior record, was not violent and was in love with his wife," Howard says. "Six months prior to the shooting, Dana had told her husband she needed some space. The father painted a picture of a distraught young man who had become severely depressed over the breakup with his wife."

Gregory had withdrawn from his friends and lost all interest in life and Howard portrayed him as the distraught husband devastated by the affair. He argued that his client suffered from "irresistible impulse" which is insanity under Virginia law. He maintained that Gregory snapped when he walked in on his wife in the arms of her lover, killing LaBove almost instantly after repeatedly firing his gun.

Friends at the trial testified that LaBove was a ladies man. On this night,

Gregory followed LaBove and Dana when they left a local bar. "To control the situation, he took along a gun," Howard explains. "When he arrived outside LaBove's cottage they were having the time of their life."

According to Howard, Gregory was "hoping that by confronting them he could put an end to the relationship." With that action going on, it was difficult for him to refrain from acting out. "He shot Howard at least three or four times," Howard says. "Ted's whole world seemed to crumble when he saw his wife in those circumstances. It was a violent couple of minutes."

Gregory was initially found guilty in a Loudoun County court of attempted murder of his estranged wife, and the jury recommended a sentence of seven years. Howard moved for a new trial, claiming that certain testimony by a defense psychiatrist on Gregory's state of mind was improperly kept from the jury. The presiding judge agreed.

After being awarded a new trial, Howard was successful in obtaining a change of venue. The second trial was held in Westmoreland County about 100 miles away. There, Gregory was found innocent. Blair Howard called witnesses to support his defense of insanity. A number of horsemen and steeplechase riders who had worked with Ted Gregory testified to his physical and emotional deterioration after his wife left him. They also told the jury that everyone in Middleburg knew about his wife's relationship with LaBove.

But the case was not over yet. There was still the charge of first-degree murder that could send him to prison for life. Because they were still married during the first two trials, Monique Dana, by law, could not testify against her so-called husband. Once the divorce became final, Loudoun County came after Gregory again.

When Dana filed for divorce Howard filed a cross complaint charging her with adultery.

During the divorce proceedings, Howard noticed Dana's attorney was going to take the deposition of the chief investigator at the crime scene. Neither Dana nor the lawyer attended the deposition. The investigator recalled when he entered the cottage that night, he asked Dana what they had been doing. She said that she had been sitting on the bed talking with LaBove and Gregory came in and announced he was going to kill them both. "All of this with her panties on the floor and the sheets all rumpled up," Howard says.

She later changed her story and admitted to the investigator that they had been making love when her husband entered the room.

The investigator didn't testify at the Westmoreland trial. So in the Rappahannock County trial, Howard declared in his opening statements "I will prove to you she lied." He acknowledges this was a risky statement to make to a jury. When Mo Dana took the stand and told the jury the second version, Howard asked if she had ever told her story differently.

Dana adamantly replied "No!" He confronted her with her original statement in which she denied ever making such a statement?"She was indignant," Howard says. "I got her locked in. Then I turned and pointed my finger at the investigator and asked her if she had told him she had been sitting on the bed with LaBove."

Howard summed it all up to the jury. "If she lied about that how can you trust her?"

"That was a devastating blow to the prosecution," Howard says.

In characterizing his client to the jury, Blair Howard quoted from Shakespeare's Othello.

"Of one that loved not wisely, but too well; of one not easily jealous, but, being wrought, Perplexed in the extreme."

Gregory's father and brother wept and the normally complacent Gregory wiped his eyes. He eventually was convicted of voluntary manslaughter after a six-man, six-woman jury deliberated for four hours. They rejected the first degree murder charge and agreed with the defense that the horse trainer had shot LaBove, described during the trial as Gregory's best friend, in "the sudden heat of passion upon reasonable provocation."

The jury recommended a fine of $1,000 and no jail sentence. Ted Gregory paid the fine and walked out of the court a free man. Many of his Virginia neighbors said that if he had shot and killed a horse, it would have been an entirely different outcome.

"During the trial, people around here whispered that he would probably get away with it," said one Middleburg resident. "In Virginia, there's this old southern mindset. They don't think it's a crime if you shoot somebody when you catch them in bed like that. It was a wonderful piece of gossip. But very little was given to the morality of it."

"The point is," Howard says, "this wasn't a true love deal, this was Tuesday night after a few beers."

Blair Howard also was (pardon the expression) attached to the well-publicized 1994 Lorena and John Bobbitt fiasco. But he wasn't the only hero in the story. There was another Middleburg "connection" as well.

"It made medical history when they sewed him back together," Howard says. "That seemed to get lost in the worldwide coverage of the act itself and the controversy it created."

Lorena Bobbitt had already gone through two lawyers and was worried sick. She was about to stand trial for malicious wounding after slicing off her husband's penis and tossing it out her car window in nearby Manassas, Virginia.

Howard's secretary took "three or four" anonymous phone calls from a woman with a Spanish accent. She would never leave her name. By this time, the defrocked John Bobbit had been tried and acquitted of marital rape.

When Howard and Mrs. Bobbitt finally "connected" he says, "I knew it was Lorena immediately when she asked if I had heard of her case." They met at 5 one evening and talked for four hours. "It was obvious she was upset, she was devastated by her husband's acquittal and felt that people didn't believe her. She felt her husband's exoneration was a total injustice."

Mrs. Bobbitt related how her husband had done horrible things to her, including grabbing her hair and assaulting her in front of customers at the nail salon where she worked. Witnesses testified that her husband verbally abused her in front of customers who were having a manicure.

"I listened to her and told her, if what you told me happened then maybe we can do something," he says.

Howard needed people to speak on the record and they were not hard to find. Three former clients told of bruises they observed on Lorena. Others said she had shown up at work with heavy makeup to cover the black and blue marks. John Wayne Bobbitt had shoved her around and had sexually abused her during the marriage. He also made the mistake of bragging about it to some of his workout buddies at a local gym.

"He told them about roughing her up while they were having sex," Howard says. John's buddies were called at the trial and spoke of his boasts.

"The chief detective went to John's house to interview him. The detective confided to Howard about his initial encounter with John. According to Blair Howard, Bobbitt "took forever answering the door. The investigator said John explained he was busy writing his autobiography. It was obvious to the jury that John was delighted by his sudden celebrity status."

"While John denied ever assaulting his wife, his Marine Corps records told a different story," Howard relates. "A Marine corps counselor not only testified that John had acknowledged abusing his wife, but had acknowledged assaulting her in writing on a form he completed for the counselor."

In the courtroom, Howard brought forth expert testimony that Lorena suffered from post traumatic stress disorder. "The characteristics of this disorder are loss of self-esteem," Howard explains, "withdrawal from friends, loss of interest in usual activities and reliving a traumatic event. Lorena testified that the traumatic event in her marriage was when John forcibly raped her after she withdrew from sexual relations with him following all the abuse."

On the night of the knife incident, "She was sleeping in a separate bedroom and planning to move out the next day," Howard continues. "John came in late after a night of drinking and carousing. He came into her room and wanted roughhouse sex. She relived the trauma of the previous rape and suddenly snapped."

Howard says the psychologist defined all the characteristics of post traumatic stress disorder and suffering from the disorder when exposed to a similar violet event. "You need witnesses to confirm that she indeed demonstrated those characteristics and was emotionally overwhelmed by her husband's abuse," he says. "After the jury heard from numerous co-workers, clients, and neighbors about John's cruel abuse, the conclusion became simple."

Not guilty, by reason of insanity.

And one end note to that other "connection." Dr. Jim Sehn, a urologist, lives in Middleburg and practices in Manassas. He received the call to put John Bobbitt back together again. "Serendipity happens," Sehn says, "even for the country doctors, who are nevertheless subject to the roulette of an ER schedule. Mr. Bobbitt was a gratifying surgical result, which hopefully was a one off event for me."

———————————

It was a cool Friday evening in September, 1998, the last game of the season of twilight polo at Great Meadow over in The Plains. It was fancier than usual and was aptly called "The Last Divot," a charity match between teams from Scotland and the U.S. People from the area bring a tailgate and visit from car to car and watch, but on this night a big wedding size white tent was set up on one side of the arena, which looks down upon the action. The invitation called for tartans. Some men came in kilts and women wore Scottish sashes. The festivities started about 6:30-ish. With the Cadillac dealers as one of the sponsors, a couple of sleek luxury cars were parked strategically. A small tent for drinks was set up next to the larger tent. There were bagpipe players from St. Andrew's Pipe and Drum Band. The round tables in the tent were covered in dark hunter green and decorated with tartan. The dinner was cold chicken, wild rice salad and several other side dishes.

No haggis in sight.

At halftime there were a few highlights of Highland Games. Listed on the honorary committee was Nick Arundel, publisher of a highly successful string of local papers who is also the founder of Great Meadow; Lt. Gov. Donald Beyer (a no-show) and State Delegate Andy Guest. Actor Robert Duvall, who lives just a stone's throw away, also was a no show as was invitee Senator John Warner. Everyone under the tent was having a gay old time, all to benefit the American Cancer Society and The Virginia Therapeutic Riding Center.

And get this. Before the start of the match, announcer Tommy Monaco asked for a moment of silence for "Diana, the Princess of Wales, Mother Teresa and our own Roberto." Breaking that silence, he barked (a la "Let's Get Ready to Rumble") "Okay, are you ready for some polo?" Following the match, won by the U.S. team by a 10-8 margin, there was a dance with music by the Rusty Nut Blues Band. But, who the hell was Roberto?

Well... Roberto was the Argentinean polo playing lover of arms heiress Susan Cummings, until she pumped four fatal blasts from a Walther Semi

Automatic 9-mm (a gift from her father) into him over breakfast just a week before the charity polo match.

Cummings and Villegas were living together at her 339-acre farm over in Warrenton. Her wealthy father, Sam Cummings (owner of Interarms, Inc.) purchased the farm in 1984 and it was held by Susan (pronounced Suzanne) and her twin sister, Diana in the name of "Ashland Farm Partnership." It was bought in two large parcels and at that time the price would have been under $2 million.

Susan had only been playing polo for two years. She started by taking lessons at the Willow Run Polo School and assembled a competitive team with Roberto as the four-goal professional, one of the best players in the area.

In 1990, he won the national USPA President's Cup playing on the Rappahannock team. According to an unwritten code, the polo players are normally paid monthly based upon the number of goals they are rated. With a four-goal rating that meant Roberto would have been paid $4,000 a month by Cummings. The cost of a polo pony can range from $1,500 to $100,000 depending on experience. But evidentially, he did more than knock polo balls between goal posts for her.

According to friends, the relationship started to unravel at the end of the summer cookout, known as an *asado* in his native country. The guests were gossiping as usual. This time it was about the handsome, two-timing Roberto. Word was that he was cheating on Susan, his wealthy patron.

"My impression was that he was not being very cool about it at all," said one guest. "Everyone knew."

The asado is very popular both in Argentina and with this Virginia polo crowd. It was held on Saturday, July 26 at the farm rented by Dr. Steve Seager and his wife, Doris. The Seager's two children, daughter Fiona and son Adair, also played polo. Dr. Seager came to the U.S. from Dublin in the late 1960s when he took up polo. He is rated as an A player, which is essentially 0. A veterinarian who specializes in research, he serves as the polo club's veterinary advisor and also in that role with the United States Polo Association. The name of his team with his children is Tullyroan, and they all like to fox hunt as well.

The Seagers hosted the asado for no special reason, according to both of them. "It's just something everyone in the polo club does from time to time," Doris said at the time.

"We roasted two sheep and ate it all down to the bones," Dr. Seager relates, pronouncing the word ate as "et." Roberto did all the cooking that night. Many people said he made a marvelous oil and vinegar type of sauce to go with it.

Susan Cummings was also at the party and even though there was gossip about them splitting, they were together that night. Everyone was asked to bring along a covered dish to compliment the main course.

"Some people came after playing polo and so they were maybe a bit late," Doris Seager says. The dress was casual. Some guests went swimming, others sat outside on bales of hay and at picnic tables. There were about 150 in attendance. It was well after dark, the weather was good. A local two page newsletter called the Polo Pony Press reported on the party and indicated that perhaps a few of the players went skinny dipping.

A local photographer who frequently covers the polo circuit knew Susan and Roberto.

"At the beginning of the summer all the photos that I would take of them, they would be close together and standing next to each other," says the photographer. "But toward the end of the summer I noticed in all my photos there was either a space between them or someone else was standing in between them."

About a week before the murder, this same photographer spotted Roberto one Friday night at Mosby's Tavern in Middleburg with a "young dark haired" woman she didn't know.

"I don't know if they were on a date or had just met there that night or what," the photographer said at the time. "But there was definitely some tension between them."

Richard Varge, president of the Great Meadow Polo Club, did not see the possibility that there could be another woman. He had spotted Roberto and Susan just several days before the murder holding hands at a social event. He acted surprised and shocked as such a notion. Those on the polo circuit who knew Cummings described her as "very quiet and sweet."

"I met her on several occasions," said one woman. "She seemed to be very polite. She had a quiet voice and I was struck when she called me "Mrs." Another woman who has played polo for many years and bought horses from Roberto said "he appeared to have very good manners, he was not impetuous. There is a great deal of controversy over the Argentine pros. I saw him enough to say with confidence that he didn't lose his temper on the field."

To this day there are still two very powerful camps in this case--Roberto's amigos and Susan's allies. Was he a brutish cad or wasn't he?

One owner/player says "he was a paid professional and could be a bad ass. These guys are rough, like boxers. They're tough, they can't be like sissies."

Speculation was floating through the thick damp air the night of that asado that Roberto had another woman. The scent of cigars hung in the air, mingling with the smell of sweaty horses and the hint of the heavy cologne that some of the players prefer. "He rode the horses hard, just like he rode his women, " said horse trader Jerry Perry of Lafayette, La. "And then he put them away sweating."

Between the time of the murder and the night of the charity polo match, friends had gathered in Middleburg for Roberto's funeral, which was organized by Varge and financed by donations. Roberto's red helmet was placed in a back pew as the coffin was rolled in at St. Stephen's Catholic Church.

Father James Muldowney conducted Roberto's funeral, assisted by Custer

Cassidy (the same man seen jogging into the post office each day with his Popeye-type hat) as deacon. Most of the 100 mourners were dressed in black with a splash of color on a silk tie or scarf with the polo pony motif. At least half a dozen media types were there, including a television crew. Roberto's former girlfriend of four years, Kelli Quinn, read the A.E. Housman poem "To An Athlete Dying Young." Suzi Worsham, one of his first sponsors, read Kipling's short story "The Maltese Cat." Written through the eyes of the pony, it mentions "men riding with their necks for sale."

William Ylvisaker, well known in polo circles from Palm Beach to Virginia, delivered the eulogy. Roberto had played for him. He talked of the times on the polo field when they were losing the match.Roberto would say "come on Uncle Bill, we'll win the game." And then he would score three more goals for the victory. The next morning, Roberto's body was flown back to Argentina, the cost of $8,000 paid for by the Argentine Embassy, according to Varge.

At the Scotland/U.S. charity polo match, Kelli Quinn looked the saddest of all.She had dark circles under her eyes. She was standing alone and told me "polo will never be the same for me."

Susan eventually was indicted on a charge of first-degree murder.When the preliminary hearing began, she was the last to enter the small Fauquier County courtroom over in Warrenton and stood by the door with her twin sister, Diana. She wore black jeans, a dark sweatshirt and jacket over a white turtleneck. She appeared to be calm and somewhat animated. When her name was called she walked down a few steps into the main part of the courtroom and stood with Blair Howard. The trial was set for the following May. The defendant asked for a jury trial and the judge said that would not be a problem.Upon leaving the courtroom, Howard would only say that it was "clearly self defense."

The first-degree murder trial of Susan Cummings took placed in a courtroom packed with not just friends and curious residents but reporters from CBS, The New York Times, Argentina and Great Britain, where the tabloids latched on to the story of the world famous arms dealer's daughter.

From the start, Howard claimed Susan shot the dashing polo player because he was abusive, and only after he came at her with a knife in the kitchen that morning. He announced in his 40-minute opening statement that several former girlfriends would testify that Roberto had a violent and abusive history.

The prosecution alleged that Susan elaborately laid the groundwork for the self-defense strategy even before she pulled the trigger. They said she purposely made a false abuse complaint to the sheriff's office days before she shot Roberto to establish his violent history.

Assistant Commonwealth Attorney Kevin Casey had been with the prosecutor's office for eight years, but this was his first murder case. He gave a three-minute opening statement and chose to rely on just the facts, saying that Susan shot Roberto in anger (not fear) "not once, not twice, not three times, but four times. He was seated at the kitchen table having breakfast. We would ask you to find her guilty of murder."

Cummings was the third of about 20 witnesses for the defense. She said Roberto became angry when she told him their relationship was over.He wanted to marry her, she said, and have children with her. If she refused, he promised to kill her, she told the court. "I felt fear of my life, I thought, 'This is it.' This man is going to kill me." According to her testimony, Roberto lunged at her and slashed her arm with a bone-handled knife.

During cross-examination, the prosecution pointed out that he had been sitting eating breakfast and not fighting with the defendant. They called an expert witness who testified that cuts found on her arms did not come from any fight as she had claimed, but more likely were self-inflicted.

Susan's formal complaint against Roberto at the Fauquier Sheriff's office said that he had shown signs of aggression during the past six months and threatened her on several occasions. Still, she had never requested a restraining order.

The prosecution presented a recorded 9-1-1 call on which Cummings reported "a shot man, and he's dead." She was asked if she had killed the man and said "I had a gun, yes he tried to kill me," and then she said she needed to speak to a lawyer. Sgt. Cuno Anderson, the first deputy on the murder scene, saw bright red blood on Cummings arm (making the point that the victim's blood had

started to dry) and said when she refused to answer questions, he handcuffed her.

A member of the rescue squad treated the scratches on Susan's arm, which did not need bandages. She accused her lover of inflicting the cuts with a six-inch bone handled knife he had won in a polo match. But Jack Daniel, a former state medical examiner, said "it seemed unlikely" the cuts were inflicted by someone trying to torture Ms. Cummings and that the scratches "are consistent with wounds that have been self-inflicted."

Casey went on to illustrate that Roberto was sitting at the kitchen table eating breakfast when he was shot. Investigator Erich Junger performed a trajectory analysis and brought a foam mannequin into court with red dowels to illustrate the point.

The highlight of the trial was clearly when Susan Cummings took the stand on the third day and told of her fear of Roberto. She said they had been arguing when Roberto drew a knife and grabbed her throat with his free hand. According to Susan, he slowly cut her arm and told her he was going to teach her a lesson. She begged him to stop and said she should make them some coffee so they could talk. After getting up from the table she went to the sink. She said she heard his chair scrape across the kitchen floor and thought he was coming at her. She grabbed a gun from inside a kitchen cabinet and shot him.

"I felt fear of my life. I thought, 'This is it. This man is going to kill me.'"

She told the court she wanted to get out of the relationship. "He wanted children. He wanted to get married. I said I had no intention of having his children. He said if I didn't agree he would kill me."

By the fourth day, the defense presented a parade of witnesses, including former employers and two former girlfriends who spoke of Roberto's dark side and violent temper. One woman, Kim Volaire, said that he had choked her during sex. "I was scared. I knew it wasn't right." Argentine native Brett Skipper, an employer 15 years ago, told of the time Roberto held a knife to his throat and said "I'm going to kill you" and then turned and walked away.

Closing statements on the fifth day brought Kevin Casey back, with blood splatter evidence saying that Cummings staged the self defense by taking a knife from her upstairs bedroom and then coldly getting a gun and killing him as he ate.

Howard argued that Roberto had crossed the line of violence, holding her and cutting her and that her fear propelled her. The jury began deliberations that afternoon.

On the sixth day, as the throng of media waited on the courthouse steps in the first sun in a dozen days, the jury continued deliberations. Susan, her sister, Diana, and their mother, Irma Cummings, sat in an empty half dark courtroom waiting. They would occasionally go outside to a courtyard to escape reporters. The attorneys hung out inside. Several members of the media ate lunch at one of the small cafes in the four-block country town. Shortly after lunch, the call went out…the jury was back.

Mrs. Cummings sat in the front row center with her daughter Diana on her right side. They held hands. Susan Cummings was wearing a black and brown blazer (it was oddly black on the back and brown on the front) and beige slacks. The judge ordered he would tolerate no outbursts. A friend of the family extended a comforting pat on the hand to Mrs. Cummings.

Then came the verdict…Guilty of voluntary manslaughter, not guilty of use of a firearm. Family members were brought to the stand to testify before sentencing.

Diana Cummings, who is blond and animated and almost the direct opposite of Susan, was dressed in black jeans and a black top. Really, all three have that so-called European look. And all three speak with a French accent. The girls were born in Monte Carlo with swish summers in Switzerland. Diana pleaded "we have always been together, in the same schools and never apart. We plan to be together forever. She has her set of horses and she takes care of them. I have mine and I take care of them." She said she had never known her sister to be violent. "Never, never."

Irma Cummings, also was in black jeans and a black top, with polka dot blazer. She's a regal looking woman with a classic blunt cut, straight chin-length gray hair. She was trying to act composed but seemed a bit confused, perhaps because she is accustomed to speaking French. When asked the first question "what is your relationship with Susan?" she said, "Oh we have a good relationship." And then she had to be prompted. "Is she your daughter?"

She said they were good twins and "played together and had no real major problems." She said that in the summertime in Switzerland between the ages of three and 16, Susan would bring home stray dogs and animals. "Both of my children were very, very attracted to animals."

Mrs. Cummings noted that her husband was "a good father, but traveling a lot. Gone for six months a year, but not in a row." And since leaving home, both girls would visit several times a year. The judge dismissed the jury, then hastily called them back in when he realized he had mistakenly forgotten to allow the lawyers to speak before his final sentencing.

Howard spoke first, saying that Susan had not a single misdemeanor or criminal offence in her life and the shooting was an act of provocation. He mentioned her as someone who rescues animals and said of Roberto, "the best predictor of future violence is past violence. His history is replete with violence, knives and threats."

Howard, as usual, dressed down in khaki pants and navy blazer. There would be no fancy handmade suits for this lawyer. By dressing in this horse country "uniform," he more easily identified local members of the jury as "one of us" and "not one of them." Howard's courtroom method once again worked magic. He had the jury lapping it up.

"This is not about animals," prosecutor Casey said. She is not here because she shot a dog or cat." This involves "two human beings. One of them is no longer here. One of them is not here because of Ms. Cummings' temper."

When the jury came back a little more than one hour later, everyone sat in the same places. Her mother heaved a heavy sigh of relief with the announcement of a 60-day sentence and $2,500 fine. She kept looking around the room, as if she was wondering "could this be right. Did I hear it right?"

As Susan Cummings stepped outside the courthouse in the late afternoon May sunshine, her eyes sparkled as she spoke to the gathered press. "I'd like everyone to know how appreciative I am. I feel very happy."

The reaction to the verdict and sentencing even within the courthouse was stunned shock. One Fauquier County employee was perplexed and said her fellow workers were equally as confused. Another longtime resident asked "how do you want that $2,500 in singles or 20s," noting what a paltry sum it would be for Susan.

On top of it all, her father had recently passed away and word was that she would soon inherit more than $100 million.

The mother of a 30--year-old man convicted and sentenced to forty years on drug felony charges of possession and use of heroin in the same courtroom seven years ago was outraged. "My son wasn't hurting anyone but himself. And this woman kills someone and gets 60 days?"

Polo enthusiast Richard Varge, who organized Roberto's funeral, was furious when he heard the news. I saw him that afternoon at the Middleburg Post Office (where else?). "Jesus Christ," he said.At his office the next day he added, "I didn't know how you could get that light of a sentence for killing someone in cold blood. I didn't think the jury knew who Roberto was. The defense painted a picture of him that was totally inaccurate. They depicted him as a devil. The entire polo community loved him for his kindness. He protected her when he played with her. It was obvious that he loved and admired her. He was a gentle man."

Varge viewed the trial as a "sales presentation. You take a gamble, it was an open and shut case. I view her as a sociopath. I view her as having no conscience. She opened fire and emptied her gun. She is a cold bitch."

Polo player Jean Marie Turon runs the Willow Run Polo School and was one of Roberto's closest friends. He testified at the trial and later reacted with a shrug. "I can't get Roberto back. I was trying to get the best for him and talking to everyone. I'm going to miss him every day. Thirty days or 60 days, after you kill a person?"

Juan Salinas-Bentley, a polo player who won the National President's Cup with Roberto back in 1991, took what might appear to be a more reasonable approach. He learned of the sentence while getting coffee in a local country store. "I thought maybe the clerk had gotten it wrong." He said Roberto was a serious prankster and "pushed things to the end. He would turn around and say 'If that horse doesn't stand still, I'm going to break his leg.'"

"It's a crapshoot," Salinas-Bentley said. "The jury probably said we're not going to let her walk free and clear, but she doesn't deserve 5-10 years. I taught her [Susan] her first [polo] lesson. She was just a kind sweet woman. I couldn't imagine her doing something like that. Deep down she must have had some fear and just snapped."

"She had a caretaker personality," Varge said. "She bought the horses, and with her in control, she had the ability to call all the shots." In social situations Varge said Susan had "no affect at all, she was just flat. She was warm to animals and cold towards people." As far as the violent part of the crime, he said "everyone knew she was unusual. But polo had definitely brought her out a bit."

"I knew them both together," Varge said, adding that he doubted she would even try to play polo again. "I don't think she will try to come back."

Blair Howard simply said there would be no appeal and asked that Susan be allowed to remain free on bond to attend her father's memorial service in Washington at the National Presbyterian Chapel on Nebraska Ave. He said she would turn herself in on Saturday, May 16 at 6 p.m.

About a hundred people attended the memorial service. Susan didn't cry, but quietly greeted the guests. Sam Cummings' old friend, Eric Fleisher, delivered the eulogy. The organ solo was "Jesus, Joy of Man's Desiring." The Hymn was "A Mighty Fortress is Our God." The Lord's Prayer and the Prayer of Thanksgiving also were read.

A reception followed in the chic Kalorama section of Washington. Late in the afternoon Susan and Blair Howard made the one-hour drive west toward Warrenton and the jail. Her mood was described as "reflective."

"She made a mistake and perhaps there was some alternative but clearly she was in fear and obviously they [the jury] could relate to that," Howard said. Susan Cummings walked the short distance from an unmarked car into the jailhouse.She was carrying a copy of a book by Lenore Walker, The Battered Woman, clearly a Howard prop for the three photographers on hand. (But only one noticed it. A detail I noted in reporting the murder for People magazine to Sarah Skolnik, the Washington bureau chief.)

The inmates from the second floor were taunting the heiress. "Welcome to the club," they shouted. "Welcome to the club."

For now, it may be the only club in Fauquier County where she is welcome. Polo club President Peter Arundel later said "in this club, she would not be welcome. Right or wrong it has deeply hurt the members of the polo community. We are outraged, saddened and angered. Her return would only stir up those feelings. We all have so much fun doing this."

Susan was in a cell by herself at the two-story brick Fauquier County Adult Detention Center in Warrenton. The jail is certified to hold up to 120 inmates. The officer to inmate ratio is one-to-three.When Susan was there, there were 56 inmates, with only three women. Other inmates were moved out and on several occasions family members were seen bringing in food.

She wore a prison issue orange jumpsuit. The minimum-security jail is brick and steel with bars on the windows and for each cell. The walls are two-toned tan at the top and gray at the bottom. Susan was given the opportunity to wash dishes or floors to earn "good behavior" points.The jail has a library and a legal library.

A prison guard saw Susan a couple of times. He described her demeanor as "not a happy camper; she's in jail." He said she had a visitor on Sunday, but he didn't know who it was. Ultimately she spent only two weeks in jail, in what many described as a pampered semi-vacation.

"I was so happy when Susan and the defense smiled at the sentence," one juror said later. "They thanked us silently across the courtroom for the slap on the wrist sentence." This juror was the last to agree to voluntary manslaughter instead of acquittal. "I think I'll send Susan one rose for every day she's in jail, if the sheriff will let me. After all, as the defense said, But for the Grace of God..."

Marian Bruffy, foreman of the jury, begged to differ.

"Honestly, I think that if Blair Howard had told the jury that Susan

Cummings was out of the country on the day of the murder and that Roberto Villegas had likely committed suicide, at least two of the jurors would have agreed with him."

William Douglas Carter and Carole Vandergrift Carter were already divorced in August, 1987 but were still quarreling over the settlement in a Loudoun County courtroom. A point of dissension included their $2.3 million 210-acre Greenwood Farm in Aldie, just east of Middleburg.

The argument became grim when a .38 caliber bullet was fired into her neck by her ex-husband, the well-to-do president of a communications company. The divorce, granted in February, 1987 in the same court system, had included a ruling that Mr. Carter was guilty of adultery with his wife's foster daughter since 1977. Mrs. Carter also maintained he had a nasty temper and owned two guns.

Following the shooting, which she survived, Mr. Carter took off for Saratoga Springs, the August playground of many Middleburg residents who flock to upstate New York for a month of horse racing and parties almost every night. Carter was arrested in Saratoga and returned to stand trial.

During the bond hearing preceding the trial, it was revealed that Carter could not procure the $250,000 bail on top of the $75,000 cash he was required to post in New York. It turned out that he had a $1.2 million lien against the farm and owed the Internal Revenue Service $900,000 in addition to other mortgage and maintenance expenses.

Doug Carter, 55, eventually got his day in court. His 50-year-old ex-wife, now a four-time divorcee, testified during the trial that he had on rubber gloves and tried to make her shooting look like a suicide. When she regained consciousness, she was able to write his name in blood on the floor before she was discovered by two houseguests and rushed to the hospital.

And guess what? Blair Howard, one of his defense attorneys, argued that Mrs. Carter couldn't possibly identify the person who shot her because she didn't have her glasses on and it was dark in the room.

The jury didn't buy his explanation that on the night of the shooting, Carter was driving to Saratoga. In March of 1988, Carter had been convicted of malicious wounding and the illegal use of a firearm and sentenced to twelve years in jail.

Just like F. Lee Bailey and Perry Mason, Blair Howard doesn't win every case.

CHAPTER 9

BEST BLOOM

Margaret Gardner has surrounded herself with many dogs and meticulously kept gardens, including a collection of 200 dwarf evergreens, knows as "The Pygmy Pinetum".

Melmore Garden

In shady corners, here and there,
Old-fashioned fairies take the air.
The slopes and flowers still hold their own
And little twigs to trees are grown.
But footsteps, leisurely or light,
Which once were heard, are silent quite,
So with the years, we slip away
To join "the snows of yesterday".

—*G. A. Carrington , December 1927*

*T*here are four garden clubs in the Middleburg area: The Middleburg Garden Club, the Upperville Garden Club, the Piedmont Garden Club and the Fauquier Loudoun Garden Club.

There's a certain formality to it all. One never asks to join, rather one waits to be invited. (Some are still waiting.) When the minutes are read, the ladies are always referred to as Mrs. so and so. First names are never used. Tea is served, and advice on everything from weeds to conservation to flower arranging is offered.

At each meeting the members are encouraged to bring an arrangement and "Best Bloom"—something that is blooming in your garden at that time of year. The arrangements usually have a theme. For example, "Modern Water— using a Creative Vertical Arrangement Like a Small Fountain" or "Thanksgiving Centerpiece." Points are gathered throughout the year and a year-end award is given in each category.

But it's not all ladies luncheons and blossoms. One group asks members to "bring a gaily wrapped gift for a child's Christmas for needy children." There are seed exchanges and many local beautification efforts around the countryside.

The 1958 handbook of the Fauquier Loudoun Garden Club, which is affiliated with the Garden Club of America and The Garden Club of Virginia, noted that: "the 1915 purpose of the club is as appropriate today as it was 43 years ago. The purpose of this Club is to increase the pleasure of country life by the exchange of ideas and information on gardening subjects."

For some, acceptance into such a group of blue-blooded horticulturists may define a leg up on the social ladder. Some of the gardeners here are members of the garden club by choice. Others are not members of the garden club, by choice.

Gardening in Middleburg is taken seriously.

Very seriously.

Mary Ramey Cunningham is the "Grand Dame" of the local garden clubs. Born in 1905 not far from Middleburg, she has been a member of the Piedmont Garden Club for over 60 years. She is also a member of the Fauquier-Loudoun Garden Club.

"I'm such a native that I've been introduced around at parties as a native so much that I feel like I'm Pocahontas with feathers in my hair," she says one day, sitting in her downstairs library. Among the garden clubbers, Mary Cunningham is revered for her vast knowledge on flowers, gardening, shrubs and local history. And while she no longer maintains a garden, she regularly attends the meetings of both clubs and customarily contributes tips and recommendations.

The shelves of her basement library are lined with the classics. It smells musty and damp, but in a good way. The room has a slate floor and handsome pine beams and panels. The books include seventeen volumes of the work of Guy De Maupassant, *Famous Women of the French Court* and four volumes of

The Memoirs of Napoleon Bonaparte by Bourrienne.

She describes the Piedmont Garden Club as "an independent club, and to me that's charming. We do what a garden club should." They also serve as hostesses and help decorate one of the houses each year for the Garden Club of Virginia Tour.

Asked if one club is perhaps snootier than the other, she laughs. "There's a lot of crossover [of members], a lot of combined interest," she says. Many are members of several clubs. She says her mother and grandmother also were devoted gardeners.

In the early 1960s, the Virginia Department of Transportation announced plans to put Interstate 66 smack through the center of her family farm. She fought back. "It meant farming couldn't go on," she says. "They proposed to pay us per square foot or something like that. So, I went to court and got damages and then sold the other side."

She now lives on the remaining 135 acres in a house she and her husband bought for $1. They moved it to its current location and refurbished it. The wide pine walls were painted "a color pink we can't talk about," she says.

She cherishes living in an old house. "An old house has a soul. And I never regretted one penny of that dollar."

Joan Moore is an earthy type in every sense of the word and an earth mother to say the very least. While married to former husband Victor duPont, she had eight children. During her 24 years of marriage, she never picked up a spade. Instead she "dug postholes and tended to Hereford, hogs and horses". With children grown and gone, she is now snuggled into a charming place she calls Chipmunk Hill on ten acres in Upperville.

"Polly Rowley (the undisputed local Genius of gardening) once said to me, 'Joan, look at the Florabunda whatever,' and I looked around and ooh-aahed in one direction and she said to me 'no, no over here.'"

Joanie (as she is fondly known around here) says, "I may not know the Latin names. But I know what I like and I just go with it."

First she consulted with a local landscape designer, Lisbeth Prins, to consider the contour of the land. She wanted to recreate the feeling of the western United States, where she had spent nine years in Jackson Hole "on a pilgrimage, to discover myself."

She incorporated a dry rock gulch and the sound of water, which to all serious gardeners is a quintessential element. At the time of our visit in late summer, drifts of black-eyed susans (Rudbeckia 'Goldstrum' for lovers of the Latin) swayed in the breeze.

The featured component of her garden is in the courtyard off her cozy living room. An immense steel sculpture is mounted on the southern wall. When she met the artist and sculptor Neil Rizos, he spoke of a recurring dream about antelope. "I asked him to use that dream," she explains, adding that she wanted it expanded to incorporate her family.

One of her eight children, Philip, was killed at age 21 in a horrific accident involving a fire while serving as a Marine. And so, standing in front of the sculpture, simply titled "Family," she explains that "Philip leads the way." There's Victor, Sam, Joanie, Westley, David, Mimi and Turner. (The males have antlers, the females do not.)

She doesn't belong to a garden club. She has her own theories. She subscribes loosely to feng shui- the Chinese theory that placement in your home, office and garden will bring "ba-gua" energy flow. "You either know that things feel right or they don't," she says. "Some people just have a sense of what feels right."

Seven Springs Farm is the definition of what should be right in Middleburg. It is old (with a circa 1790 stone house), charming and unpretentious. The gardens are in complete context with the house.

At this 160-acre oasis that Elaine Burden shares with Childs Frick Burden, her husband of 25 years, let there be no doubt that tradition prevails. It lives on not just in her graceful gardens, but in her lifestyle devoted to animals, preservation and conservation.

Elaine began gardening in the early 1980s with a long garden that was about three feet wide filled with iris, peonies and daylilies. "I re-did the entire thing," she explains, sitting in her Palm Beach-inspired pastel sunroom, overlooking the back garden. Her Welsh Corgis, Jasmine and Ivy Geranium, are at her feet. The majestic Blue Ridge Mountains are in full, glorious unobstructed view beyond. That first border grew from three feet wide to twelve feet wide and 110 feet long. It's now a classical English style "mixed border" brimming with trees, shrubs, annuals and bulbs. On the west end are the "cool" colors: yellow, white and blue, and then moving along past a teak bench midway the colors become awash in "warm" colors of red, purple and pink.

The key to what makes this a classic is in the broad aged stones that align this part of the garden. Where another gardener may have used brick, maybe even old brick, it wouldn't work here, out of context. These are old stones, found on the farm, where it has been said that soldiers marched nearby during the Civil War. In the back part of the house, a small cannonball was found lodged near a second floor window.

Elaine has installed a tiny culinary herb garden right outside her kitchen door with parsley and nasturtiums (which she uses as a garnish when serving cold summer soups). There is Macintosh apple tree espalier against an adjacent smokehouse. And a secret garden with a knot of box and dwarf barberry.

There is also a formal garden, which is planted "informally," according to Elaine, with azaleas, rhododendron, Hilleri holly and boxwood. A separate boxwood parterre is planted with pink tulips in the spring and throughout from one "room" to another an arbor drips with moonflowers, clematis paniculata, or in one case, a weeping blue atlas cedar. In the water garden, which provides sanctuary for goldfish and frogs, there are lotus and tropical water lilies. All around are customized birdhouses for bluebirds, titmice and other fine-feathered friends.

Mrs. Burden is president of the Fauquier Loudoun Garden Club, co-chairman of the Garden Club of Virginia's Program and Lecture Committee, the retired chairman of the Garden Club of Virginia Horticulture Committee and the former president and now vice president of the Middleburg Beautification and Preservation Society.

In case you think this is all title and hot air, think again.

Through the conservation efforts of the Garden Club of Virginia, there are no billboards along the highways. And as you stroll down the brick sidewalks in Middleburg, take a look around and notice the potted plants on the corner. And if you stop to rest on a teak bench that has a running fox on it, you can also thank Elaine Burden.

Polly Rowley is the undisputed master of gardening in the Middleburg domain.Her knowledge of plants and placement is encyclopedic. At her Cold Crick Farm on 60 acres just outside of town, she created an oasis. And at The Hill School, she designed, installed and still oversees the maintenance of a 130-acre arboretum. Her garden design excels because it's fluid and graceful. Large mounds of grasses flourish in just the right place. A small dry stone wall she built curves down a slope and wraps around a bed of dwarf evergreens. She establishes the plants within the landscape, instead of moving the landscape to accommodate her vision. Nothing is ever out of context.

The terrain at the school was developed by Rowley to render a handsome campus and to furnish a teaching tool for the students and the community. A classic hedgerow includes native shrubs, a haven for wildlife creatures. More than 600 trees and shrubs have been planted. Some were installed for the variety of leaf shapes—ash, maple and gingko—to educate the children. For color, she added honey locust, smoketree and variegated giant dogwood. For their blooms, the children will find redbud (a favorite in these parts), cherry and Donald Wyman crabapple.

The two playing fields are called Acer (the Latin for maple) and Quercus (Latin for oak). There are six or more varieties of each tree so the students can study the subtle differences. "At the same time they can begin to develop a comfortable use of the Latin names," says Rowley, a member of two local garden clubs who also serves on several national committees. "Though this appears to be a daunting task for many adults, children love the opportunity to exercise the use of unusual names. The fact is that more and more children come from families that are no longer in touch with the land through farming, it's important to create an atmosphere that promotes a sense of appreciation and respect for the natural environment."

Missy Janes is the daughter of Polly Rowley, so she comes by her horticulture knowledge naturally. In 1990, she and her husband, Bill Janes, renovated a house on 13 acres that adjoins her mother's farm. They call it, appropriately enough, The Pond House. They often "commute" back and forth on a golf cart.

Missy's approach to gardening and the land always adds another dimension. She doesn't just plant a vegetable garden. Instead it's a children's vegetable garden, where 13--year-old daughter Maxie has a bamboo teepee overflowing with gourd vines. There are also dinosaur gourds, lablab beans, sweet potato vine and red runner beans. And of course, there are pumpkins.

"I guess if I think back, there was always an orchard and a garden, we lived off the land," Janes says. "It all formulated my thinking that the landscape should provide and be pleasing at the same time." Older teenage son Pack looks out over the land form his custom-built treehouse surrounded by tulip poplars.

Several times a year, Missy produces various "events" at The Pond House and each time it involves children. The activities often center around a large pre-Civil War stone bank barn that has been renovated. A French country Tudor style henhouse provides shelter for designer chickens such as Aracauna (they lay blue eggs and are often referred to as the Martha Stewart chickens.), Silver Spindled Hamburg, Rhode Island Red and Brown Leghorns.

In early June, a Junior Cross Country event is held in honor of Eve Fout and Hank Woolman, who have taught so many children and ponies to love and appreciate the sport of foxhunting. The event also includes the Middleburg Orange County Beagles. There are classes for the smallest of children on ponies and competition for the older children in pair races. The jumps are all made of pine trees, hay bales, post and rails. But Missy's creativity (which is almost unmatched in these parts) bursts forth with a canoe as a jump, and an old sofa as another.

She has no trouble gathering volunteers to help with the Cross Country event, as mothers line up to judge the fences and help fill out the entry blanks. Fathers who might otherwise rush off to work in Washington take the day off to serve as scorekeepers.

At the end of the day, everyone gets a ribbon: fastest time, best turned out, clean round and other "fun Awards at the judge's discretion."

For a Halloween birthday party one year, all the children came in costumes and carved pumpkins at the large pine table in the center of the barn. Then they roasted marshmallows on a bonfire outside, all the while sipping hot apple cider.

At Christmas, the Janes' have hosted a sing-a-long for families. The children decorate the barn. A large tree is brought in and they make "ornaments" of oranges and lady apples. Pine garlands are hung from the rafters. The children are invited at 5 p.m. for mini hamburgers, cheddar and Swiss fondue with apples, pears and carrot and celery slices and best of all--decorate your own cookies.

The parents and other friends are invited to join in at 7 p.m. for spiced roast beef and mini- Yorkshire puddings, pumpkin biscuits with smoked turkey and homemade cranberry chutney, crab and corn fritters, smoked salmon, potato and mushroom tartlets and assorted desserts.

Hot spiced and cold cider along with hot chocolate and spring water was served with a luscious chocolate Yule log and lots of candy canes, while the children play Christmas Carols on their string instruments in the loft and later an adult group performs folk music in one corner.

What does all this have to do with gardening?

It's about a love of the land and the lifestyle and preserving it for the next generation.

Evidently, this philosophy has worked.

Each year the Middleburg Garden Club sponsors The Christmas Greens Show at the Emmanuel Episcopal Church Parish House. There are prizes (Jefferson Cups) for design such as "Christmas In The Virginia Hunt Country," either traditional or creative. "An arrangement for a hunt board to be viewed from one side only. Middleburg Garden Club members only. A trophy in memory of Nanette White and Francis Foreman will be awarded for the best arrangement in this class."

Other design categories for "Celebrating Christmas Around The Country" include a Santa Fe Christmas, an Arizona Christmas, a Montana Christmas" and so on. There also are awards in the Horticulture classes: needled evergreens, broadleaf evergreens, hollies, cacti, succulents, forced bulbs, houseplants and topiary.

The rules state that "children are encouraged to exhibit."

Several years ago, Grandmother Polly Rowley and granddaughter Maxine Janes went out in the woods and gathered all sorts of pines and pinecones. "She won a couple of times." Rowley says, "and now she calls and says 'Polly, you need to help me with my exhibit.'"

This is a good one…Martha Chapman is a member of the Piedmont Garden club. In between chauffeuring children to school and other activities, she attends the monthly meetings and serves as hostess for an outdoor picnic luncheon when it's her turn. There's just one twist here. She's not the gardener in the family.

Henry O. "Chip" Chapman, a Monday through Friday Washington, D.C. real estate businessman says "I'd join if it weren't all women."

He says he was also fascinated with gardening watching his mother Scottie Chapman in her garden several miles away where he grew up. "When I became a home owner out here things changed," he says. When living in Washington he had a "tiny garden." Once in the country, he started with a perennial bed 25 feet long against a stone wall. And each year he adds five more feet.

"Basically," he notes, "the soil stinks. So mainly what I do is manual labor, I have replaced the clay with eight inches of top soil and now it's easier. For me it's a place to blow off steam. That's what I enjoy, spending a couple of hours in the garden. It's a physical thing." He has planted lupines, delphiniums and, like all gardeners, has had some mistakes. "I planted some things too close." So he is constantly dividing and moving.

"In the long range, in my retirement, this is what I'll do," he says of his wife, Martha. "I can't get her to plant a flower. She won't even do the annuals. But she's great at flower arranging."

"He's happy over there," she explains one day from her car phone. "And, I don't get near it."

Mary Scott has been a member of the Piedmont Garden Club off and on since moving to the area in 1975. It's been off and on because for 13 years, she spent Monday through Friday living in New York City when husband Willard took his weather shtick to NBC's Today Show.

"We came back to the country for every weekend during that time, except once," she says. He would commute early Monday morning. She had a standing Monday morning tennis date and would follow later in the day. They would return to their 15-acre home called "The Old Ground" each Friday.

Mary loves flowers and herbs. "I also have a cutting garden," she says, while taking a walking tour one morning. She raises dahlias, daffodils and tulips and "lots of lilies." There's a larger border around the swimming pool. "Basically, I'll see something that's pretty," she explains, "and I order it."

Once while on a trip to Mexico she admired a pergola and took a photo. "I came back and had it built and planted it with wisteria. Some told me it wouldn't work so fast, but in five years, I had shade."

Husband Willard also has a hand in the gardening. He has a small apple orchard with varieties of Lode, Red Delicious, Yellow Delicious, Grimes Golden, Red Rome Beauty, Fuji and Johnny Apple Tree. "Willard is especially proud of this as it's a cutting from the original Johnny Appleseed trees," Mary says.

He also raises peaches and strawberries and cures his own hams, as well. When the hogs are slaughtered each February, Willard rubs them with salt and, according to Mary, "pats them and loves them" and then hangs them in the smokehouse. They used to have chickens, but it got to be too much. "We had brown eggs," Mary says. "He would take them to NBC and sell them. He enjoys all that. He leaves no stone unturned as far as country life [is concerned]."

When Margaret "Meg" Gardner latches on to a subject, she goes well beyond total immersion. For example, she has a fascination with Lawrence of Arabia. She has a collection of hundreds of books on the subject. But beyond that, while reading his letters, if there's a book mentioned that he liked to read, she tracks that book down and reads it, too, like "Lady Into Fox" by David Garnett published in 1928. "You get to know more about a subject if you read everything they read," she says.

In 1994, she became enamored with the colorful glass Christmas ornaments made by Christopher Radko. She started a collection, now numbering over

2,500, which is one of the largest in the United States. She converted an old barn into a gallery to house the collection with glass cases lining the walls. A totally adorned tree is displayed year-round.

An avid foxhunter for 50 years, she served as Joint Master of the Middleburg Hunt for 10 years. Horses were an interest she shared with her late husband, Gary, who was killed in his Cessna 320C while flying back from Saratoga in August, 1994. Local artist Jean Bowman Morgan also died in the crash along with two people on the ground when the plane slammed into their home in Waynesboro, Pa. It was reported that the impact ignited a fuel tank. At that point, Meg tore down all the barns.

"I didn't want to wake up every morning and walk out and see the horses and all," she said. That's when she decided to take up gardening.

"I got tired of pulling weeds where everyone parked," she says. As usual she jumped in full speed ahead. She started with a parterre outside her kitchen door. This geometric section includes plants that are native to the area such as: *Picea pungens* 'Koster', grown with *Picea glauca* "Conica," along with a tree called Cunninghamia lanceolata, which was named in honor of James Cunningham, who discovered the tree in 1702.

One gets a first glimpse of Meg Gardner's personality, at times whimsical and at other times downright serious, driving up to Wingfield Farm. There appears to be a flock of sheep grazing on the hilltop. They are in fact custom-made faux sheep made of wire (built right on the farm, which we will get to in a minute).

At the crest of the hill, a sculpture of a goddess is surrounded by pillars set in a square of bricks and stones surrounded by maple trees and *Ilex glabra* or inkberry shrubs. Next comes "The Urn Garden," a circular brick path surrounding a variety of rock plants. A large willow and tall evergreens, along with rose bushes, make this a favorite spot for this British native to have afternoon tea.

Down a steep brick walkway to the very bottom, a square gazebo is flanked on each side by two horse head sculptures, which she calls "The Four Horses of the Apocalypse."

One level up, a pool of spouting fish is bordered by what is called prison pines, loosely interpreted to symbolize escaping a prison wall. Along the next level called "The Appian Way" is a narrow garden of pines. And on the end is a statue of David with the head of Goliath resting at the base. In an unexplained occurrence, according to Meg, the water that sometimes pools on the statue has a reddish tinge, almost looking like blood. It's there on the day of our walkabout.

And there's more.

Not only did Meg want to dig deep into gardening, with masses of books on the subject in her kitchen sitting room, she also became fascinated with dwarf evergreens. This collection, which includes well over 200 varieties, is known as

"The Pygmy Pinetum."

Around a corner we come upon "The Hunt," a topiary project in the works. One can see the outlines of the yews also known as *Taxus baccata*: a fox and the horses in full gallop. One shrub didn't make it and Meg (with that dry British humor) installed a grave marker that reads "Here Lies Lucy."

She is always working on new elements. An octagon structure will eventually hold steel cutouts of people that are to be hand-painted. The cutouts swivel in the wind. "It's Swedish," she says, showing the page of a magazine that inspired the edifice.

In the back, a custom-designed chicken house, "The Hen Hilton, By Appointment to the Prince of Hanover," is adorned with a regal-looking antique plaque, a gift from a friend. And then there's a workshop Meg has outfitted for Dan Baker, the on-site artisan who has created so many of the extraordinary pieces here. She refers to him as "Dan Dan the painter man."

He has painted portraits of most of her 15 dogs. (Remember, when she decides she likes something…) They come in all sizes, including a flock of teacup poodles with names like Tuffer-Tuffer, Muffer-Muffer, Fluffer-Fluffer and Nuffer-Nuffer. Then there are the usual mixed breed types: K-Mart, Scruffy and Slob Dog (an overweight hound type), and two ferocious guard dogs, Dolly, a Rottweiler, and Ginger, a Doberman.

Although not a member of the garden club, Meg has opened her garden on many occasions. "If it brings enjoyment to others, then I like it," she says. "Everyone keeps asking me when am I going to give up making gardens? The answer to that is: when I run out of space."

Somehow that's not a surprise.

CHAPTER 10

NEVER A DULL MOMENT

Celeste and Henry Wheelwright at the Cakewalk.

*T*here's the story of one dearly departed Middleburg hostess who was having a cocktail party when the bartender had the gall to drop dead moments before the festivities were to begin. She ordered the remaining help not to call the rescue squad because her guests would be arriving shortly, reasoning that the poor soul couldn't be helped anyway, so why ruin the occasion?

The same woman once taught her 13-year-old grandson how to make a perfect Whiskey Sour on the theory that it was a necessary part of his liberal arts education, along with art appreciation and opera.

Seventy-something William Edward Grant, Sr. also learned to mix drinks at a tender age. "My mom put me to work when I was 12 years old," he recalls. He started cutting grass and then worked as a butler and learned to cook for Morris

Paris, who once owned Marley Farm. "When I was 16, he asked me if I wanted to learn to mix drinks," he says in a gravelly voice.

He is now a freelance bartender, following a 29-year career as assistant supply manager with the Washington-based Institute for Defense Analysis, a division of the Pentagon. As one of several older black residents, he supplements his income pouring drinks and passing ham biscuits at dinner parties, weddings and other social occasions. He charges $85 for the first four hours and $10 an hour after that.

Known as "Mister Grant," he brings along his own supplies to your party: cocktail shaker, corkscrew and swizzle sticks. He loves to talk about the good old days in Middleburg when Ethel Garrett, a grand dame at Chilly Bleak Farm, would gather all the help on the front lawn and pass out Christmas gifts. "She was a beautiful woman," he recalls. "She gave good things, candy and scarves."

Mister Grant also arrives with a medley of drink recipes. There's just one hitch here, though. He occasionally drinks his mistakes during the course of the party and may need a ride home.

He offers libations like The Moth Ball--guaranteed to keep you warm in the winter--and his own Blueberry Liquor, made with the juice of the blueberries he grows at his home near Rectortown.

THE MOTH BALL

Mix apple cider with 105 proof white lighting (also known as moonshine) and heat it up. Ratio to be determined at your own risk.

MISTER GRANT'S BLUEBERRY LIQUOR

Mix two cups of sugar with two cups of blueberry juice and melt them together. Mix with one fifth of the very cheapest vodka you can buy. Let it "set" for ten days before serving.

The timbre of boogie woogie, ragtime and stride resonates in the late evening summer air on the Saturday after Labor Day for the Goose Creek Jass and Ragtime Society's annual celebration. It's a scene that would rival anything F. Scott Fitzgerald may have envisioned in East Egg.

Middleburg does not have a "social season" like Palm Beach or the Hamptons. That's part of the attraction... the Middleburg mystique. This, after all, is the country. Understated yet elegant is invariably the norm. There's no such thing as a splashy ball and no flashy ladies luncheons either. However, there is never a dull moment.

Holmes Morison, a member of the long line (now six generations) of the Dulany family, lived at Welbourne, an elegant mansion in Upperville. He learned to appreciate the sounds of the enchanting 1920s: Bunk Johnson, King Oliver, Jelly Roll Morton and the New Orleans greats. His wife, the former Sally Harris, who lived at Stoke (another grand dwelling) near Aldie, shared his enthusiasm for the music.

When he died in 1972, family members wanted to have a classic jazz funeral but didn't have the time to organize it. Two years later, his son, Nat Morison, had that memorial service at Trinity Church. Members of the group report that "with a rolling of drums, the band played a funeral dirge for the processional, seated themselves in the chancel and played each hymn during the service, and then led the recessional with a blaring of trumpets and joyous music to celebrate the ascent of a loved one to join God in His Heaven."

Those gathered on May 11, 1974 returned to Welbourne for a reception. (And by the way, Welbourne is now a Bed and Breakfast run by that same Nat Morison and his wife, Sherry. At the end of the day, there were 14 people in the music room, and they made plans to re-group the following year.

They first assembled on the banks of the nearby Goose Creek with a 78 RPM Victrola to play their music. Using the aged subscription dance notion, they invited friends and asked them to chip in toward the expenses and bring their own refreshments. They adopted the name and used the original spelling of the word jass.

From then on, they would meet on alternate years at Welbourne and Stoke. When it's held at Welbourne it's called a "Cakewalk" and when it's held at Stoke they call it the "Stoke, Stomp and Strut." Members of the group include many members of the Morison family, such as the patriarchs Nat and George, who arrive in black tie. Gloria Armfield (the dynamo real estate broker at Armfield, Miller and Ripley Real Estate) and Howard Armfield (of the insurance agency Armfield, Harrison and Thomas); Gray and Anne Coyner, Tish and Martin Fleming, Barbara and Toby Merchant (owner of The Plains Pharmacy) and George Scheulen (owner of Scheulen, Patchett and Edwards Accoutants) and his wife, Barbara.

Musicians from all over the country are now flown in for the party, like The Boilermaker Jazz Band from Pittsburgh and Terry Waldo and his Gotham City Jazz Band from New York.Lovely Natalie Lamb from New York sings the blues of Ma Rainey and Bessie Smith.

A small dance floor is set up in front of the porch at the circa 1775 Welbourne manor house, which defines shabby gentility. When guests walk around to the side for the barbecue supper, one need only glance up at the gutters and wood trim. (Suffice to say they could use some attention, but this is also part of the charm.)

When the party is at Stoke, the dance floor is set up on the vast terrace of the Italianate villa owned by George Morison. An adjacent arbor drips with wisteria and children play hide and seek in a boxwood garden.

Everyone brings a lawn chair or blanket. Friends form their own picnic on the lawn. Bunny Nesbit has been attending for well over 20 years. She usually brings cold sliced London Broil, served with French bread and horseradish sauce. "I marinate it in whatever I happen to have (bourbon, spices, herbs, sherry, ketchup, minced garlic) for a good 12-18 hours," she says. "And then cook it on the hottest grill possible for five minutes on each side and slice on a diagonal very thin after it cools."

Others in her party supply sun dried tomato and basil pesto cheese torte, smoked salmon, assorted cheeses with crackers, fruit, deviled eggs and ham biscuits (a staple in these parts and we will get to those later).

"I also bring wine, beer, champagne, and the usual bourbon and vodka," says Bunny. (Set- ups are provided by a fleet of freelance bartenders.) "We just all come together and bring something we think everyone will enjoy. It's like a small neighborhood party within a larger party.Good people, good music, good food and drink, good time." And all that *jass*.

For an exquisite fall cocktail party for friends and neighbors at Oakwood, Nicky Perry sends out a simple invitation in autumn colors of yellows and orange. Two torches at the entrance to the driveway lead the way for guests. Valet car parkers are waiting by the house. Nicky greets friends just inside the front door of her federal-style brick home. A bartender takes drink orders. Party food of sliced beef with horseradish sauce, hot crabmeat dip, and ham biscuits are served in the dining room.

Ruth Scott, a long-time fixture in the area, does freelance catering work to coordinate the food and the help for many parties. Ruth is also sexton at Middleburg Emmanuel Episcopal Church. "She helped me arrange for the ham biscuits," Nicky says. "And there're a number of women who do this but we used Jerry Ann Dade. Her biscuits are wonderful."

Indeed, they are famous in these parts. When Senator John Warner married Elizabeth Taylor in December, 1976 on a hillside at his farm called Atoka, Jerry Ann Dade made her ham biscuits for the reception.

The classic bite-size delicacy is a staple at many Middleburg parties, from the tailgate to wedding receptions and cocktail parties.

Jerry worked for "The Senator" for 20 years and when he sold the farm to Susan and George Carnercio, Jerry Ann stayed on. In her off time, she makes the biscuits. "One time I did 500 when someone was having a cattle sale at his farm," she says. She charges $3.50 per dozen, without the ham, which, by the way, simply must be Virginia country ham.

"Years ago, they started out as what is called a beaten biscuit," she explains. "Some people make an angel biscuit, with yeast. It's a bit lighter. But I make the baking powder biscuits." She rattles the recipe off the top of her head.

HAM BISCUITS
Makes two dozen

2 ½ cups flour
6 Tablespoons Crisco shortening
2/3 cup milk
3 teaspoons baking powder

Mix until it sticks together and then roll out on a floured surface. Use a1½ inch cookie cutter (Sold at the Gourmet Kitchen Plus in Middleburg). Bake on an ungreased cookie sheet for seven to 10 minutes or until the tops are brown in a 400-degree oven. Once cooled, cut in half and spread sparingly with butter. Add several paper-thin slices of Virginia Country ham the same size as the biscuit.

The Hunt Breakfast, to the uninitiated, is a misnomer. It never takes place in the morning. Rather, it's offered following the hunt and sometimes doesn't begin until four or five in the afternoon.

Zohar Ben-Dov, an Israeli-born real estate investor, moved to the area from New York in 1985. He exercises his passion for the sport five days a week. His wife, Lisa, often joins him, but divides her time between riding and playing tennis and working on a number of charity events.

On the third weekend in November, the Ben-Dovs entertain about 450 guests at their 400-acre Kinross Farm for an annual Hunt Breakfast.

"Since we hunt with many different groups, we invite all our hunting friends and a few others," Lisa says. Their farm bridges the Piedmont Hunt territory and the Orange County Hunt territory. The 80-plus riders of the Orange County Hunt meet at 10 a.m., finish about 2 p.m. and then join the others in the main house for the breakfast. Etiquette dictates that all riders should never wear their black or Pink coats inside, so the riders change into what is called a hacking jacket of tweed. It's also a no-no to ever wear spurs inside; they must be removed. (There are a few who should take note here; they've been spotted in spurs in the dining room.)

Lisa and Zohar greet the riders and offer them a "stirrup-cup," a drink before the hunt. "We have either sherry or port and for those who don't drink,

I offer apple cider," Lisa said.Led by huntsman Adrian Smith, the hunt's famous ring neck red foxhounds make their way down the long drive.

"I like to keep it simplistically elegant," Lisa says. With such a large guest list, she hires a caterer to execute her recipes. The theme for the table setting is different each year. "One year it was silver," Lisa says. The centerpiece was the Middleburg Hunt Cup, won by their steeplechase horse, David's Passing. A silver horn of plenty held the muffins. Another year, the motif was equestrian with the Ben-Dovs' collection of antique boot pulls, hunting whips and spurs surrounding a saddle and a mass of fall flowers.

Copper colors prevailed another year. Antique pots encircled by oranges, corn, and pears that had been spray-painted copper bronze stood out on a tablecloth that was salmon and hunter green. The plates are always black, Lisa's signature touch, because "the food looks so attractive on a black plate," she said. The napkins were salmon.

Each year they have a different cookie, a paper thin fall leaf or the fun black cows with the white center...exact duplicates of the Belted Galloway cows that the Ben-Dovs breed and raise. And two different dessert puddings that are positively scrumptious.

CROISSANT CUSTARD WITH APPLES
(Makes 8 servings)

3 apples-peeled and chopped
1/2 cup brown sugar
2 ounces rum
2 croissants cut into small squares
1/4 cup currants

Custard
1 quart half-and half
6 eggs
2 Tablespoons vanilla
1 cup + 6 Tablespoons sugar

Garnish
1 cup whipping cream
2 Tablespoons confectioner's sugar

Preheat oven to 350 degrees. Place chopped apples on a tray and sprinkle with the rum and brown sugar. Bake approximately 45 minutes until the sugar is melted and apples are tender. Place croissants on another baking sheet and bake until lightly browned, about 15 minutes.

Place custard ingredients in a bowl and beat with whisk until well mixed. Strain. Place equal amounts of the croissant and apple pieces in individual or large ovenproof dishes and mix in currants. Pour custard to top of large soufflé dish and put in another container and fill with water to come half way to the sides of soufflé dish. Bake 45 minutes until set. Whip cream and add sugar. Garnish each serving with a generous amount of the whipped cream.

BANANA PUDDING
(Makes 8 servings)

Custard
8 egg yolks
1/2 cup sugar
4 cups half-and-half
1 teaspoon grated lemon rind
1 teaspoon vanilla

Put ingredients in top of double boiler over simmering water. Whisk constantly until slightly thickened. Cool.

Layer a bowl with alternating layers of vanilla wagers and sliced bananas (using six bananas and 3/4 box vanilla wafers), covering each layer with the custard.

Make your favorite banana pudding, alternating banana slices and vanilla wafers and substituting half-and-half for the milk and using a vanilla bean for seasoning. Serve with whipped cream: one pint whipped cream with two tablespoons Myers rum.

———————————

There are very few people who could get four Episcopal priests together in the same room for anything except something pious. Since 1972, Alice and Angus Thuermer have a divine Christmas caroling party, which could be called "Oh Come All Ye Faithful."

In the second floor of their home, a converted Dutch Colonial barn, partygoers unite for an event with a Scottish flair. Men and women are urged to wear tartan. The eggnog is served from a sparkling silver punch bowl.

Angus MacLean Thuermer is a towering figure (6-foot-2) and traces his Scottish heritage to his eponymous maternal grandfather, who was from the Isle of Skye. Angus worked for the CIA (in the clandestine services) for 26 years and served as official spokesman for four Directors. He always introduced himself as "The Spooksman." Through the years, he and Alice have lived in India, West Africa and Germany, where he served as chief of base in Berlin and had a television in his office focused on Checkpoint Charlie. They have traveled to all corners of the world. Now in their early 80s, in one recent year, they went to London for a week of theatre, up the Yangtze River, down the Mississippi on the Delta Queen, took a ship to Antarctica and attended a family reunion in Yellowstone Park.

Through the years, Alice has worked as a writer and a copy editor at the Indianapolis Star and a reporter for the Associated Press in Chicago. They make an adorable couple; she is "just five feet tall."

Their cast of fascinating friends for the Caroling Party includes Barbara and Harry Rositzke, (he worked as head of Soviet operations at "The Agency"), Ambassador Richard Viets (who served in Tanzania and Jordan) and his wife, Dielle Fleischmann (as in margarine), Kim and Brit Hume(who both run the Washington bureau of Fox News and spend weekends at their country home in—what else—Hume) and Sally and Dick Irish (who both served in the Peace Corps in The Philippines).

The highlight of the evening comes when Angus stands beside the foot pedaled reed organ (purchased from some missionaries in West Africa) to lead the gathering for carols.For "We Three Kings," the Reverends Neale Morgan (retired from Middleburg Emmanuel), Robert Davenport (Trinity Church in Upperville), Douglas MacCaleb (Christ Church in Winchester and in full tartan kilt) and Mark Andrus (Emmanuel in Middleburg) take center stage. It's anything but a Silent Night.

ALICE THUERMER'S EGGNOG
(Makes about 100 punch cups)

15 eggs
1 ¼ cups sugar
2 ½ cups bourbon
½ plus 1/3 cup dark rum
5 cups heavy cream, whipped
6 ¼cups milk

Separate eggs. Keep whites aside. Beat yokes till lemon-

colored, adding sugar gradually. Fold in bourbon and rum. ·
Just before serving, add milk, the heavy cream, whipped and
the egg whites beaten till stiff but not dry.
Enjoy.

———————

Diana and Josh Muss have an annual open house on New Year's Day. "It
started out years ago as a get-together to watch football and cure hangovers,"
Diana says. It's evolved (as parties do), and in recent years, the Orange County
Hunt has met at their 180-acre Fox Valley Farm and it's also been a Hunt
Breakfast.

The guest list includes friends from the country but also friends from
Washington, such as former Senator Richard Stone and wife Marlene, local
television personalities Paul Berry and Barbara Harrison, as well as Chris
Wallace--a nationally known ABC television journalist--and his wife, Lorraine.

Diana staggers the afternoon arrival time of the 65 guests, so everyone isn't
alighting at the same time. The menu consists of grilled beef tenderloin with
condiments of horseradish cream and apricot chutney, sweet potatoes with
honey and butter and mushrooms in Madeira cream. Her specialties just for the
occasion are scalloped oysters and black-eyed pea vinaigrette--for good luck
throughout the New Year.

SCALLOPED OYSTERS
(Makes 8 servings)

Clean 1-pint oysters (save and strain liquid from oysters)
Cracker crumbs, coarsely crushed
½ stick butter
1 cup (plus) half and half
Salt and pepper

Butter 1½ quart casserole. Place a layer of crumbs (which have
been moistened with half-and-half) on the bottom of dish.
Add a layer of oysters, dot oysters with butter, salt and pepper.
Cover this layer with crumbs and repeat to make two layers.
Finish by pouring the remaining cream over top layer. Bake at
350 degrees for 40 minutes.

GOOD LUCK BLACK EYED PEAS
(Makes 8 servings)

2½ cups dried black-eyed peas
Fresh ground salt
Fresh ground black pepper
2 bay leaves
Fresh parsley
5 garlic cloves
1 large onion cut into large pieces
½ pound bacon, cut into two inch pieces

Cover the peas with about two to three inches of water along with salt, pepper, bay leaves, parsley, garlic, onion and bacon. Cover and cook over medium heat until peas are tender, about 45-60 minutes. To be served piping hot from a chafing dish.

The community spirit extends beyond the Hunt Breakfasts and the cocktail parties in Middleburg. Men and women who are often seen at these various "dos" can be found several times a year with their sleeves rolled up toiling in the kitchens at the Trinity Episcopal Church.

Ten times a year, a group of dedicated volunteers led by Neil Peddicord makes lunch for 600 needy people for a Washington-based organization called So Others Might Eat (SOME).Women like Stephanie Knapp, who lives atop a nearby hillside in a lovely home called Four Winds, comes to chop and dice for a rice and vegetable dish.

""We have a debt that goes forward for people who are less fortunate than ourselves," she says simply. Harriet Condon, Helen McCarty, DeeDee Cady, Debbie Weisman, Sarah Sisk and Edie Smart labor in the kitchen. "So many have helped in the 14 years we have been doing this," Neil says. Missy Janes, Barry Groom, Jackie Eldridge, Joan Elliot, Dorothy Gow, Kerry Dale, Marsha Keech and Alice Falkner bring a total of 50 dozen brownies. (One time the girls at Foxcroft brought ten dozen brownies.) Mark Smith and Jimmy Hatcher load up the church van with the food. And finally, Neil and Ann MacLeod head to O Street in Northwest Washington, not far from the Capitol.

"We are commanded to let our faith show through in our work," Stephanie says.

RICE AND VEGETABLES
(Six hundred servings)

50 pounds of rice
24 pounds of carrots
24 bunches of celery
1 dozen, 36-ounces packages of frozen, chopped spinach
12 pounds of butter
1 dozen, 46-ounce cans of chicken broth

Get six helpers together, wash celery and carrots and chop ugly ends off. Slice up carrots and celery using one bunch each for each of the 24 heavy foil trays. Use ½ package of thawed spinach. Use between two or three cups of raw dry rice and stir with the vegetables, then smooth it out in bottom of pan. Add salt and pepper and two sticks of butter. Add ½ can of broth, plus ¾ can of water, which has already been heated together. Cover with heavy foil as tightly as possible and bake at 350 degrees for about one hour or more.

———————

The tailgate season begins in February with the "unsanctioned" (that means point-to-point races sponsored by the various hunts) and ends with the fall steeplechase circuit, recognized by the National Steeplechase and Hunt Association. In between are horse shows and polo matches.

The highlight, of course, would be the Middleburg spring and fall races at Glenwood Park or the Virginia Gold Cup at Great Meadow, a resplendent parade of fancy fashion and sleek automobiles. Add to that fast horses and loose women (some might amend that to women on the loose), though sometimes the horses get loose, too.

Often, several people will go in together and buy a parking space at the races. Everyone brings something. For this I offer a phantom tailgate, put together with recipes and tips from a group of friends.

DOC SAFFER'S ULTIMATE
BLOODY MARY ADDITIVE

1 quart vodka
1 bottle of whole peppercorns
1 lemon

3 empty Worcestershire bottles

In an empty vodka bottle, pour contents of one bottle of peppercorns (This is the basic flavor so if you have a favorite, use it). Peel outer skin from lemon and put it in with peppercorns. Fill the bottle with vodka. Let it sit for three months. Turn bottle over several times every four weeks to mix. At the end of three months, run liquid through a coffee filter, and transfer contents to empty Worcestershire bottles. Add three drops (this is potent stuff) to a Bloody Mary cocktail and you will experience the Ultimate Bloody Mary!

JANA LEEPSON'S MUSHROOM PATE

1 pound mushrooms
1 large onion
2 cloves garlic
1 pound tofu
3/4 cup ground almonds
2 Tablespoons minced parsley
2 Tablespoons soy sauce
1/2 teaspoon thyme
Dash of white pepper and cayenne

Saute mushrooms, onion and garlic in butter. Mix all ingredients in food processor and refrigerate before serving. Garnish with fresh parsley.

SUSAN WALLACE'S PASTA SALAD
WITH SUNDRIED TOMATOES
(Makes 8 servings)

2 cups sundried tomatoes in herbs and olive oil
1 pound box of pasta (penne, fusili or rotini are the best) cooked according to package direction, drain and cool
1/2 cup fresh herbs (basil, oregano)
1 clove garlic, finely minced
Salt and pepper to taste

Slice tomato pieces length wise in 1/4 inch strips. Combine

cooked pasta with tomatoes, 1/2-cup olive oil from tomato jar, herbs, salt, pepper and garlic. Toss to coat pasta well and serve.

FIONA HUGHES'S SCOTCH EGGS
(Makes 10 servings)

10 peeled hard-boiled jumbo eggs
2 pounds ground pork
Flour
2 eggs
1 cup fresh breadcrumbs

To taste: sage, thyme, garlic
1/2 teaspoon white pepper
1/2 teaspoon black pepper
1 teaspoon salt

Cooking:
1 beaten egg
1 cup fresh breadcrumbs

In a food processor mix pork, raw eggs, breadcrumbs and seasonings until pork is finely ground. Roll hardboiled egg in flour and then sausage mixture. Dip in egg and then roll in breadcrumbs. Fry, either in deep fat or keep turning in shallow fat, until brown all over. Serve cold with favorite mustard, relish or chutney.

MARTHA CHAPMAN'S FRIED CHICKEN

For the fried chicken I called upon my friend Martha Chapman, mother of three—including twin daughters—and much too busy too cook. This was the message she left on my voice mail.
I have only one recipe for fried chicken—that is, you drive west on Route 50 and take a left where the sign says Atoka. Veer right immediately and park your car on the right at the Atoka store. Take out $8.99 from your wallet and walk into the store and order one bucket of chicken. It's awesome and

the latest rage."

Okay. And for an additional main course, Linda Young, my good friend and excellent administrative manager, orders a side of smoked salmon. But this isn't just any old salmon. Andi Marr, another friend, has a business called "Just The Best Scottish Smoked Salmon." This delicacy is flown to Dulles Airport from the coastal village of Achiltibuie in the Highlands direct to your front door. Linda embellishes the platter with capers, finely chopped onions, wedges of lemon and party-size pumpernickel bread.

FRANNY KANSTEINER'S
LUSCIOUS LEMON SQUARES
(Makes 24 servings)

Make the shortbread crust first:
1 cup flour
1/2 cup butter
1/4 cup sugar

Blend well and press into a 7 x 11 x 1 1/2-inch pan. Bake at 325 degrees for 20 minutes or until browned lightly on top.

For the filling:
1 cup sugar
2 eggs lightly beaten
3 Tablespoons lemon juice
1/2 teaspoon lemon rind
1/2 teaspoon salt
2 Tablespoon flour
1/2 teaspoon baking powder
Confectioner's sugar

Mix sugar, eggs, lemon juice and rind, salt, flour and baking soda. Pour over hot shortbread crust and bake for 25 more minutes at 325 degrees. Remove from oven, cool in pan and sprinkle with confectioner's sugar and cut into squares.

On Memorial Day weekend, the countryside is crawling with visitors, also known as tourists, for two major charity events. For over 40 years the Hunt Country Stable Tour sponsored by Trinity Episcopal Church in Upperville offers a tour of the major farms. Among the 14 stops on the tour are the Mellon estate, Rokeby, the Robert Johnsons' Salamander Farm and the Middleburg Agricultural Research and Extension Center (MARE), a 419-acre working farm donated in 1949 by Paul Mellon to Virginia Tech for research on the nutritional care of horses. Proceeds from the tour, as much as $50,000 a year, benefit the church's many outreach programs.

At the Emmanuel Episcopal Church in Delaplane, Mary Scott leads a group of 100 volunteers for the annual Strawberry Festival, held at nearby Sky Meadows State Park. Now in its eighth year, they have raised $60,000 in one weekend for their outreach program. The atmosphere is "simple" according to Mary. "We have an egg and spoon race for the children, a cake walk and tug of war." And, of course, there are tons of strawberries, all locally grown. There are fresh strawberries and strawberry sundaes. And, what would a Strawberry Festival be without a strawberry pie? And who better to help his wife with all of this than television's favorite weatherman, Willard Scott?

WILLARD SCOTT'S STRAWBERRY PIE

1 baked pie shell
1 quart strawberries
1 cup sugar
1/4 teaspoon salt
1/4 cup water
3 Tablespoons cornstarch
1/4 cup water

Wash and hull strawberries. Chill all but 1 cup, mash this cupful, and add to it the sugar, salt and 1/4 cup water heat to boiling. Blend cornstarch with water, combine this with boiling mixture, cook and stir until clear. Add chilled berries; pour into baked pie shell and chill.

———————

Before moving to Washington, young Sarah Smothers would have a very special birthday each year. About one month before her birthday, she and her mother, Lorraine, would start thinking about the "theme." For her fifth birthday in June, 1992, the theme was a "Rainbow Unicorn" high tea.

Lorraine (now Mrs. Chris Wallace) orders the invitations from Pretty Paper in Richmond. "They fax me a couple of samples and I go over it with Sarah and she decides," she says. The invitations are mailed two weeks in advance. She buys the party favors and games at G Whillikers Toys in Warrenton. The girls received gold garlands and the boys got gold crowns. Everyone got a goodie bag of mini-trolls, super balls, card games, My Little Pony fruit snacks and a bubble wand. A fresh supply of homemade bubbles is on hand for them to play with out in the vast; meticulously kept back yard that looks like an English postcard.

Lorraine makes a trip to a craft store and buys Lilliputian size baskets, which she spray paints and makes little centerpieces with carnations for the children's table. Then, she says, "I buy big bolts of pink and white tulle. I staple it to the three trees in the grove where we set up the children's table."

The girls (all in pretty summer dresses) are set up at a miniature makeup table. They can primp with play lipstick and nail polish. The boys get rubber stamps to play with and make designs on paper. Sarah's younger brother, Remmick, is also among the guests. He celebrates his birthday in October, with just as much pomp.

The children play on the swing set in the back yard or blow bubbles. Sarah's father, comedian Dick Smothers, is on hand to play games such as Unicorn Hoops, in which parents are positioned on a baseline, while the children run a relay gathering hoops on their unicorn horns. And of course Dick Smothers records the entire event on videotape! Uncle Tommy Smothers demonstrates his famous yo-yo tricks.

A British game called Pass The Parcel, which Lorraine learned as a child while attending boarding school, involves all the children sitting in a large circle on the grass. A tape cassette with music is played and when the music stops, whoever has the parcel gets to open it up. The package contains little individually wrapped presents, one after another, in one big present.

"We encourage the parents to come and stay," Lorraine says. "We like them to play games and have a good time too." For the adults, tea sandwiches of cucumber, egg salad and cream cheese with green olives, currant scones and clotted cream. All are arranged attractively on a silver tray on the table covered with a perfectly pressed floral linen cloth.

The sandwiches and scones, as well as Sarah's birthday cake (sponge cake with cream icing and raspberries), are done by Donna Draisey, who owns the downtown Middleburg restaurant and business, The Country Sampler and Details Catering and Special Events. Lorraine makes her ice tea using an herbal tea with no caffeine such as mango or watermelon mixed in equal parts with fresh lemonade and a splash of pineapple juice. Fresh mint is served on the side. An English flavor prevails throughout the party.

The children sit at a long table in the grove. Peanut butter and jelly and egg salad sandwiches are served on a silver tray. Carrot and celery sticks are offered and then it's time for the cake. Lorraine, never one to miss a detail, helps cut the cake and has individual cups of ice cream ready for each guest.

The presents are opened and the children gather up their goodies and yet another lovely birthday party slowly draws to a close. During the week following her party, Sarah sits down at her small desk and creates colorful thank you notes of construction paper and sends them to all her little friends. A future gracious hostess... just like her mother.

BUBBLE MIX

This recipe comes from Elna McMann
of G Whillikers Toys in Warrenton:

2 cups Joy dishwashing detergent
6 cups water
3/4 Karo light corn syrup

Combine, shake and let settle for four hours. For best results use only Joy and Karo brands. It's non-toxic, but not for human consumption.

PINWHEEL TEA SANDWICHES

For these sandwiches, Donna Draisey of Details Catering in Middleburg recommends using one loaf of unsliced white bread with your favorite sandwich fillings: smooth butter or cream cheese mixtures are especially good. Try peanut butter and jelly for the children. Chopped cucumber and egg salad can also be used. Remove outer crust from bread and slice horizontally in 1/2-inch thickness. Gently roll with a rolling pin. Spread filling over bread and roll up. Chill. Slice before serving.

This is from Donna Draisey of Details Catering in Middleburg, too.

BIRTHDAY CAKE
(Makes 20-25 servings)

9 eggs, lukewarm
1 1/2 cups sugar
1 Tablespoon vanilla
2 (scant) cups sifted flour
6 Tablespoons melted butter

Preheat oven to 350 degrees. Beat eggs and one cup sugar at medium speed for seven minutes and add remaining sugar and beat until lemon colored and forms a ribbon. Add vanilla and fold in sifted flour. Then fold in melted butter. Pour into greased and floured 12-inch cake pan and bake until tester inserted in center comes out clean, 35-40 minutes. Remove from pan and cool on rack.

Filling:
3 cups fresh raspberries

Frosting:
1 1/2 pound cream cheese, room temperature
1/2 pound unsalted butter, room temperature
2 Tablespoons vanilla
8 ounces imported white chocolate, melted and cooled
5-6 cups confectioner's sugar

Beat the cream cheese and butter until smooth, add vanilla and chocolate. Blend in sugar until frosting is proper consistency to spread.

Soaking syrup:
1 1/2 cups water
3/4 cup sugar
1/2 cup favorite liqueur, optional

To assemble: using a serrated knife, cut cake into four layers. Place bottom layer on cake plate and brush with soaking syrup. Spread with frosting. Top with next layer and brush with syrup. Cover with fresh raspberries, leaving a 1/4-inch border. Top with third layer and brush with syrup, spread with frosting. Brush remaining layers with syrup and place on top. Frost sides and top and decorate with fresh flowers.

The invitation from Diana and Bert Firestone defines their June garden party...exquisite. It makes this initial statement of refinement with the green and white racing silks used by Newstead Farm.

For the Firestones and their daughter Alison, horses are a way of life.

They've owned many major thoroughbred racehorses, including Genuine Risk, the first filly in 65 years to win the Kentucky Derby and the only filly ever to place in all three Triple Crown events. In addition to their race horse interests from New York to California, all three Firestones ride on the horse show circuit, including trips to Europe, where Alison competes on the international tour.

They love to sample the local cuisine along the way. "Diana and I and maybe a few friends like to eat at nice restaurants," Bert says, "And Alison has her own friends she goes out with."Alison will be a leading contender for the U.S. Olympic team before the 2004 Games in Athens.

When the annual Upperville Colt and Horse Show takes place in early June, not far from their 400-acre farm, Diana says, "it's a great way to entertain all our friends we see all year."

Indeed, there are over 400 guests invited for a garden dinner party. The guest list, which Diana works on throughout the year, includes their horsey friends in town for the show as well as a cross section of friends, neighbors, folks from church, and local politicians. Tutti Perricone, owner of Back Street Cafe and Catering, assists the Firestones in orchestrating the event. Six weeks before the guests arrive, Bert meets with Tutti to formulate the menu. "We like to have something that everyone would like," he says.

"It always includes beef tenderloin," Tutti adds. "It's one of his favorites." The tenderloin is served with two sauces, horseradish and roasted red pepper mayonnaise, along with fresh tri-color ribbon pasta, sautéed polenta crab cakes, Italian sausage ratatouille and another Firestone favorite, fresh asparagus. The Firestones preview the wine and choose the local Piedmont Vineyards, appropriately named Hunt Country White Chardonnay.

The party is the most elaborate entertaining done by the Firestones all year. When they are not traveling, they like to have small dinner parties for 8-10 guests in their formal dining room. And when the three happen to be home for dinner in the summer, "we like to grill a steak and have some sliced tomatoes." And for dessert? "Apple pie," Bert adds.

Tutti, a Middleburg native, started working in a local restaurant as a dishwasher, then waitress and finally bookkeeper. She opened her own business 10 years ago. On the day of the party, her husband, Vince Perricone, locks up his print shop (where the invitations were produced) and drives a refrigerated truck out to the farm and works with the crew in the cooking tent.

But for this affair Tutti takes center stage.

"I never had formal training in cooking," she says, "I learned a lot through observation. I love food, we have a personal relationship." She also has a personal relationship with music--a gospel singer as a young girl and now a star in countless local productions, she is known as a "culinary diva."After setting up tables all day, giving instructions to the 30 waiters and waitresses and preparing a feast, she changes clothes and joins the jazz trio in the gazebo by the pool for a set of songs.

The community spirit carries on with many local products incorporated. The salad baby greens were grown by a nearby farmer. Middleburg's Lowelands Farm French Tarragon Vinegar was used for the dressing and their Honey of a Mustard was part of the antipasto display assembled by Middleburg floral designer Markey Love.

Markey, a gardener and flower arranger for 15 years, uses an etageres a fleurs (three- tiered plant stand) to construct an impressive antipasto presentation. She gathers Bells of Ireland, lilies, roses, dianthus, and lemon leaf and mini cypress from various sources, for the floral accents. Then she adds potted herbs, salade savoie, ropes of garlic, salami, smoked cheeses and proscuitto ham along with bowls of olives and baskets of fresh Parmesan cheese. She and Tutti complete the look with two-foot wide terra cotta pots for the salad and large beehive shaped pots for the homemade foccacia bread and herbed breadsticks.

The Italian essence in the food is completed with the centerpieces Markey designs the day before at her downtown Middleburg workshop, using terra cotta pots with red dianthus and aromatic herbs particularly basil, oregano and "for the feathery effect fennel," Markey adds.

"Everything color-wise is very simple because of the setting. We don't want to upstage the backdrop," Diana explains. Hence, the tablecloths are white with large squares of their racing green in the center. All of this comes together against a majestic setting. The gardens, circa early 1800s, stretch out on terraces very much like one might see in the hillsides of Italy. A series of rooms lead down to a reflecting pool with a bronze sculpture "Joy of the Waters." All of this overlooking a large pond as ladies in linen dresses sip white wine and oooh and aaaaah at the perennial flowers.

Bert Firestone greets the guests at the appointed hour of 7 p.m. Diana runs late after riding in the show, but not without good results. She is often in the winner's circle in the Amateur Owner Hunter classes. Men in blue blazers with silk ties of horses, spurs, and foxes (with a few tennis racquets and ducks thrown in for good measure) mingle and mix and perhaps drink the favorite local bourbon, Virginia Gentleman.

Torch and tree lights installed for the evening lead the way to a ravishing dessert table brimming with miniature cannolis, lemon torta profiteroles and strawberry Grand Marnier tarts (with local strawberries, of course.). The tent on hold in case of rain is clearly not needed as the party comes to a graceful conclusion. At this time of year, when the Virginia farmers are focused on the weather forecast while making hay, the threat of rain is real.

"We're just lucky with the weather," Bert Firestone says, smiling and looking off in the distance to the Blue Ridge Mountains.

(Facing page, top left, clockwise) Sally Bolton, Donna Hackman, Shannon Davis and Tempe Weinbach, Lauren and Rene Woolcott, The Coach Stop was once a local gathering place, Former Hill School headmaster Tom Northrup

(Top left, clockwise) Tyler Gore, Kathie Hoerner and Tim Hoerner, Jimmy Hatcher and Carolyn Douglas, Sheryl Bills Heckler Wood and Dot Smithwick

CHAPTER 11

REAL...ESTATES

Each place in Middleburg has a story all its own.

*T*here's the story one real estate broker tells of the "tire kicker." It seems the visitor in question was reading the Sunday "Country Properties" classifieds in *The Washington Post* and decided it might be "fun" to spend the afternoon in Middleburg. He called and made an appointment. The broker showed him all around.

The last stop on the "tour" took them down a charming dirt country lane and across a cattle guard. There was a gate to open and close as they drove up into the farm. The visitor politely obliged since the broker was behind the wheel.

At the end of the look-around, the man from the city confessed. He appreciated the time and effort, but really didn't have any interest in purchasing. He just thought a day in the country might be "fun."

When the visitor got out to open the gate as they departed the estate, the broker drove off, leaving him stranded.

He says he just thought that might be "fun" as well.

Real Estate broker Phil Thomas has been a commanding presence since 1967 at the main intersection of Washington and Madison Streets, just steps from the only traffic light in town. (And no, he's not the drive-away broker described above, although he and several others did relate to the story.) He has listed and sold just about every major piece of property in the area at least once, sometimes more. In 1999, his company listed and sold 64 properties totaling over $75 million. Thomas and Talbot Real Estate is also an exclusive affiliate of Christie's Great Estates International.

Phil served as agent for lease between Hubert B. Phipps and Phoebe Phipps and John F. Kennedy and Jacqueline Kennedy. The date on the Kennedy lease for a house near Atoka is May 15, 1963, and the cost was $2,000 for two months. The original is framed and hangs on his office wall, along with numerous maps of the countryside. Phil can go on for hours with stories on properties and the provenance of each estate.

When Phil first started to sell real estate, a 300- to 500-acre place would go for $300 to $500 per acre, including "proper improvements, manor house, etc." Over 30 years later, the average price is $15,000 per acre.

He began with an office in the basement of the Middleburg Bank in 1962. At the time, there was just one other serious competitor up the street, John Talbot. "We were at each other's throats all the time," Phil says over lunch in The Tap Room at The Red Fox. "We didn't even dare take a vacation for fear the other would get some business. So we decided to make a deal."

They formed Thomas and Talbot Real Estate in 1967. Then they needed an office, but there was just one problem.

"We didn't have any money," he relates. "We were flat broke. There was an antique shop in the building at the time, Raymond Bates. He wanted to sell. John knew a lawyer, Wilber Hall in Leesburg. He was the dean of lawyers. He handled trusts for people. We didn't have any money at all, but we told him we wanted to borrow 100 percent of the mortgage money. No, actually we told him we wanted to borrow 110 percent, because we wanted to make improvements. A few points and we got it."

About five years later, John Talbot wanted out. Again, Thomas made a sweet deal. "I wrote him a check and refinanced the building and I'm still here," he says. "It's been fun. And I learned a lot from John."

His immense private office looks more like a den or library and resembles a page out of coffee table book defining the English or Scottish country look. The walls are finished in a glazed hunter green. He sits in a lofty swivel red leather chair behind an antique desk with red leather top. Old sporting paintings adorn the walls. There's an antique globe and several collections: pigs and one of miniature soldiers. There are oriental rugs and a red leather couch with needlepoint pillows. A coffee table brims with photo albums of properties and books on everything from hunting to carriage driving, a diversion he shares with his wife Patricia (Patti) Thomas, an attorney and member of the Town Council.

It hasn't all been effortless. "It's been feast or famine," he says. During one recession he lived in one of two apartments above the office. "In each decade a different engine is the driving force of the real estate market," he says.

In the 1960s, he met up with an investor named James S. Abrams, who made money with a pharmaceutical company that manufactured birth control pills. "These places out here were pretty tattered at the time," Phil relates. "He bought some of them and fixed them up and resold them."

Of course, Middleburg has always been popular with the horse crowd, and these days, it's the high tech crowd. "They have a great deal of wealth and they want to live in a protected area," he says.

———————

When Jack Kent Cooke arrived in Middleburg in the late 1970s, he was one of the wealthiest men in America. A Canadian by birth, he'd made his original fortune in the radio business in partnership with fellow media mogul Lord Roy Thomson.

A few years before relocating to Virginia, Cooke had divorced his first wife and "love of his life" Jeanne after over 40 years of marriage. By then a billionaire, Cooke had also made a fortune at the dawn of the cable television industry and was also one of the originators of pay per view sports television as a promoter of several of Muhammad Ali's major fights. He was an owner of the Triple-A minor league baseball team in Toronto and soon expanded his sports interests to include ownership of the Los Angeles Lakers basketball team and the Los Angeles Kings hockey team, building the arena known as "The Fabulous Forum" in Inglewood, Calif. He also held a minority interest in the Washington Redskins football team, but was unable to take part in their day-to-day operation because of his involvement in the NBA and NHL.

After the divorce, one that included a then record $42 million settlement (negotiated, by the way, by Judge Joseph Wapner of television's "The People's Court") to his wife, Cooke divested himself of the basketball and hockey holdings in order to become the operating owner of the Redskins.

The team trained at a site near Dulles airport only 35 miles from Middleburg and Cooke decided the Virginia countryside was the perfect base of operations for his wide variety of investments. This included the team, major real estate holdings in Phoenix and ownership of the 77-story Chrysler Building in New York City, which he bought for over $80 million in 1979 and then spent another

$30 million in renovations.In 1985, he paid $176 million to purchase The *Los Angeles Daily News*.

In Middleburg, Cooke bought Heronwood, a property of about 50 acres, with a main house that is remarkable model of Georgian architecture, part of which dates to the 1700s. He promptly renamed it Fallingbrook in recollection of a rather well-to-do section of his hometown Toronto, where he had always aspired to live. Records indicated he had paid $1.3 million. A sales brochure at the time had described it as "secluded in the heart of Piedmont hunt country, a classic gentleman's equestrian estate." How fitting, since as time went on, journalists in Washington eventually fondly referred to this colorful character as "The Squire."

On his first night in his new house, there was a terrible thunderstorm and the lights went out. Cooke, a voracious reader of all literature, went into his new library, which featured exquisitely detailed shelves, marble floor and fireplace. He lit all the candles he could find and took down a book.

"It just wouldn't have been right without reading a book about Thomas Jefferson," he told more than one person.

The stone manor house's principal rooms open to an imposing grand hall. From here French doors open to an expansive rear terrace overlooking the lawns and gardens with a coveted view of the Blue Ridge Mountains beyond. It adjoins the property of the late Paul Mellon, who reportedly invited Cooke for a Sunday luncheon to meet Prince Charles and his ravishing wife Diana. But Cooke allegedly sent his regrets in favor of watching his beloved football team.

A master suite includes dual baths and dressing rooms (always of utmost importance for Cooke, with more on that later). There were two other bedrooms and a two-bedroom staff suite as well as self-contained apartments on the first floor. At the time there was a caretaker's residence and a guest house/office.

The grounds display one of the finest examples of topiary work in America. The gardens have been featured in a number of magazines though the years. One time, when I visited him on a scouting mission for House and Garden magazine, he rode his Tennessee walking horse through the manicured front lawn pointing out the various sections.

The boxwoods and yews were trained and pruned into various shapes, including nine-foot boxwood peacocks. The panorama combines weeping willow and fruit trees, arbors, fish and lily ponds and one of Cooke's favorite spots, a secret garden. There's also a heated swimming pool.

It was during his rather lonely days here that Cooke had a romance and a brief second marriage to artist Jean Maxwell Williams Wilson, also known as Jeanne Two.

The outbuildings included a gardener's cottage, guesthouse, pool house, potting house and sheds. There was also a broodmare barn for eight mares and a horse barn with seven stalls and a small tack building with two run-in sheds for horses. All of which would change for the better when Robert Smith purchased it for $1.7 million in 1983.

Smith (along with his brother-in-law Robert Kogod) owns the venture started by his late father, Charles E. Smith Commercial Realty L. P. and Charles E. Smith Residential Realty, Inc. As heads of the largest real estate development group in Virginia, with houses and apartments all over the map, the brothers-in-law net worth is $900 million as reported recently by Virginia Business Magazine.

When Smith first moved to the area, neighbors held their breath. If a man who had overseen the likes of suburban Washington's glass and concrete Crystal City transformed into a residential cash cow, they wondered what might do in the country?

Not to worry. Instead, Smith added to the land holdings, went back to the original name of Heronwood and transformed it into an unsullied retreat of about 600 acres. He called on Blackburn Architects in Washington, D.C. to design an addition to the main house and an artist's studio for his wife, Clarice.

Over a 10-year period, this firm went on to design a 20-stall broodmare barn, a 16-stall yearling barn, three two-stall isolation barns, a hay barn, a service storage building, grooms quarters, an apartment and vehicle service and storage areas and a farm manager's residence.

His property also came to include what is called the Grafton estate, once owned by revered Archibald C. Randolph, a Master of Foxhounds and sporting gentleman. "When he died," Phil Thomas explains, "he (Randolph) left it to his son and not his wife." According to Phil, Theo Randolph didn't want to pay the $500 per acre asking price.

"She had her lip all poked out about it," Phil says.

The land passed through a number of hands before it was purchased eventually by Bob Smith. The house at Grafton is in the classical revival style of architecture and it was built in the 1920's.It had been empty for a number of years before Smith bought it, and had deteriorated significantly. Termites and dry rot had devoured the house and a significant portion of the exterior walls had to be replaced. The house was rebuilt from the roof down. Before reconstruction began, the center of the house sagged six inches.

The old mansion was eventually converted into a farm office and four staff apartments. And the estate office (Robert Smith's office) was expanded. "It probably would have been cheaper for Mr. Smith to tear it down, but knowing the historic significance and the sensitivity of the community, he chose to restore it," says one local intimately familiar with the project.

The Smith holdings also include the historic and hallowed Upperville Horse Show grounds, once the very definition of shabby gentility, with leaking and creaking green and white frame official's stands. It's the oldest horse show in the United States and a very significant stop on the national circuit in early June.

The place was clearly in need of a facelift.

"One day, Bob Smith leaned over and asked me 'if it's so important why is it falling down?'" Phil Thomas recalls. Smith offered to do the repairs if members of the community would participate. "He said he would match dollar for dollar the money raised," Phil says. "So I went out and asked some people and all I got was 'Oh I'm strapped right now' or 'I'll get back to you.'"

Much to his credit, Smith took over the entire project. Now, skillful replacements (also done by the Blackburn firm) can hardly be recognized from the original structures.

Smith's horse racing interests through the years have produced a number of stakes winners, including the champion sprinter Rubiano and Kamar, a broodmare of the year.Now in his early 70s, Smith sold off all his horse interests by the late 1990s.

Meanwhile, Jack Kent Cooke moved on to Kent Farms in the early '80s. This was originally part of a farm called Atoka, owned by Senator John Warner, who also served on the board of The Washington Redskins. Warner and Cooke cut a private deal for the 183 acres.

Cooke built a modern house he named Far Acres, designed in the "style" of Frank Floyd Wright, and it was reported to have cost $1.8 million. It had one master suite bedroom (17 x 18) with a fireplace and a sitting area of equal size, and a boatload of closets, which Cooke loved to show off to visitors. It also includes his and her bathrooms with marble tops, whirlpool tubs and dressing rooms. But "his" dressing room is 11 X 32 and "hers" is 11 X 20.

The 5,900-square foot residence opened into a vaulted living room with Italian slate floors. The west side—all in glass—faces the Blue Ridge Mountains. Cooke loved to invite guests for a sunset cocktail in the adjoining sunroom.

While living at Kent Farms, Cooke married Suzanne Martin in July, 1987. Things started to get rather dicey and spicy out here.Pregnant when they were married, she had agreed to have an abortion, something she later said she'd done, but then reneged on her promise.

At one point, they had a terrible fight and she claimed she was forced out of their car along a country road and had to walk several miles in the dark to get home. Their daughter, Jacqueline, was born in January, 1988 while Cooke was in San Diego wallowing in his Redskins' Super Bowl victory. Seventy-three days after they were married, he filed for divorce. In spite of a pre-nuptial agreement, the court ordered child support payments of $29,000 a year.

The sunroom opened to the heated pool, site of many aquatic frolics and splash parties not only with Suzanne but also the next Mrs. Cooke, a beauty named Marlena Chalmers, who also just so happened to be one of Suzanne's old friends.

Known as the "Bolivian Bombshell," Marlena married Cooke in May, 1990. Not only had she once been convicted of conspiring to import cocaine, she'd spent over three months in prison. Her most notorious incident came in September, 1993 when she was stopped by the police in Georgetown at 1 a.m. with a 20-something young man perched on the hood of her sleek Jaguar.

Mr. Cooke died in April, 1997 at age 84. Marlena had been cut from his will, but she appealed and eventually went off into the sunset with a cool $20 million. To his only daughter Jacqueline, he left $5 million. And for her mother, Suzanne, not a bloody dime, as he might have said.

The outbuildings at Kent Farms include a pool/guest house and a two-story manager's house with five bedrooms. Add also a two-story tenant house with four bedrooms and yet another two-story tenant house with three bedrooms. (Need we mention all these outbuildings have more bedrooms than the main house?) And then there was the farm office complex, a 7,000-square foot converted barn from which "The Squire" ran his businesses. It included a reception area, boardroom, kitchen and computer rooms.

For horse lovers, the horseshoe-shaped stone stable with 12 stalls, tack room, office and feed rooms is the signature attraction. An apartment above has a great room, kitchen, bath and deck.

And, oh, almost forgot, it all includes your own polo field. Once known as Phipps Field after the legendary businessman and horse breeder Hubert B. Phipps. Cooke renamed it Kent Field and it is now known as Goose Creek Polo Field.

Patricia Brennan purchased the farm from the Cooke Estate in April, 2000 for $3.1 million, for her daughter, Maureen Brennan, an avid equestrienne. When she came to Virginia to look at the place, Maureen says she got a certain feeling or aura when driving up the long winding entrance. "I knew right away before I even saw the barns or anything," she says one day over lunch. After she looked around Kent Farm, she had Mary Ann McGowan, an agent with Thomas and Talbot, drive up the entrance again, just to make sure about that feeling.

Originally from Long Island, where she operated a hunter and jumper farm, Maureen, in her mid-30s, came to this area to be in a real horseman's community. "I was unprepared to be as awe struck on a daily basis at the beauty of the countryside in this part of the world. For me, preservation of the land has become a meaningful and important issue."

She has since renamed it Foxmount Farm, "the name of my paternal grandfather's family home/farm in Waterford, Ireland," she says. She is now breeding, raising, training, showing and selling Dutch Warmbloods.

"I am blessed to have parents that both emotionally and financially support, sponsor and encourage my dreams," Maureen says.

She has made only minor cosmetic changes, such as improving the entrance and fencing some fields. "I am trying to leave the environment as untouched as possible. For example, there are several wooded acres that I will allow to remain for wildlife to flourish."

In one of those unique Middleburg moments, I sent Maureen an email and asked about her move to the area. Her response was touching. She had truly captured the essence of this community after only a few months of living here.

"My move to the Middleburg area has positively affected my life on so many levels. I feel that I have both broadened and deepened my horsemanship skills. Life is supposed to be enjoyed and I truly have a sense of appreciating life and having fun.I made a conscious decision when I arrived that I would not say 'No' to any invitation.Thus far, I have honored my 'don't say no' motto and it has allowed me to have so many wonderful new experiences that I previously would have never imagined.This all may sound corny but I feel that relocating to Virginia has been a very significant part of my journey in my life. I love traditions and I can surely get my fill here. I love that Middleburg looks and has a feel of "Main Street USA" including the local friendly bank, bakery, hardware and book stores, etc.

"I love when someone asks, 'What do you do?'They don't mean where do you work? They mean, 'do you hunt, ride steeplechase horses, show jump or play polo?'"

Right next door to Kent Farms is the place known as Atoka Farm. This is the 557-acre estate that once belonged to Senator John Warner, known not only for his political achievements but also as the sixth husband of Elizabeth Taylor.

Warner was formerly married to Catherine Mellon, the daughter of the late Paul Mellon and that is how he came to own this historic property. It was on this farm where he married Taylor in 1976 and also hosted his political parties known as the Atoka Country Suppers.

Named for a Cherokee Indian chief, the main house, built of field stone, dates to 1816 with a number of renovations since that time. It has been referred to as a modified version of the classic elongated Virginia farmhouse to maximize the view and the sunlight.

There are old fireplaces with antique mantels and pegged oak floors. The 7,000-square foot house has five bedrooms with five bathrooms and two half baths. The entrance hall has a terra cotta floor and is 14 x 15 feet. The living room has a handsome black marble fireplace, custom cherry cabinetry and oak floors.

Outside, in a renovated barn, there's a heated indoor pool, where the Senator once hung symbolic flags of his career from the rafters—Secretary of the Navy, the Bicentennial, the U.S. Senate. There's a tennis court, a stone and log office and four tenant houses. Add to that a barn with seven stalls and an indoor exercise area, and a smaller barn with four stalls. Liz Taylor and Warner divorced in 1982.

In 1994, Atoka sold for a recorded price of $3.7 million as a weekend retreat for Jorge J. Carnicero and his wife, Susan. His Vienna, Virginia business, IntraDyne, offers technology solutions. Known as "George," he has served as president of the Washington International Horse Show for several years.

Hermen Greenberg serves as a vice president and a very active member of the board of same show. He has opened his Middleburg home on several occasions on behalf of the show, including a luncheon one year in honor of Zsa Zsa Gabor, who felt so at home by the end of the afternoon that she took her shoes off and put her feet up.

The Washington, D.C. real estate developer and his striking wife, Monica, bought Rutledge Farm in the mid-1980s. According to Regardie's Power Magazine, his Southern Engineering, Inc., has built 20,000 houses in the area and his estimated net worth is between $200-300 million.

Through the years, Monica has ridden in the ladies sidesaddle classes at many of the major shows in Virginia and at Washington, cutting quite the elegant figure on her horses.

They have since lovingly and meticulously restored the circa 1800 stone house, which has been featured in *House and Garden* and *Veranda* magazines. They added a carriage house (garage with apartment above but made to look like an old carriage house) and an addition to the main house. There was an existing porch on the rear that was enclosed and extended across the back.

The Greenbergs have furnished the house with period pieces all dated from 1820 to 1840. She worked with her friend and designer Irma Hariton. Everything down to the wide stenciled pine floorboards and even the lamps (which have no lampshades) is authentic. Dana Westring, a local decorative artist with international clientele, did a mural of Rutledge on a downstairs wall. Her numerous collections of Auguste Edourat silhouettes adorn the walls and displays of her cotton and straw bonnets and hand-made quilted petticoats grace the bedrooms upstairs.

With over 128 acres, in 2000 it was assessed for tax purposes at over $3 million. They have an extensive thoroughbred business, with numerous stables and an indoor arena. They have ten broodmares, some in foal to famous stallions such as Deputy Minister, one of the leading sires in the country. They raise and sell yearlings on the open market at the prestigious auctions of Keeneland and Saratoga--the Christies and Sotheby's of horsedom. They've bred and raised Colonial Affair, who won the 1993 Belmont Stakes (the final leg of the Triple Crown) and the Whitney Stakes at Saratoga. They bred Battle Mountain, a stakes winner who won over $400,000, and Clever Clever, another stakes winner.

Horses also have always been of utmost importance at Llangollen, which stretches out over 1,100 acres. It's often referred to as one of the most famous estates in the area. Roy Ash, the current owner, started Litton Industries, served as the CEO of Sara Lee, and was the treasurer for the 1984 Los Angles Olympic Games.

Built in 1830, it changed owners several times before John Hay Whitney and his legendary wife, Liz Tippet, purchased it in 1930. If the walls could talk here, they'd tell of the wild hunt balls thrown by Liz Tippet. And of the time she brought her favorite horse into the great room or the 35 dogs that lived here full time. (The most beloved ones were kept in her deep freezer when they passed on.) And of the well-known visitors: Doris Duke, Elsa Maxwell, Eddie Arcaro, Prince Aly Khan (who gave Liz away when she later married Richard Lunn), Bing Crosby, ambassadors and politicians from Washington.

Ash and his wife, Lila, are no strangers to life inside the Washington Beltway. He once served as director of the Office of Management and Budget under President Richard Nixon. They bought the house in 1989 for $6.9 million and did restorations under the guidance of decorator Phyllis Nee that took five years. The house is now 13,000 square feet. There's a horseshoe stable (where Liz Tippet kept a black bear in one stall when he wasn't chained to a tree), training barns, cattle barns, cemetery, private fire engines and more.

During the decorating and remodeling, Nee made discoveries all along the way. There were snakeskins in the basement and a walk-in safe for silver and jewelry now used as a wine cellar. All the walnut wood used for the new floors and free-floating staircase is from trees salvaged from the property. They've never brought a horse into the great room, but they do continue the traditions at Llangollen.

From his real estate transactions over the years, Phil Thomas has maintained a friendship with many of his clients. And as a result, he has visited many of them at their other homes in far-off places.

Such has been the case with Jeffrey Steiner, the chairman of Fairchild Corporation, which makes aviation parts. A native of Austria, Steiner has homes in the Hamptons, Manhattan, London and Paris. And Phil and Patti have visited him in the south of France too.

Phil met Steiner when he was in the area looking at property with his son, Eric, a polo player. He ended up buying Foxlease for $5.7 million. "One of the first things he did to help preserve the way of life was to place a permanent fox hunting easement on the farm," Phil says, ever mindful of the way of life in Middleburg. "I think that is so commendable."

Once owned by the Archbolds, a well-known family in Washington, D.C. Their estate, Hillandale, with a Tuscan-style mansion on the edge of Georgetown, was a landmark where sheep once grazed.

They also owned a country place—Foxlease Farm. The main house, known as "The Hut," was originally a rather rustic structure in the woods. When John Archbold decided to expand, he chose none other than Middleburg's most famous architect, Billy Dew, to design it. He envisioned a series of pavilions that are linked by transition rooms. It grew to include a massive music room (complete with commercial size organ from Hillandale) the most extraordinary chamber of the house; it extends to 30 by 64 feet. A number of benefit concerts have taken place here through the years. The room lends itself to such a setting with five sets of French doors that open to a Pennsylvania flagstone terrace similar to the loggia entrances at a theatre.

From the music room a visitor passes into the fountain room, a round room covered with a sky light with a water statue called "Dancing Boy" as the center attraction. A cupola above leads to a minstrel gallery. There're three gargoyles attached said to represent John Archbold, Billy Dew and the contractor's superintendent. From here, a visitor goes to a rather small, yet comfortable living room.

The main dining room is lofty and looks fit for a troop of knights in shining armor to appear for a meal. There are large straight-back chairs and a long hand carved dining table. The ceiling measures 22 feet high and there's a walk-in fireplace, which has been described as a duplicate of a Tuscan kitchen. There's a separate dining room for the staff.

The octagonal library is paneled in walnut. And a master bedroom has an adjacent spa pavilion lined with shimmering gold tiles.There are a total of nine extra bedrooms for guests.

As if nine extra bedrooms aren't enough for friends and guests, then there's "The Spook House," with an apartment. It was named after the designer, Charles Addams, a well-known writer and stage designer and illustrator. A friend of John Archbold, he did the first conceptual designs of this square two-story building.

There's the usual pool, stables and manager's quarters at Chilton too. Built in 1929 by a well-known local horseman Arthur White, it was once owned by Hobart Taylor, an African American attorney from Washington and Executive Vice Chairman of the President's Commission on Equal Employment Opportunity in the Kennedy and Johnson administrations. He has been credited with coining the phrase "affirmative action."

"I don't think he had a very good time here," says Marc Leepson, a writer and current owner along with his wife, Janna. "Some folks in the '60s and '70s cruelly referred to Chilton as Chitlins."

The Leepsons bought the 67 acres for $1.7 in 1988. They moved here from her family's 200-acre farm in the eastern part of the next county over, Prince William. The mega-mall known as Potomac Mills was one mile away.

"We wanted to be someplace where we weren't surrounded by development," he says, "And still be in the Washington area." At first the barns were a bonus. "It was the house, we liked. It had the location and the house itself."

But along came two children, a boy and a girl. And we know about those little girls and their ponies. She grew into a horse lover. So the barns came in handy.

The 15-room stone Colonial has a center hall that runs the length of the house. A paneled living room has a secret door to a small guestroom and bath. It's in this room where Mark Leepson does his writing.

As for Janna's creativity, she's redone a cottage into an artist's studio. They've also renovated the kitchen. "When we moved in, there were only two light bulbs in the kitchen," he says. "And all the appliances were Westinghouse and all of them were outdated. One of the previous owners was a member of the board of Westinghouse." In addition they converted an outdated butler's pantry into a playroom.

The 180-acre property called Stoneleigh has been restored a number of times. In 1987, it was recognized for the excellence in the restoration of an historic residence.

In the late 1990s, Mary B. Schwab, a niece of financial mogul Charles Schwab, purchased it for $3 million and she has since added more acreage. The circa 1832 fieldstone Colonial was once again refurbished in 2000, combining historic importance with contemporary comfort. Through the years, the details include five fireplaces, hand-carved moldings and pine floors bought from a 200-year-old property. A state-of-the-art kitchen, marble counters and extensive cabinets are de rigueur. All of this overlooks a breathtaking three-acre lake fed by a string of ponds.

The landscape has been updated with gardens, walkways and trees installed. And of course, there's a pool. The horse facilities here are extensive, with barns, paddocks and schooling areas. Her show jumpers are in training with Joe Fargis, a gold medalist at the Los Angeles Olympics in 1984, and Schwab follows the "A" circuit from Wellington in Florida to the Hamptons. She even added a comfortable cottage for Fargis on the property.

One of the most historically significant properties in the area is Piedmont Vineyards. This ochre-colored manor house, called Waverly, dates to 1740 and has what one architect called "some Greek Revival roots to it." Now 143 acres, it has been designated a Virginia Historic Landmark.

During the 1940s, Elizabeth and Thomas Furness hired David Adler, a Chicago architect, to do some work on the nine rooms and six fireplaces. He ultimately designed a new rear entrance garden with a maze with American boxwood and a gazebo and arbor.

Adler said the house was much too full of character to touch. He did, however, draw some stencils for the front veranda, which are still intact to this day. The Furness's daughter, Elizabeth Worrall, eventually took over the vineyard, which was established in 1973. A grand and graceful lady of remarkable style, she entertained lavishly both in the main house and the adjoining winery and tasting area located in a bank barn.

In 1998, Baron Gerhard von Finck and his tall dazzling blond wife, Caroline, purchased the vineyard for a recorded $2.2 million. A descendant of an old and aristocratic German family, Gerhard had a few race horses at a nearby farm called Meadow Grove before he moved on to grapes.

With 25 acres planted with Chardonnay and Semillon, Piedmont Wine has been served at The White House. In early 2000, Gerhard took several bottles of wine to London for the International Wine Challenge, known as the 'Oscars' of the wine world. With more than 1,200 entries from 31 countries, he came back with a gold medal.

"We're not talking about The Governors Cup or some local competition," Phil Thomas says, "We're talking the world, and that was fantastic."

"I always loved wine, not beer, and I am hoping to transform a hobby operation into a real business by 2004," Gerhard says. "By this time, we should have 30 acres fully planted in chardonnay and cabernet sauvignon, giving us about 7,200 cases of wine per year [up from 3,000 cases presently] if there is no major natural disaster."

In addition, he is planning to convert the main house into a bed and breakfast. "The B&B and the winery would complement each other well," he adds.

When Phil and his wife Patti were married in 1989, Gerhard, a director of the German Jockey Club, invited them to visit him in Baden-Baden. They all went to the races and a string of lavish parties. "Gerhard asked us where we were going to end up on our honeymoon trip," Phil says. "I told him we were going to Venice and what day we would be there."

On the appointed day, Phil says he never dreamed Gerhard would show up. But when he was standing in the lobby of the hotel, he recognized a familiar step behind him. The three spent several days together sightseeing and having a grand time. This included a stay at the Excelsior Hotel on the island of Lido.

Toward the end of the stay Phil says, "Gerhard told me, 'When I get married, this is where I want to be.'" Two years later, they were back for a wedding that, according to Phil, was like something out of a movie. "We went in a flotilla of boats up The Grand Canal."

That's also what the Middleburg Mystique is all about.

"There's such a broad spectrum of people here," Phil says. "For a local like me to be involved in this high end real estate and meet these people and families and backgrounds is fascinating. I really still enjoy it."

Then he stands up from the couch, leans against the doorway, and reflects on the tales he's heard and the people he's met. "This is not West Virginia, where everyone could be their own third cousin. This is a very cosmopolitan and international community. They all have interesting stories."

CHAPTER 12

ℰASEMENT 𝒟OES ℐT

One of the most elegant examples of renovations took place in the late nineties at the 265-acre Snake Hill Farm, now known as The Goodstone Inn.

*T*he last one in wants to burn the bridges.

It's all about sprawl, easements and electric gates.

It's the hot button topic in these parts. In the early 1990s, Disney threatened to move into the next county, not far from sacred Civil War battlefields with a $650 million 3,000-acre history theme park. Protesters simply sprang out of the woodwork. T-shirts and bumper stickers shouted "F--- The Mouse." The anti-sprawl crowd pleaded it was all in good taste and asserted it stood for Fight The Mouse. But...please. Eventually the Disney types all went back to Anaheim and Orlando with their rat tails between their legs.

The battle was won, but the war persists. Bumper stickers now proclaim "Middleburg Says No To Sprawl." It's emotional and complex.

Dozens of organizations have arisen to fight everything from large scale housing communities, to preserving hedgerows, minimizing outdoor lighting and halting a controversial bypass around Middleburg. Everyone likes to talk about the good old days and names like Randolph, Mellon and Ohrstrom are mentioned. But times have changed and who will carry on the traditions and preserve the character and lifestyle? Will it all endure?

The Piedmont Environmental Council (PEC) is by far the most highly visible of these groups. The non-profit group was formed in 1972 "to promote and protect the Virginia Piedmont's rural economy, natural resources, history and beauty." It covers nine counties and deals with "land use policy, land conservation, transportation, water quality, historic preservation and environmental issues."

They were a strong force in the Disney battle. Among their original objectives: "It can bolster those officials in positions of responsibility who are willing to stand up to opposing interests. It can, through timely legal action, assure strict compliance with zoning and other laws and regulations."

The mighty PEC claims a membership base of 3,000 and a very influential and often affluent 36-member board from nine counties. One of its most gallant endeavors took place in October, 2000 with the purchase of the 1,292-acre Ovoka Farm in nearby Paris, a verdant valley that that is a positively pristine swath of resplendent farmland.

Owned by Middleburg realtor Phil Thomas, who inherited it from his father, it was on the market for 10 years and listed at $12 million. A group of 100 (now referred to as "conservation buyers") banded together to buy the property for $6 million, with Mr. Thomas donating an additional "gift" in a somewhat complex agreement. Portions of it were then resold to the National Park Service and Sky Meadows State Park.

John T. (Til) Hazel is one of the largest developers in the area. In what some would call a contradiction to his business, he owns a sprawling estate not far away. In 1988, he told a reporter from *The Washington Post,* that Middleburg had "gobs of money. I am just appalled at how much money is available for expensive land, and housing and horses." In other words, the land is not available for him to develop cookie-cutter communities with the McMansions he's put up all around the Washington area. Yet another set of bumper sticker shouts, "Middleburg, If You're Not Rich You're Not Welcome."

The PEC officially notes that for several years they had been "working with other individuals and organizations as a part of a much larger effort to reduce truck traffic and place more land in voluntary conservation easements."

Among those involved is the second generation of the Ohrstrom Family, committed to preserving the integrity of the land. Their support is financial as well as philosophical and their convictions are powerful.

Chris Ohrstrom says the most meaningful way to safeguard the character of this territory is open space preservation. "That can be accomplished a number of ways," he says. "Adequate zoning, which will always be under fire. Scenic easements (and browbeating your friends to do so). And third, demographics tending toward extremely wealthy people who can afford large unused areas of land and non-performing assets are helpful, though newly rich people tend to build vulgar and large houses."

"It's called NIMBY," says another long time resident, who takes exception. "Not In My Back Yard." A neighbor tells me, "It's hard to please the old guard no matter what you do."

Easements. That's the buzzword. At cocktail parties, over lunch or standing in line at the Safeway, people ask, "Is that place in easement?" It's almost like you have a contagious disease if you own a large parcel of land and you haven't put your land in easement.

In 1966, the Virginia Outdoors Foundation was devised by the General Assembly to "conserve and protect Virginia's scenic, scientific, natural, historic, recreational and open-space areas for the benefit of the public." In simple terms they define an easement as: "a legal agreement between a landowner and a public body or conservation group. The parties agree to protect the open-space and natural resource values of the land. The easement runs with the land and is recorded in the local courthouse. Each easement is tailored to reflect the conservation values of the property and the individual goals of the landowner."

The easement then restricts the dreaded large-scale sub-division. The land can be sold or passed to heirs and the easement is everlasting. "All land I own is in or in process of going into scenic easement through donation of the development rights to VOF," Chris Ohrstrom says.

Chris Ohrstrom and wife, Lila (daughter of Bonnie and Charles Matheson--long time residents) have meticulously restored Lee Hall, an 1818-1835 vernacular Virginia house. He is an expert on historic paints and wallpaper and owns a business involving both. Their house had been abandoned since the 1940s and then was dismantled and reassembled on site with sympathetic alterations to make it livable. "I tried to make it look as if it has always been here," he says. It has a number of outbuildings: an 1850 granary, 1840 smokehouse, 1850 dairy, 1820 kitchen, 1850 corncrib wagon barn-a reassembled using standing seam or wood shingle roofs.

They are putting up a guest cottage, an abandoned 1820 house from the North Carolina/Virginia border. "One must accept that some change is inevitable," he says. "Try to focus on what is good here not the few ugly houses." He has gone about this by also purchasing the farm next door and building in the vernacular style.

When he finishes Montrose next door. It will look exactly the same as it does now but shaggier, with more habitat. He, like many others, feels that an important way of preserving the character of this area is to encourage all new construction to maintain the flavor of the Piedmont vernacular.

"This may be any one of styles dating from 1740-1940, but there's a certain traditional style, which was popular here until the advent of the raised ranch in the '50s and '60s, " he says. "These are structures with symmetric fenestration of divided light, double hung sash, simple gabled rooflines and either stone, stucco or weather board siding." Recently some extremely vulgar manifestations of new wealth have blotted the countryside. "These tend to be huge domiciles using architectural traditions that are unheard of here," says one neighbor.

"It's one thing for these people to come in here and built houses," says another native. "But let's make them pretty."One local architect adds, "There should be a big box law."

One new dwelling that was highly criticized was the 17,170 square foot house built in the early 1990s by Stephen M. Wolf. Chairman and CEO of United Airlines, he later joined USAirways as CEO. He and his striking blonde wife, Delores, bought the 143-acre property (he has since added more acreage) formerly owned by the Final Exit Duo of Betty Bruce and Justin Bowersock (See Chapter 13, Death in the Afternoon). It was on this farm where they committed suicide.

At the time it was the largest house to be built in the area, with final costs estimated at $5.3 million, complete with a ten-car garage.They have no horses and no horse interest.

Ambassador Charles Whitehouse was formerly the chairman of the PEC. He worries about "the complete ignorance" of people moving to the country and those that don't "engage in the activities of the countryside."

He tells the story of one wealthy new landowner with a large pond. Whitehouse asked the new owner if he was going to stock the pond for the farm help to fish.

"Why would I want to do that?" the new landowner asked.

It's a long time custom here, as Whitehouse pointed out, "They're unfamiliar, they come here and don't know how life is lived here."

"Stop manicuring everything. And ban electric gates. That stuff is pure Southern California," Chris Ohrstrom says. "I personally will not go to a party at the house of anyone who has metal gates. If they are that unfriendly, I do not want to know them. Also, I refuse to have any intercourse with these people who are building monstrosities and gating them."

The mechanical gates "have the opposite result of their intended effect," according to long- time resident Charlie Matheson. "Their very presence, I think invites the very kind of unsavory characters to break in. It creates an image of over the top wealth. It's very un-country and unwelcoming."

"It changes the dynamic and makes those who have lived here forever shy away," says another long time resident, who begs anonymity. This person works on a number of charities and doesn't want to offend new arrivals. "It's a double edged sword. You need the funds, but you wish it was the same."

The other contradiction comes from lifelong residents comfortably ensconced in the ancestral home. After years of living off the interest of inherited money and not working, they now find themselves forced to sell off portions of the family property to pay rising real estate taxes. And the next thing that happens is a big new house going up on those sliced off acres.

Wolf may have been one of the first ones to install the dreaded electric gates. One of the wealthiest African-American entrepreneurs, Robert Johnson, founder and chairman of Black Entertainment Enterprises, which he sold for $3 billion to Viacom, installed an electric gate. Johnson and his attractive wife, Sheila, purchased the 133-acre Salamander Farm in 1996 for over $4 million. Once owned by the former governor of Rhode Island, Bruce Sundlun, and later by Bill Ylvisaker, a wealthy polo player from Wellington, Florida, this farm has a handsome stone manor house with a guest house, manager's house and a charming old courtyard stable in matching stone. It had been a very popular part of the Memorial Day weekend Hunt Country Stable Tour sponsored by the Trinity Episcopal Church several times. The Johnsons have been generous donors to many local causes, especially those that are horse-related.

However, with an intense interest in show horses, the Johnsons added a new stable and indoor riding arena, which offended the design sensibilities of some. They added not just an electric gate, but also outdoor lighting that one neighbor complains "Lights up like a Holiday Inn off I-95."

Minimizing outdoor lighting is part of the mantra of the 600-plus members of Goose Creek Association (GCA), a 30-year-old non-profit devoted to protecting the "Goose Creek watershed and other environmentally critical areas in Loudoun and Fauquier counties. Development is steam-rolling our way and unless plans are made to control growth, this unique and historic landscape could turn into a crowded and congested carbon copy of the areas further east."

Missy Janes wrote guidelines for becoming a steward of the land. "Minimize mowing and bush-hogging," she writes. "Allow areas of taller grass to encourage grasshoppers, butterflies, earthworms, micro-organisms and healthier soil." She continues with recommendations to preserve hedgerows, settle for dirt roads, plan entrances to blend in with the neighboring landscape and plant trees and shrubs as a buffer to buildings."

One resident tells of the "city slicker" who moved to Middleburg and promptly replaced all the three-board fencing with four-board fencing, perhaps for aesthetic reasons. There's one problem. The fawns are unable to negotiate these high fences and cannot get through. No matter what kind of perceived danger or nuisance the deer might pose, it's unpopular to set such a trap. "I'm sure these people just thought it was nifty to put up that fence because it cost a lot of money. They didn't even consider the animals," says one.

The same philosophy holds true with using an industrial strength leaf blower in the fall and winter. "Leave the leaves where they drop" is the mantra.

On decreasing outdoor lighting, Missy Janes continues "the night sky is a special attraction in the country. Lights confuse plants and animals that live by nocturnal schedule or navigate in the dark. Over-lighting is contributing to the suburbanization of the country and is not in keeping with its rural character." She advises to "direct light toward the ground with shields to control unnecessary up-lighting, burn off when not needed and refrain from over-lighting entrances."

Greg Ryan, a highly successful businessman and amateur steeplechase rider, started coming to Middleburg while still in college in the early 1980s. "Middleburg was the place to be for a young rider," says Greg, who is in his early 40s and was named one of People Magazine's 100 most eligible bachelors in 2000. "I started riding for trainers like Oliver Brown and Mike Pierson and eventually started to get on horses for Dot Smithwick."

A well-known horsewoman, Smithwick owns Sunnybank, a 2,000-acre farm that adjoins the steeplechase course, Glenwood Park. In the fall of 1986, Smithwick sold 213 acres called Creekside to Greg.

"She didn't have to sell it to me. She didn't have any financial reasons," he says. "We were just good neighbors and friends." They signed the contact in the paddock of the Middleburg races. He was wearing racing silks and getting ready to ride. He has won 127 steeplechase races.)They had one lawyer do the deal.

"I like it because it's at the end of a dirt road and it's old Virginia. It's like going back in time." The house is circa 1780 and was stucco over fieldstone. "Back then," he explains, "stone was considered a poor man's house." He has since renovated the house, knocked out walls and opened the kitchen. There is a spring house, which this perpetual playboy uses as a bunk house for friends to "crash after parties after the races." And a two-bedroom guest house.

"It is not a place with pillared gates with eagles on top," he says, adding that he didn't want a show place with a manicured lawn and a white fence. "There are stone walls with some barb wire and there's still some coon hunting around here." (In his free time he likes to hunt just about anything and he also likes to play paintball.)

When talking about the big box houses or those who might want to close their land to the hunt he says, "this is America, you can do what you want. However, I also feel you shouldn't impose your will on other people. If you don't want to fox hunt, fine, but don't complain about it to everyone else."

He is trying to preserve the down-home country feel of his place and has no outdoor lights. "This is not Greenwich, Connecticut."

Jane and Hudnall Ware have 50 acres with a house and a barn they call Waverly Farm. She's heavily into horses and says, "Hudnall was slow to accept moving here." They had lived on a smaller place and before than spent time in London. Once the real estate agent drove them down a dirt road into the back of the property she says, "he got it. He understood the open space all around."

Hudnall has had a number of business ventures and is a partner in the Memphis BBQ with five restaurants and two franchisees.

"We can't afford to be huge landowners, but we are of like mind and it's like having your home next to a park." They plan to put their piece of property into easement. At the same time, she understands the flip side of not putting your property into a perpetual situation. "My family has a 1,000-acre farm in Madison County, Georgia and we have to think about what our grandchildren will want to do. The land value will go up and they might not want to keep the farm."

Ed Moore, a financial advisor, and wife Margaret bought a house in the village of Upperville for the same reasons, "It's the protection factor," he says. "We realized that with Mellon on one side and a few others we'd be safe. It's the almighty dollar."

Residents of Middleburg went into a swivet early in 2000 over the pending sale of the Pettibone estate on the edge of the village to a developer. Jane and Hudnall went to the meetings about the controversy. "I wanted to see what it was all about," she says. "You can't take away people's rights to sell their land, you have to be prepared to put your money where your mouth is and form a land trust." (The property in question was eventually bought by a group of conservationists.)

On this Chris Ohrstrom agrees. "Pony up and buy the land yourself. If you do not own it you have no real say in what goes on. This after all, is America and property rights must be respected."

"I don't stuff envelopes," Jane says of her conservation sympathies. "I have two small children. I'm not opposed to sitting at a polling station though. My recent thoughts are to educate myself on both sides. You can't bitch about it [land being sold] and one person can't buy it all," she says, after dropping her youngest at preschool one morning. "I know one thing, I love it here. I can take my child to nursery school in a horse van and I'm normal."

Maggie Mangano is forming her own interpretation at preserving the character of the landscape. She and husband Frank bought 350 acres called Sunridge-Erwin Farm for $3.5 million from Paul Mellon in April, 1994. It includes a stone house and more outbuildings than anyone can count. But the showpiece of the property is a handsome horseshoe barn fashioned in the Normandy style. At the time, Mellon was just beginning to downsize his thoroughbred race horse interests. He had used the barn for his string of yearlings. It's now home to many champion show horses.

"We used to come down from Ohio on the weekends and look at property in the area," she explains over a pancake breakfast at The Coach Stop. "We looked at a zillion places including Jack Kent Cooke's with a horseshoe barn." But before they even moved in, Frank Mangano keeled over and died from a heart attack in June, 1994. Maggie, with two young children, was left to sort out his extensive business interests in radio stations and newspapers.

Since then, she bought an additional seventy acres to square off her property lines. She is striving to "keep the farm as it was [with Mellon]. I don't want it to be slick and I want to keep the wild places," much like the Goose Creek

Association endorses. But she is torn and points out that "when I came here, all the fence lines were trimmed, so now at least, I am not trimming around the tree pens."

She offers another view of the automated gate debate. "Even though the road says private lane, tourists would drive up anyway. I don't want to take a walk and all of a sudden there's someone there and I don't know who they are."

She frequently contributes to many of the preservation organizations. "I hope I will live out my days on this farm. I love the architecture and the way tradition takes precedence. I don't fox hunt but I'm supportive. When I came here, I wanted to abide by the courtesy of riding through and I intend to continue."

Sandy Lerner is one very outspoken landowner who does not abide by the custom of allowing the hunt through her property. She is an animal rights advocate. As the co-founder (with her former husband, Leonard Bosack) of the computer network Cisco Systems, she came from California with buckets of money. A 1998 article in, The Washington Post reported she had $80 million in stock from the company.

Young (early 40s) and captivating, she's had a number of suitors. She has been photographed in Forbes magazine, posing nude on top of her beloved shire horse. She also had purple hair for a while, no doubt a result of her business interest in Urban Decay, the cosmetic company she owns. It caters to defiant-oriented youth with lip gloss and nail polish colors and names such as: Gash, Radium, Roach and Asphyxia.

"Lerner's personality is as hard-edged as her dress and manner," according to a 1997 report on the internet from Lingua Franca, Inc. "She is being sued by her horse trainer and former close friend, Patricia Holmes, with whom she developed the first Urban Decay color, Bruise. Holmes claims Lerner breached an oral contract to share ownership of the company.

"She didn't have a role in the company, and my gardener didn't have a role either," says Lerner. "She hung on for a while, kind of in a groupie status, because she was my friend and she had my horses.""

In 1996, she paid $7 million for the 793-acre Ayrshire Farm with a forty-two room stone mansion and then promptly closed the property to the Piedmont Fox Hounds. (The very group all wrapped up in the hit and run accident involving Joint Master Randy Waterman and the Katz family.)

"She's entitled to her opinion on blood sports," says one forty-year resident, "But it's odd that she would want to live here. She could move somewhere else where there is no fox hunting."

One neighbor's rendition on such a deed is to "treat those who close their land to the hunt coldly. Do not speak to them. Hopefully they will not like it here and move away. The hunt is vital to keeping habitat intact."

Lerner's own cold shoulder to the hunt may have had some fallout when she later purchased a historic building in the village of Upperville. She planned to transform the 178-year old Carr House, named for the village's founder, John Carr, into a pub and restaurant. Too commercial, some outraged locals complained.But after months and months of legal battles, she won.

A woman of her convictions, some people are now slowly accepting her straightforward philosophy. An article in The Washington Post in 1998, said, "she is the first to own up to her one-and-only-ness. She doesn't mind her absent-mindedness. She revels in her rarity, wallows in her weirdness, capitalizes on her craziness." She has hosted a fundraiser for the PEC and a number of benefits for the local humane shelters. She has done millions of dollars in renovations of the houses and barns and planted 250 new trees.

She has rebuilt historic stone walls. These walls could possibly date to the Civil War--often referred to around here as "The War or The War Between The States." The history of the farm says "during the Civil War, on June 21, 1863, a portion of the battle of Upperville was fought across Ayrshire, and the farm was a refuge for John S. Mosby, the Grey Ghost of the Confederacy and his partisan rangers." She has frequently hosted Civil War re-enactments at Ayrshire.

Her favorite horse is the Shire, known as one of the tallest horses in the world. She has noted that these horses could carry 400 pounds of knight and armor into battle or a joust. She uses them for carriage driving in pleasure events like horse shows and has appeared in the Middleburg Christmas parade.

She's fond of the Highland Cow, those adorable longhaired brown, fuzzy bovines from Scotland. She says they're environmentally friendly. "When the English pushed the Scots and their Highland cattle off the farms following the battle of Culloden in 1746, the English sheep that replaced the cows cropped the grass far closer, and the change proved devastating to the fragile moorlands."

Her foray into cattle was not her first. Raised by two aunts, she spent time on a cattle ranch in California. At age nine she bought her first steer, then sold it and bought two more. When she entered college at California State College-Chico, she had thirty head of cattle.

Lerner's devotion to anything Anglophile extends to literature. She bought Chawton House in Hampshire, England in 1992, the fifty-room manor house not far from where writer Jane Austin once lived. She established the Centre for the Study of Early English Women's Writing with one of the world's largest collections of novels written by women between 1600 and 1830.

It was also an uphill battle, much like the battle she waged for the pub in Upperville. It seems the British locals of Chawton Village—population 310—didn't take too kindly to her renovations, which were years in the process.

"As the news of Lerner's acquisition spread, so did the rumors, eagerly pounced on by the British press. It was written that the house was to become an English branch of Euro Disney—or worse, a lesbian commune. Opposition to the restoration reached its peak over the fate of a set of badgers living in an abandoned swimming pool on the estate, according to a 1997 report by Lingua Franca, Inc. "Badgers are a protected species in Britain, and when word got out that Lerner's team planned to destroy the pool—a 1930s addition to the Chawton grounds—the local badger-rights society was called in to raise a ruckus.

Here in Virginia, she set aside thirty-five acres for organic vegetables: sweet corn, potatoes, cabbage, squash, onions, tomatoes, watermelons and pumpkins, some of which will be offered at her pub, once it opens. She's raising free-range organically-fed holiday turkeys, certified by the Virginia Department of Agriculture. They sell for $2.50 per pound.

Such fancy farming, though, is driving the every-day farmer out of business. "The land is so expensive that farming is so expensive," says Charles Whitehouse. "It doesn't make sense for a $5,000 steer to walk around on your $15,000 acre."

One young cattleman believes firmly in the future of farming. Mike Barreda and wife Leslie Grayson started Blue Ridge Beef in the late 1990s. They leased back 200 acres of the 500-acre family owned Blue Ridge Farm, built in the 1930s by Cary T. Grayson as a thoroughbred stud farm in the grandest style. "He was a southern gentleman," Barreda explains. "He was a physician from Culpeper and was the White House doctor for Woodrow Wilson. He had married very well. The horses were a passion and a hobby."

The estate was incorporated to avoid death taxes and, says Barreda, "over time the family wasn't was interested in the risk of horses." To keep things on the up and up among the nine remaining shareholders, it was decided he and his wife (one of the nine) would lease back part of the farm.

"It's my personal focus as a steward of the land to grow grass and the cattle are a means to harvest it," he says one sunny morning. He's sitting in his living room with three-year-old daughter Mia on his lap. There are cats, dogs and toys all over. She has a new toy cell phone. He's the caregiver. Wife Lisa works as director of the Northern Virginia office at the Virginia Outdoors Foundation. He's wearing jeans with big red suspenders. Until we go outside for a walk, he has no socks and shoes. His left toes are painted purple—the work of Mia no doubt. (One can only wonder if it's an Urban Decay nail polish product from neighbor Sandy Lerner.)

With his method of alternative agriculture there's no erosion of the soil, no herbicides and no pesticides. "It's offensive that they feed grain as much as they do. Cattle are adapted over evolution to eat just grass. Grain is erosive and a chemical intensive crop."

He has sixty head at a time and sells seven a year slaughtered that gross $11,000 each. He sells an additional thirty live, at the Marshall Livestock auction on a Tuesday. (Hint: a fascinating event to visit)They bring about $1 a pound.

He questions every assumption about farming. And cites the mindset that something is done a certain way because it's always been done that way, "Like daddy did it." He has a linguistics degree from UC-Santa Cruz and was once an environmental writer in Washington, D.C. He now reads voraciously about farming.

The cattle are trained to graze an area and move on. He has a rotating movable system of fences. There are no bare spots on the land. He does the same thing with hens, which produce eggs and roosters that are slaughtered. There is a moving "Poultry Palace." He calls chickens "lawn ornaments" and adds, "I don't care what others say, there is an aesthetic. If you're going to be doing this every day, it's like having your office the way you want it." So he has exotic black breeds like Dark Cornish and Blush Star hens.

"I mail-order roosters specifically for making them into roasters," he explains, "The vast majority of all animals that are butchered for quality meat are male. Roosters are cheaper than hens because most people don't want roosters. The breed I get to make into roasters is called "Buff Orpingtons." I get them because when they are young I can easily differentiate my black hens from the buff colored roaster roosters. And, that way I don't mistakenly butcher butch-looking hens."

He likes this breed for eating "partly because the small feathers left over after plucking don't show up against the white skin. The main reason commercial fryers/roasters are white is because these pinfeathers don't show after plucking," he says. He describes his method of slaughter as "nontraumatic" for the bird. "Traumatized animals release hormones like adrenaline into their bodies, which seem to affect the flavor of the meat."

Mike and Mia take a walk in the field to see the chickens. He says there are no other children in her playgroup with fathers who are farmers, a somewhat sad commentary on the times. "There are some who are employed by the big estates, but that's all." So he invites the children over to see a tractor and help bottle feed the calves. "I have a standing list of women who want to see a cow being born too."

In addition to the costs, Barreda believes one reason more young people haven't gone into farming are the parents saying "don't get on that tractor." Or, "It's too dangerous, don't do that."

Barreda is also a board member of the Goose Creek Association and a strong advocate for slow growth. He perceives a 75 percent chance of making his business a success. "When people come from the city and say it's so restful out here, it makes me laugh. I don't have any leisure time."

Shelby Bonnie plans to carry on an illustrious tradition. His grandmother, Theo Randolph, was one of the grandest sportswomen in all the countryside. A Master of the Piedmont Fox Hounds until her death, she served as president of the Upperville Colt and Horse Show and was a founding member of the Washington International Horse Show. She adored horses and dogs and fell in love with this area when she boarded at Foxcroft School from her home in Boston. During breaks from school she would visit her uncle, General George

S. Patton, a Master of the Cobbler Mountain Hunt, not far away in Markham.

She and husband Dr. A. C. Randolph bred Thoroughbreds and many fine and famous show horses as well as steeplechase horses Bon Nouvel, Walrus, Salem and Quiet Flight. She was often fondly referred to around here as the "Kingfish" in her role as mistress of Oakley, the site of two Civil War battles. She also possessed an enormous flock of turkeys, which were a coveted gift to both employees and friends at Thanksgiving and Christmas. In addition, she raised pigs, chickens and her beloved Norwich terriers and longhaired dachshunds.

She was an outspoken woman, although frequently preceding her statements on the ability of a certain horse or something like that with, "But my dear..." Friends, employees, neighbors alike respected this decorated horsewoman. She left her estates, Oakley and Salem totaling 600 acres in Upperville to her grandson.

"We had a very special relationship," Shelby says. "When I was young I would visit her and she'd be looking out the windows and I'd be walking all around her farm." Shelby, also a horse lover, is anything but the spoiled grandson. He received his MBA from Harvard Business School where he won the Rollins Award for overall contribution to the school. He also earned a bachelor's degree in commerce, with distinction, from the University of Virginia. He was a managing director at Tiger Management, a New York-based investment firm, and worked in mergers and acquisitions at Morgan Stanley.

He then joined a company called CNET in 1993 and was its first major investor. CNET Networks, Inc. is a global media company that creates content-driven Internet marketplaces for consumers and businesses and is among the most trusted source of information on computers, the Internet and technology.

Fortune magazine has listed Shelby Bonnie as one of the 40 wealthiest Americans under 40 years old, with a net worth estimated at $403 million. In February, 2000, CNET acquired mySimon, the Internet's largest comparison shopping service with more than 200 categories and over 2,000 merchants. CNET also produces award-winning content for television and radio with programs on CNBC and in national syndication, as well as nearly one hundred countries around the world. CNET has investments in cash and marketable securities that are valued at more than $1 billion, including its approximate 12 percent stake in NBC Internet, Inc.

Shelby Bonnie held positions as Chief Financial Officer and Chief Operating Officer prior to being promoted to Vice Chairman in 1999. By March, 2000, he was named Chief Executive Officer. "At this stage in the company's evolution, there is a great opportunity for me to assume management of the organization and take it to the next level." Bonnie said at the time.

He's putting a tremendous amount of time and money into renovations at Oakley, which boasts an 1857 manor house with pre-Civil War heritage. "It's stucco over brick," he explains and we've taken all the stucco off, re-pointed the brick and now recovered it in stucco. It's been an enormous amount of work and has taken two years."

Miles and miles of dry stone walls have been meticulously reset. And more miles of board fences have been repaired and painted. Part of his holdings include the Salem Farm where the historic Upperville Grand Prix Jumping finals are held each June. He's restored a house there, as well. "I feel a responsibility to my grandmother and the area.

"It resonates of a texture and flavor of very few places in the world," Shelby says. "In a world where things are homogenized, there is a wonderful sense of history and beauty [here]." And what does he feel is the most important way to preserve the character of the area? "I'm a very big believer in easements. People need to come together and not divide up farms. The land is expensive and scarce."

Moses Thompson bought a segment of land with an 1805 Italianate-Victorian stone house to renovate with barns and tenant house from Donald Graham, the chairman of The Washington Post Company. Graham continues to own the 600-acre family farm, Glen Welby, where he and his family visit on weekends and during the summer.

Moses owns Team Technologies, Inc., an international consulting firm, specializing in Third World countries with clients such as the World Bank and United Nations. He travels throughout the world and is an enthusiastic fox hunter.

The son of two Baptist ministers, he relates the wide-open spaces and riding to hounds to religion. "The early morning hunts have served as a form of secular theology. A time to rejoice, give thanks and praise the Creator.Like a monastic order, the field of riders in black coats and turned out with military craft, ceremoniously move off in the morning mist and with each hunt recreate an ancient ritual."

A member of the Orange County Hunt, he was awarded a "mask" one fine fall day. An honor for any follower of the sport, he was told it was a "trophy for your new home."

His wife, Holli, was a former vice president for fine jewelry and watches at Chanel in New York and Paris before discovering the Virginia countryside. They are board members of the Mosby Heritage Area Association, led by President Margaret Littleton. This group was formed in 1995 "to increase awareness of the historic, cultural and natural qualities of a unique part of Northern Virginia."

This 1,600-square mile sector was the first heritage area in Virginia; it's cultural and historic in nature encompassing Native Americans as well as Revolutionary and Civil War periods. It loosely follows the trail of the cherished Confederate cavalryman John Singleton Mosby—also known as The Grey Ghost—along Route 50 from Ashby's Gap near Paris to the Mount Zion Old School Baptist Church near Lenah.

The Association has a series of recorded cassettes for driving tours and maps. They host lectures: "Thomas Lee of Strafford Hall" and seminars"Art of Command for the Civil War-Mosby Rangers 43rd Battalion Virginia Cavalry" and have published *Profiting from Preservation*.

"We loved it here and wanted to put down roots," Holli says. "Every year they get deeper and we bought this big old house and we want to be here forever."

"When I first came here in 1990, it was difficult for new people to get involved in these issues," Moses says. "But in ten years as the pressure and threat has increased, the community has made room for this next generation. It's also been a change for the next generation of locals, the expectations are much greater to provide leadership."

Contemplating all the preservation groups Thompson says, "it's clear that we are determined not to become a culture based on bypasses or drive-throughs. However, the problem is not so much what we do not want to become, instead our challenge is in deciphering what alternative vision of the future we wish to propose."

The list of "Stewards of the Land" continues. Molly and Clarke Ohrstrom put long hours and funds into a holiday gala for the PEC hosted in the horseshoe barn at Llangollen Farm, once owned by Liz Tippett Whitney. Former president of Litton Industries and director of the Office of Management and Budget under Nixon, Roy Ash and wife Lila Ash graciously offered it for the event. Gold Star sponsors had a table of ten guests for $5,000.

Harry Darlington IV, known as Skipper or Skip, is the third generation of his family to live at the sprawling Chilly Bleak Farm. His grandmother, Ethel A. Shields, first married Harry Darlington Jr. in 1931 at the age of 42. She remarried George A. Garrett, an investment banker. They lived in Washington and the Middleburg area and she was often referred to as a "prominent hostess."

Skip's father, Harry III, was best known as a member of Admiral Byrd's 1940s Antarctic expedition. In 1947, Jennie and Harry Jr. went on another trek to the Antarctic financed in part with $50,000 from The New York Times. Mrs. Darlington's reports were published in the paper and she later wrote a book called "My Antarctic Honeymoon".

The family business continues with prized Charolais and Angus beef cattle. And Skip, who owns 203 acres, is now Involved in a high-altitude environmental research business in The Plains called Sky Calypso. His sister, Cynthia Darlington Beyer, maintains an adjacent 113acres.

One of the most elegant examples of renovation took place in the late 1990s at the 265-acre Snake Hill Farm, which has been in continuous use for over 250 years. It has been transformed into a beautiful inn. Now known as The Goodstone Inn, it is operated as a livestock breeding operation including farm fresh eggs for the inn's kitchen, which are hand-dated by the estate manager. Fourteen guestrooms and suites are decorated in the English and French country style. They include the carriage house, a former stable, now with four drop-dead stunning rooms and a gorgeous great room. Other accommodations include the Dutch cottage, Spring house and the French farm cottage.

The current name dates back to the Goodwin family who owned it in the early 1900s and had a dairy called Goodstone. The family built a mansion, also called Goodstone that was ravished in a 1939 fire. The only portion of the original structure is the ivy-covered façade now a breathtaking site near the classic old swimming pool, bathhouses and arbors, which had been added in 1943. This has now become the site of a number of weddings.

Frederick Warburg, who bought the estate in 1943, was a member of the well-known New York banking family that helped finance the Harriman railroads. The Warburgs rebuilt a manor house to replace the Goodstone mansion after the fire.

The Warburgs came to the farm during the foxhunting season and used it off and on as a second home. It continued as a full-time dairy and horse farm during their ownership. It was during this time that the estate was renamed as the Snake Hill Farm, because of the long winding dirt Snake Hill Road around the farm, not far from Goose Creek.

Mark Tate, a co-owner of The Coach Stop Restaurant and a member of the town council, serves on the Open Space Outreach Committee. He's working with others on Conservation Investment Districts "to permit property owners to invest in conservation of open spaces within the boundaries of that district."

The list of groups goes on: there's the Land Trust Alliance, the American Farmland Trust and the Land Trust of Virginia. Susan Young, a teacher at the Hill School, and a third-generation Middleburger, put together the Wancopin Creek Watershed Neighbors for a water quality monitoring project with science teacher Ben Hren.

In the predominantly African-American neighborhood called St. Louis, six churches bought two and a half acres along Snake Hill Road to build five houses for Habitat for Humanity. Reverend Joseph Biniek of St. Stephen's Catholic Church told The Washington Post in November, 2000 "It speaks so well of the community and the churches working together to make an impact."

Cricket Whitner, a native of Upperville, serves on the Steering Committee of the Route 50 Corridor Coalition, which is lead by artist Susan VanWagner. This group intends to ease highway-oriented sprawl through the village of Middleburg. They've introduced a scheme called "Traffic Calming" to emend highway safety and are waging a battle against a proposed bypass. Cricket is the daughter of the late Erskine Bedford, a Master of the Piedmont Fox Hounds. She and husband Jim Whitner, a stockbroker, live on the family farm, Old Welbourne.

Benefactors and volunteers often wear several hats for several organizations, like Marsha deGarmo, who works endless hours on behalf of the Route 50 group and a political action committee called VSS--Voters To Stop Sprawl. Scott Casprowicz serves on a new entity called the Virginia League of Conservation Voters.

The Fauquier and Loudoun Garden Clubs, lead by Ann MacLeod, Sally Morison and Millicent West, with the assistance of state grants oversaw the rebuilding of one of the last four-arch stone bridges in Virginia. Built in 1801, it transverses Goose Creek about half way between Middleburg and Upperville.

Donnie Ridge, a descendent of General James A. Buchanan, who built Ayrshire Farm where Sandy Lerner now grows vegetables and raises Shire Horses, spearheads a group to raise $350,000 to breathe new life into Buchanan Hall--once donated to the village of Upperville now offered as a self sustaining center. Built in 1933, it has been the site of some great parties (particularly at Halloween), community gatherings and performances of the Middleburg Players and family reunions.

When Linda and Bob Newton of Roundaway Farm discovered the one-acre Rector House at a tiny crossroads called Atoka was for sale, they bought it. They'd heard a used-car dealer was thinking of buying it. Visions of a mega-gas station and convenience stores or worse--those dreaded Golden Arches--danced in their nightmares.

"The historic significance of the crossroads alone justifies its preservation. It was here in 1863 that Col. John Mosby officially organized his band of partisans into Company A, 43rd Battalion of the Virginia Cavalry," they wrote in a letter asking others to join in the effort to save the building. "On the eve of the Battle of Gettysburg, it was on the property surrounding the Caleb Rector House that General J.E.B. Stuart waited for a communiqué from General Robert E. Lee-orders that apparently delayed Stuart's arrival on the scene of this decisive battle"

Neighbors quickly united for the conservation battle and the Rector House now appropriately offers rent free office space for the Goose Creek Association, Route 50 Corridor Coalition, the Land Trust of Virginia and the John Singleton Mosby Heritage Area. They formed the Atoka Preservation Society and bought up several contiguous buildings including a beauty parlor and a tanning salon. A component of the efforts put building restrictions on additional parking and square footage.

But when the question of whether or not it should remain commercial came up, the women in the group answered with an emphatic No!!! "I think there's some who don't want to lose the beauty parlor," Linda Newton told an attentive gathering in her graceful great room at Roundaway Farm one evening. The group of thirty included neighbors John Zugschwert (known as John Z because his last name is such a mouthful), Jackie Gammons, Rebecca and Ken Tomlinson, Sally and Steve McVeigh, Valerie Dove (whose husband Guy Dove serves as treasurer and was traveling to Turkey on business), Virginia Hunter, Shane Chalke along with Mia and Donald Glickman who are in the process of renovating one of the finest places in the area called Rockburn Farm.

Rockburn Farm and Rockburn Stud were once owned by the late Hubert Phipps, a publisher and race horse breeder, who also sold the Kennedys their place. His daughter, Melissa Phipps, has renovated a 65-acre place called Creek View Farm. She added a two story clapboard addition to the circa 1759 stone house under the guidance of architectural historian George Rosenbaum.

The area is definitely changing. The young cattle farmer Michael Barreda talks about service farming and the workers who "Mow, blow and go." They cut hay for $15 per acre because these people don't have any animals to eat the grass. He predicts that "pretty soon people will realize without cattle they're spending a lot of money to bush hog. And they'll pay farmers to put cattle on their land."

"The new dot-coms don't have the same philanthropic outlook," Ambassador Whitehouse observes. "It's hard to see how the next generation is going to take this. It's difficult to analyze.

Writer David Brooks used his hometown of Wayne, Pennsylvania, as an example in his book, "Bobo's In Paradise: The Upper Class and How They Got There". He wrote about "Latte Towns" as "upscale liberal communities, often in magnificent natural settings" and about how Borders Books, The Great Harvest Bread Company and Zany Brainy found their way into town. In Middleburg, the B and A Grocery owned by the Edwards family stood on the corner of East Washington and Liberty Streets. It was actually a market. They had house charge accounts and Alice Edwards would offer up all kinds daily news, judgments and gossip.

It's been elegantly restored by Tom Carroll, a man of great rural aesthetic vision and is now The Piedmont Gourmet, where you can buy a short latte for $2. This doesn't mean that the old place was better. It's just that times are changing and thank goodness it's being done in good taste.

Finally back to those automatic gates. One evening I was bringing Won Ton soup to a friend who stays in a cottage on a large farm along Route 50, just west of town. He was recuperating from hip surgery. It was dusk as I drove up to those gawdawful gates. Not knowing the pass code, I pushed the button that says "call." But of course, I got no answer because my friend was in bed and couldn't get to the intercom button. I had to drive out and around to yet another gate and finally after much confusion got in to deliver the soup.

I asked about the gates and why the owner insists on them?

"In case the horses get loose, so they don't get out on the highway," he says.

Okay, fine. If you want to close a few gates so the horses don't get out. But why do you need a pass code to get *in*?

A Welcome to Middleburg and the Hunt Country

CHARLES S. WHITEHOUSE
REFLECTIONS OF AN OLD CODGER

An Upperville lady once said to my wife, "General Lee was a fine man, but he was from "away." As we all know, this uniquely beautiful part of Virginia is accustomed to new arrivals from "away," some from much farther away than General Lee was. I am from "away" and so is my wife, and so are most landowners in the Middleburg area, but some of us have been here a long while and, in addition to the concepts of our generation, we remember very well the attitude of our parents' generation who came here to enjoy the fox hunting and the traditional sporting life which has brightened life here for some many years.

A very significant invasion of arrivals from "away" took place in the 1920s when well-to-do Northerners—dare I say Yankees— came in significant numbers and began to purchase farms from the Virginians whose homes they had been since before the Civil War. Many were devout churchgoers. All were committed to horses, hunting, and outdoor sports. They kept the land as they found it, modernized the houses they bought, and fixed up their fencing and stone walls. They even paid for paving the road between The Plains and Middleburg! Almost all were successful in making friends with their Virginia neighbors.

Today, the situation is very different. New arrivals from "away" are often from very far away. They come because the area is beautiful and easily accessible. Many are not coming here for the foxhunting and the traditional sporting life, and therefore may not have an appreciation of the continual hard work it takes to preserve the beauty, wildlife and customs of this countryside. Many are only vaguely aware that they are the beneficiaries of the major conservation efforts made by earlier arrivals to protect open space and the rural character of the Piedmont.

These conservation efforts drew national attention when an aroused local citizenry decided that a proposed Disney "Theme Park" near Manassas would overwhelm the area with all the tourist blight that now characterizes Orlando, Florida. With the help of well-known historians like David McCullough and C. Vann Woodward,

A Welcome to Middleburg
and the Hunt Country *(cont'd.)*

a coalition led by the Piedmont Environmental Council fought Disney—and won! This campaign, however, is only the best-known battle in the war against sprawl, against the ill-conceived projects of builders and developers, and against massive projects like the Outer Beltway.

This civic activity continues to be a daily struggle in which the Piedmont Environmental Council is joined by the Goose Creek Association, the Route 50 Corridor Coalition, and a variety of other civic groups. These aggressive and capably led organizations always need new recruits. Join them. Their foes are worthy of your steel!

The major conservation project in this area is the effort to have as much land as possible protected by conservation easements, which preserve open space and restrict future development. This program has been very successful. There are more scenic easements here than anywhere in the United States! Many farms are still not protected, however, and new landowners of unprotected land can save the countryside for themselves and others by taking this step. They may also be to preserve their own land values over time and obtain substantial federal estate tax benefits. Speak with a local lawyer or call the Piedmont Environmental Council or the Virginia Outdoors Foundation for more information.

Alas, some newcomers are introducing suburban garden concepts into our countryside. They bring an obsession with clear cutting, clipping, and mowing. They profess concern for wildlife but seem determined to remove the natural habitat in which birds and animals feed and live. They find hedgerows and thickets messy and long for the tidiness of the garden they left behind elsewhere. The Virginia Native Plant Society expressed the alternative very eloquently:

> Hedgerows and unmowed edges are wildlife's highways as well as its homes and supermarkets. Natural areas provide vital travel corridors for birds, insects, toads and others amid the expanses of empty green lawn that act as barriers to animal movement and native plant dispersal.
>
> These natural places, spared the obliterating force of

A WELCOME TO MIDDLEBURG
AND THE HUNT COUNTRY *(cont'd.)*

mowers and weedeaters, can create islands of wild beauty
on your land. Plan these "let-go" places with the same care
that you give your more manicured areas and you'll find
them as rewarding as your mowed lawn and weeded garden.
Perhaps more so, as an uncut strip of lawn or field can offer
a natural succession of bloom from spring dogwoods to fall
asters.

It is interesting that some seem to forget that the "hunt country"
cachet gives additional value to all of our properties and are indifferent,
or worse, to the activities of local fox hunts. Some newcomers view
the organized local hunts with attitudes which range from bemused
tolerance to outright condemnation.

The new arrivals have moved into "hunt country," but some abhor
hoof prints on their land and seem unaware of the fact that nature
soon conceals the marks of horses' hooves. They put up new fences,
but forget about including gates and jumps that enable the hunt to
pass through. Some even bring their urban fears of strangers and a
fortress mentality to the countryside, unaware of the local traditions
of neighborliness and free (but careful) passage for the hunt.

Horses and foxhunting are an important part of the character
of this countryside. This is, after all, the home of the oldest horse
show, the oldest hunt, the oldest race track, and some of the oldest
stud farms in the country. Much of the land looks little changed from
what George Washington saw when he rode from Williamsburg to
Winchester or as he surveyed tracts of land near Rectortown. It can
be enjoyed from a car, but the Piedmont from the back of a horse
is better. People who take the trouble to get permission from their
neighbors and are punctilious about closing gates will find one of
the great joys of living here is to view large areas of open land as our
ancestors saw it.

We hope motorists will slow down and proceed carefully
past horseback riders along the roadside (and bicyclists, as well!).
Landowners who welcome the local hunt and maintain jumps and
gates on their land will receive the warm gratitude of their riding
neighbors.

A Welcome to Middleburg and the Hunt Country (cont'd.)

This is a wonderful place to live. The heavenly views of distant fields and hills, the winding dirt roads, the traditional stone walls, the scale of the houses and farm buildings are a glorious mixture of God's creation and order that Man has imposed on nature. It is not just strip mall development that can mar the countryside. A new mansion on every hilltop with paved drives and bright landscape and security lighting which may be seen for miles around can also unalterably change this gentle traditional landscape.

It is obvious that our urbanized society will yearn increasingly for solitude in natural surroundings. This means that people will continue to want to come here—not for the same reasons as the earlier arrivals from "away," but because the area is unique and wonderful. The long-time residents are not hidebound but they appreciate the uniqueness of this area and its fragility. They assume that folks come here because they like the way it is also and are, therefore, puzzled by those who want to live in "hunt country" without the hunt or the country. This is the hunt country, not suburbia. It is Middleburg and The Plains and Upperville, not McLean or Manassas or Tysons Corner. That's why we are all here. Birds and skunks and foxes may live in our unmanicured hedgerows. The hunt may come by and leave hoof prints (and probably manure) on our land. The constellations are visible at night. We have found a corner of heaven. Enjoy it and help preserve it—it will only grow rarer in our crowded modern world.

CHAPTER 13

Peter Wilson *(Photo by Janet Hitchen)*

DEATH IN THE AFTERNOON

Shelly Malone was a dazzling and vivacious horsewoman. She owned an exquisite gift shop in Middleburg called Capriole—named for a dressage maneuver somewhat like a leap or a jump. The shop specialized in all things horsey: Jack Russell calendars, mugs and key chains and other high-end gifts.

On a crisp, fall Sunday afternoon in 1992, Shelley and a friend, Erica Stumvoll, went out riding from Western View Farm near The Plains. At some point, their horses started to buck and spook, and both women fell off. When Stumvoll got up, she found Malone near a tree on her back and later claimed her horse had stepped on her friend. Five weeks after the accident, she gave a statement to local authorities that Malone was struggling for air, but showed no signs of bleeding or broken bones.

Stumvoll went for help, but evidently got lost returning. Shelly Malone died after being airlifted by helicopter to the Washington Hospital Center. Almost an hour and a half had elapsed from the time of the accident to when the rescue squad arrived.

Shelly's relatives claim that Fauquier County Sheriff Joe Higgs (the same man who oversaw the Susan Cummings murder case) has regularly acted in bad faith and blundered in the investigation encompassing her equestrian-related demise in October, 1992.

Her entire lifestyle—shop, horses and much more—were reportedly financed by Cecil Altman, a wealthy married banker from Switzerland, to the tune of $5,000 per month and sometimes more. But Altman evidently was not the only man in Malone's life. She also was involved with Steven Head, a personal fitness trainer, who claimed he made love to her just a month before she died. He also said he was so in love with her and had plans to marry her.

Shelly evidently had another type of engagement in mind; just several days before her death she had a liaison with Robin Gulick, an attorney in Warrenton. Gulick is a presence in the same Fauquier County courtroom, where Blair Howard is also seen. And then there was George Carhart Jr., who also claimed to be her boyfriend.

The cause of death was eventually found to be blunt force trauma to the chest. Tyler Gore, the local undertaker, agreed. "It was quite obvious that a horse had stepped right on the middle of her chest," he recalls.

When Shelly's family tried to string events together, very little made sense. Bloodstains were later found in her car. Jewelry was missing from her house, furniture had been removed from the premises and her diary was gone. To this day, her relatives continue to hound the local authorities, especially Sheriff Higgs, to reopen and reinvestigate the case.

On the fifth anniversary of her death, family members took out a full-page ad in *The Fauquier Citizen*. They accused George Carhart of fleeing to New York three days after the funeral, and they asked others to join them at the Old Court House to "protest this grotesque crime that is rotting the heart of Fauquier County." They urged people to visit the website for Parents Against Corruption and Cover-up. They have cooperated for an episode of Unsolved Mysteries. But life and death goes on in Middleburg…

As folks went to pick up their mail on November 7, 1994, the buzz at the post office was over the suicide of Peter Wilson, a colorful character who strutted the brick sidewalks of the village for more than 20 years. The patrician-looking British horseman would often drive through town in his white Jaguar with at least four or five exotic looking dogs hanging out the windows. He would often dine at his favorite restaurant, The Coach Stop. He usually dressed in complete riding attire, or perhaps a tweed hacking jacket of expensive origin and sometimes shorts and a designer sports shirt. He often purchased them at second hand shops or the rummage sale at the church. If the town had hired someone to promote the equestrian image of the community, Peter would have been direct from central casting.

For most of the past two decades, Peter trained horses for socialite Rose

Marie Bogley, a stylish blonde widow who adores horses, dogs, fine antiques and entertaining elegantly. She has been known to own as many two dozen dogs, two dozen cats and even more horses on her farm.

Through the years she's been escorted to one Washington affair or another by such well known men as Ambassador True Davis, Master of Fox Hounds Randy Rouse, designer Arnold Scassi, Senator John Warner, Sonny Montgomery and the former Ambassador from Iran, Ardshir Zahadi.

Peter (who was openly gay) and Rose Marie shared what appeared to be a love of animals. For many of her sumptuous hunt breakfasts and Christmas parties, he assisted her with decorations and centerpieces. His British love of horticulture would be displayed in baskets dripping with geraniums hanging around the barn. At this time of year, he'd go into the woods and gather greenery for a giant wreath filled with holly and birds displayed it at The Coach Stop.

Peter and Rose Marie also had been known to have a tiff or two.In one last confrontation, one of a series through the years, he was fired after she heard he'd abused one of her horses at the Washington International Horse Show, an annual October fixture.In previous years, they had always managed to settle their disputes. This time, he was devastated, telling many friends he didn't want to leave, that he loved living on her sprawling estate and didn't have anywhere else to go. She had given him a week to pack up and get off the property.

Peter John Wilson was born in Leicester, England March 3, 1939. According to longtime friend John Buswell, Peter came to the United States about 1956 as part of an entourage with the British Equestrian Team. After following the fall circuit of indoor horse shows (including the Washington International), Peter decided to remain here, even though he didn't have a green card.

He took a number of jobs in the horse world, first in Atlanta, with George Morris, the top teaching professional in the country, "Peter worked in Atlanta when I first met him, while I was giving a clinic," Morris said."He was a good rider and very attractive. In the past 30 years I only see him once a year and I've lost track but he was very colorful and a good horseman. But none of this surprises me. He was very high strung and emotional. I liked him, but this is not a surprise."

"I knew him for 25 years and in all those years he was always a perfect gentleman and never said a word out of place or a bad word about anyone. He was always full of fun," says Pam Dickson, owner of Fursman Kennels.

Just after his job in Atlanta, Peter took a number of jobs in the horse community up and down the East Coast. He was working on Long Island when John, also a horseman, showed up one day—out of work and wondering where to go next.

Peter had a full time job at the time, but nevertheless suggested they go to Virginia. "We put all our clothes in an old Nash Rambler and came to the Warrenton Horse Show," Buswell later recalled over breakfast in a back booth at—where else?—The Coach Stop.

"I asked him 'Aren't you going to feed the horses before you leave?' and he said, 'No, it's time these people do it themselves.' And away we went."

But when he had to move south, it took three trips with a truck and horse trailer just for the clothes. He also always wore a strong herbal oil called Patchouli, prompting one friend to recall, "I always knew if Peter had been in the bar, the aroma hung in the room."

John, who is also British, and Peter traveled around Virginia for a year and sold a horse and made enough commission to live on. "We got along very well," John said, adding that they were close but never lovers.

"Peter would get his eye on someone and work a long time in order to...shall we say for the pleasure of their company. I'm holding back, there are millions of stories. A lot of people will say, 'How dare you say that.' They didn't really know him; they just saw him with the dogs. I knew him and we talked through the years. He had a dark side."

Many thought his life story had a sort of Equus aspect to it, much like the dark play about horses and death by Peter Shaffer.

"I knew his habits, you know, Peter had bad habits," said Ronnie Sakell, a professional horseman in Charles Town, West, Virginia. "He devoured young boys. He would seduce them through riding by having them ride for him. On the negative side he would leave the horses at the drop of a hat. On the plus side he was very fastidious in the way he capable of turning the horses out, but it had to be on his schedule."

One of the people who got to know the dark side was Jim "Jimbo" Chaplin, who was 20 when he met Peter and started riding his horses. "We were lovers for eight years," said Jimbo, who lives in Orange, an hour's drive south of Middleburg, and now trains ponies and horses. "John Buswell told me he had someone for me to meet and I drove to Middleburg and ended up staying. I had no idea."

The two lived together in an unheated cottage on a farm outside of town and in the winter they would rig up a wood stove. "It was okay in the spring, summer and fall," Jimbo recalled. "But don't go there in the winter."

"I don't want to degrade this person. He was abusive to me," he said. "But he told me I was the best thing that ever happen to him."

"Nobody was ambivalent about their feelings toward Peter," said long-time Middleburg resident Jacque Dreyer. "He had a joie de vivre, he was fun-loving; maybe his fun was misdirected sometimes, but he tapped everything with great enthusiasm."

One of Peter's skills with horses was training the horse and rider for the ladies sidesaddle class at the various horse shows. Among those he helped at one time or another was socialite Monica Greenberg, who stood and spoke at a memorial service put together by his friends. She said that Peter always had something nice to say to her about the way she looked or rode.

Rose Marie Bogley liked to fox hunt and ride in the sidesaddle classes and that's how she and Peter hooked up. He conditioned her horses for both types of work. He maintained a stable at Bogley's Peace and Plenty Farm then in Middleburg in 1980 when the Fauquier County Sheriff arrested and charged him with two counts of animal abuse, a misdemeanor, involving horses (owned by others) that were under his care at another location. One horse died from starvation and the other was eventually humanely destroyed as a result of malnutrition.

Rose Marie was in London at the time and Peter Wilson could not make bail. He spent two days in jail and was released after posting $1,000.

Attorney Jonathan Lynn (now the Commonwealth Attorney for Fauquier County) represented him.Charles B. Foley was the attorney for the Commonwealth. They entered into a plea agreement, with one charge dropped and Peter pleading no contest to the other. He was sentenced to a term of twelve months in jail, with all but 30 days suspended. He was given credit for the time already served and with good behavior, served a total of twelve days.

"He should have spent two years in jail," said state humane investigator Effie Fox, who was disappointed with the outcome. She had twenty witnesses lined up to testify. "What kind of a hold did he have on her? Right after he got out of jail he went right back to her stable, riding to the hounds and showing in the gentleman's hack. Why did people allow him to continue? Animal cases never get the credibility they should."

Said one long time member of the hunt, "Everybody liked him in spite of what he was."

Fox added that during the time of her investigation in 1980, by chance she received a letter soliciting donations from the Washington Humane Society and among those listed as an honorary director was Mrs. Samuel E. Bogley.

Rose Marie Bogley came to the Washington area as a young woman from Johnstown, Pennsylvania, and took a job working on Capitol Hill."Bogley was an old Maryland family," said one woman who has known her for more than 30 years. "Sam Bogley was in the real estate business."

Mr. and Mrs. Bogley lived in Potomac, Maryland, where they rode to the hounds with the Potomac Hunt. He died as a result of a fox hunting accident with the Blue Ridge Hunt in Berryville when his horse stepped in a hole.

The Bogleys had one daughter, Hilleary, who runs an ice cream parlor called Scruffy's, named after her mother's favorite dog, a miniature shih tzu.Proceeds go to the Middleburg Humane Foundation for abused and neglected animals. She and her mother were estranged off and on and have since reconciled. At the time of Peter's death, Hilleary indicated she and her mother did not get along because of her mother's loyalty to Peter. "He was practically a member of the family for 20 years," she said.

As a widow, Rose Marie settled at first in Middleburg and later moved to Upperville. She traveled back and forth to Washington and was frequently photographed at many charity events. For her 50th birthday party at the Madison Hotel, a number of gentlemen friends got up to make a toast.

She was often seen swirling around the dance floor in a designer ball gown, traveling to the races in Saratoga, or driving to and from town in a brown and black Rolls Royce. She is still quite elegant. Her Christmas Hunt Breakfast was one of the highlights of the season, bringing together her city friends and her country friends. She also served on the board of the Washington International Horse Show, ironically enough the event that ultimately caused Peter Wilson's demise.

As a representative of the Middleburg Hunt, Wilson was eligible to ride in the Gentleman's Hunter Hack.In this event, riders are asked to walk, trot and canter their horses, and they each jump two fences. When Wilson's horse refused one of the jumps, he was thrown off. "I saw it happen," said trainer George Morris. "I knew that he had a fragile ego and it probably upset him."

According to one expert, the "horse was notorious for stopping. That's how Rose Marie got the horse. He was supposed to be used just to hack." But Peter got back on and dug in his spurs and finished the jumps.According to many at the show, he took the horse out and beat him, going far beyond the line of discipline.

"I saw the horse in the van," said Leah Palmer, who traveled with a group from the Middleburg Hunt. "He had welts on his neck and cuts on the head and I think the major part of it happened in the van. I was approached by one or two people who asked me 'Did you see the guy in the gentleman's hunter hack?'"

By Monday morning, the phone lines were buzzing in Middleburg. A number of people called Rose Marie, and she fired him. According to John Buswell, Peter was despondent. He had landed on his feet so many other times. "The looks were going and his age was coming," he said.

Wilson borrowed a gun from a blacksmith friend and told him he needed to put a horse down. On the evening of November 6, he laid down in his bed in a loft above a barn on Rose Marie's sprawling estate. He surrounded himself with his dogs, put a shotgun in his mouth and pulled the trigger. John Buswell discovered the body the next morning.

"I got there ten minutes before anybody else," said Buddy Owens a member of the Marshall rescue squad. "There were a number of people waiting near the barn. Mrs. Bogley was sitting nearby in a golf cart. It was a big room with a lot of furniture and stuff. It was an eerie feeling. The room was sort of dark. He didn't have a massive hole. There was a bit of dried blood to the side of the mouth."

The service was held five days later at the Royston Funeral Home on the main street of Middleburg. Friends had gathered the necessary funds in an account set up at the Middleburg National Bank. Rose Marie Bogley was conspicuously absent from the memorial service. There was also another hitch that some may not even know to this day. Funeral director Tyler Gore refused to handle the cremation, saying that he had been advised by his lawyer not to do it unless a next of kin could be found. Two weeks passed before a funeral home in Warrenton surrendered the ashes to John, who scattered them across the countryside.

Meanwhile, back at the Bogley farm, life went on with a long planned hunt breakfast the day after the service. Some who had attended the memorial service also attended the party.

Guests were served chili, ham, and fried apples. And nobody uttered a word about Peter Wilson. "Some people who were there probably didn't even know about what happened not too far from the main house," said one guest.

"In this town, everybody has to be forgiven for at least one thing," another observed.

All deaths are not a mystery in Middleburg.

In April, 1990, Justin DeWitt Bowersock III, a retired Washington banker, and his wife, Betty Bruce Van Antwerp Bowersock, made a final exit that stunned most of the locals.

The Bowersocks, both 82 and married for 60 years, were vibrant members of the community. Their twin daughters, Frances and Carol, volunteers for the Middleburg Rescue Squad, discovered their parents at their 143-acre Rock Hill Farm near The Plains. The Bowersocks had been 20-year members of the Hemlock Society, an organization that believes in the personal choice of suicide. They ended their lives with a lethal cocktail of Seconal, Darvocet and vodka martinis. When the Bowersocks seemingly felt the quality of their lives was faltering, they made plans to "call it a day."

Three months prior to their demise, Justin Bowersock had a series of small strokes. Then a mishap at home left him in bed with a bad back. Betty Bowersock was suffering from emphysema and was overwrought about having to give up her regular tennis game. Bank accounts and real estate had already been put in the twins' names. Everything was detailed, including a notebook with extensive commentary on their final wishes…cremation and no memorial service.

"People were incredibly supportive," Carol Bowersock, also a former mayor of Middleburg, said at the time. "There's a real sense of community about Middleburg, it involves not just the town residents but people who live all around here. It's not a place, it's a feeling." And when all the Bowersocks' wishes were carried out and their farm was sold, the new owner was none other than airline executive Stephen M. Wolf and his wife, Delores.

CHAPTER 14

ONWARD CHRISTIAN SOLDIERS

*"The Lord will guide our feet into the way of peace,
having taken away the sin of the world."*

The Book of Common Prayer, 1979

A grand gathering of the fraternity of fox hunting mourns the loss of one of
their own. *(Photo by Janet Hitchen)*

*T*yler Gore is the local undertaker.

He recognizes just about everyone. He saunters down the brick sidewalks
and stops to chat. He schmoozes and works the room at the Middleburg Business
and Professional Association meetings.

As president of Royston Funeral Home, Inc., he operates one of the oldest
businesses. "You need a sense of humor," he says. "I walk a fine line."

No problem there. This man moves gracefully from the somber dark gray
three-piece suit he wears for a funeral to the radiant blue shorts he wears for
walking and exercise to the red suit and white beard he might don as Santa
Claus at Christmas events.

Tyler Gore and wife, Peggy, came to Middleburg in 1955, just after the
Korean War. Before the war he started college as a pre-med student. "When I

was discharged from the Army, it was between semesters," he explains."So I couldn't get in school. We came to Middleburg, because my wife was from this area. The only place available for rent was an apartment above the funeral home.

"I helped Norris Royston. There was no rescue squad so I helped with that, and he talked me into staying." Then, he went back to school at Temple University and got his license and degree as a mortuary scientist.

He says his professional services begin at the time of death until the sod is laid on the grave. When he first started in the 1950s, the cost was between $795-850. Today it's about $4,500. He figures he's buried 5,000 "clients" since he started in the business, about 100 a year. "But then again in 2000, there were only 55 and I haven't had a call in two and a half weeks," he says one morning over coffee.

His clients cross all socio-economic lines. Like the time there was a shootout during an argument at a card game and two men were killed. Another image continuously haunts him--"a little girl with blonde, candlestick curls."

Like many in Middleburg, he loves to talk about the good old days. He's watched Middleburg grow and as he walks up the street, he reminisces. "This was the movie theatre," he explains about the lot next to The Red Fox Inn."And this was the post office," he says as he passes Dominion Saddlery. And so it goes as he moves up the street in between bidding good afternoon to a local realtor."Over there," he says, gesturing in the direction of the Episcopal Church, "were stables behind the church, and the cemetery was the exercise area.

"I came to Middleburg at the tail end of a good era." he says. It was the mid-1950s and he recalls a "true camaraderie of Middleburg" that crossed all financial lines. This is still true.

The Gore family has also grown with Middleburg. Son Tyler Gore, Jr. has an insurance business and daughter Donna Draisey runs a creative and successful catering business and restaurant in town.

In the village of Middleburg, Tyler Gore's accomplishments are legend. He helped to start Christmas in Middleburg, held annually on the first Saturday of December with a parade and other celebrations.

"If he says he'll get something done, he gets it done," says Cissy Bunn, a former shop owner. "It's amazing how many people he knows. He's a very resourceful man."

The lighter side of Mr. Gore is just beneath the surface, probably well guarded considering his occupation. But it bubbles up from time to time in conversation or when you see him driving up the street in his 1929 Mercedes Gazelle. He often tells people he specializes in underground condominiums.

His drollery has emerged a number of times on the stage of the Community Center with the Middleburg Players. He made his debut in 1988 as the crooked senator in "Born Yesterday" and captured the role of Inspector Barnes in the musical "Bells are Ringing."

He has served as a scoutmaster and was the first person in Middleburg to be honored as Businessman of the Year.He organized a football camp for children and helped start the Mercer Athletic Association.He's also a past president of the Middleburg Lions and a former member of the town council.

He's an unobtrusive presence at every funeral, memorial service and burial. He stands to one side silently, prepared to assist a family member or escort attendees to the proper pew.

Many funerals in Middleburg have a distinct touch: a bagpipe player, jazz band or a trooping of fox hounds.

"It's more the norm here to have church funerals, it's different than some places," says The Reverend Mark Andrus of Emmanuel Episcopal Church in Middleburg.

Located on Washington Street on the corner of Liberty, the land was purchased by four trustees in June of 1842 for $75. The brick structure, completed one year later, has been referred to as neo-Gothic and first accommodated "40 souls." In 1927, it was enlarged by about one third. There is a marble memorial tablet to Middleburg's founder Leven Powell, outlining milestones of his life (1737-1810) on the east wall. The church overflows with charm, with a long list of gifts of bibles, candlesticks, communion vessels, organ and windows. The memorial needlepoint kneelers represent an ongoing project.

"The burial often precedes the service," the pastor notes. "I don't know what that means, it's more private and that's the most difficult. Maybe they have thought about it more." Sometimes the burial is on the same day, but in the winter some might wait until spring.

When 45-year-old McKelvy Costin died suddenly while jogging on the campus at Wakefield School (where he coached sports) in August, 2000, the outpouring was phenomenal. His daughters offered "appreciations and reflections." What some might not have noticed that day as folks left the church, the organist played "On The Street Where You Live," a highlight ofKelvy's performance in My Fair Lady with The Middleburg Players. He sang it at his wedding to his wife Sandy and again on their 10th anniversary. "And believe me," his step-mother, Jean Gold says, "there wasn't a dry eye in the place."

For the funeral service of Marielle McKinney, the beloved wife of Ambassador Robert McKinney (ambassador to Switzerland and also the first ambassador to the International Nuclear Regulatory Commission as well as the long-time publisher of several newspapers in New Mexico), a quartette of strings and a quartette of singers from the Peabody Conservatory were brought to Middleburg.

And the most requested hymns?

"Joyful, Joyful, We Adore Thee; Amazing Grace; All Things Bright and Beautiful, and (of course), Onward Christian Soldiers."

Mark Andrus reminds that a funeral is a worship service and a eulogy is not a proper component. "We are not celebrating what he or she did in life," he says, adding, "More and more the case is a memorial service."

On the day Billy Dew's memorial took place, the town was nearly vacant. Friends had gathered at the Community Center. Billy Dew was Middleburg's most famous architect.

"What was happening was really a passing," says Mark Andrus, who read at the non-denominational service. "He represented a way of life that is virtually gone. It was partly about his life and also a whole way of life. People come together to reaffirm their shared history."

Indeed, looking around the room that day, it was filled with what some would call 'the old guard.' Friends and family spoke at the service, including Ambassador George McGhee, who often joined Billy and other gentlemen for a Friday lunch group.

Billy Dew was part of that post office parade. He shuffled the three blocks from his office at the other end of the village for many years. He ate breakfast at The Coach Stop every day. He was 92 when he died in the fall of 2000 and the restaurant added his favorite meal to the menu:

BILLY DEW BREAKFAST

Two Poached Eggs
Orange Juice
Toast and Marmalade
Coffee
$4.25

Billy's stamp can be seen on a number of buildings in town: the Community Center (where a standing room only memorial service was held in his honor), Middleburg Bank, Middleburg Real Estate, the Yount and Hyde Building and the very important ABC store.

A bachelor all his life, Billy cut a lean figure when dressed in black tie. He loved to dance and was often included as the "extra" man Following studies at the University of Virginia (where else?) he began work at the prestigious firm of Trenor and Fatio in Palm Beach in 1936. "They were the society architects," he told me once. His own office building on the east of town is a Federal gem.

After leaving Florida, he decided Middleburg would be a nice place to settle. "The large estates would be much like what I had done in Florida," he said. His first job in town was remodeling the Red Fox. "That was just after the big flap of cutting down the trees on Washington Street. The Red Fox had once had a drug store and a hardware store inside in part of it. The tap room in the back had been an apartment. The basement had a dirt floor."

Always a very popular extra man at parties, Billy Dew cut a mean swath on the dance floor. He played tennis well into his 80s. He read several newspapers every day and was writing a book when he died.

He once described his design philosophy. "You have to ask yourself, does it look good or doesn't it? The proof of the pudding is in the eating. It shouldn't be what one professor thought in college of what is good and bad. The clients give me a list of what they want and it evolves with the house. When I do period houses, I make an agreement that we don't stick slavishly to a particular style. Everything comes into play in the end."

For the Episcopalian service, the funeral order begins when the body or ashes are brought in. When The Reverend Richard T. C. Peard, then the rector of Trinity Church in Upperville, died at age 50, he had written his own service. His body was brought in to the church in a simple wooden casket. The hymns included one that Dick Peard had written--"Holy and Creative Spirit," now part of the hymnbook at Trinity.

The Trinity Church has been referred to as Paul Mellon's church. The church, parish house, and rectory were given to the Meade Parish by Bunny and Paul Mellon. The building was designed by the late H. Page Cross of New York (who also designed the stables and other buildings on the Mellon's farm). The architecture is an adaptation of the style of the French country churches of the 12th and 13th centuries. (The style has often mistakenly been referred to in print as English. It is not.)

"I have been greatly influenced by the simple stone churches in the villages of France and Sweden," Mrs. Mellon wrote in a 1978 letter to the church. "Although churches were small, they were landmarks in rural communities surrounded by wheat fields, flax and forests. They were used daily as havens of rest and peace for all who lived nearby. Women left small bunches of flowers from their gardens. Men prayed on their way to the fields. Strangers stopped as they passed by. The doors were open, and the bells rang the hours. The rector or priest was known to everyone. His house and garden next to the church were identical to many others in the village. Many stones inside the church had engraved on them the single word, MERCI, or translated, "Thank You." These were the gifts given by those whose prayers had been answered or who had known a great joy, and wanted to leave this mark of gratitude. This was our concept of a church in Upperville, this quiet town next to the Blue Ridge Mountains. The church, the house for the rector and the Parish Hall were begun in 1951. The church is not a Norman church, as it has often been described. It is the conventional sign of a cross, in which we incorporated ideas and designs from many different sources."

Made of Virginia sandstone, some of the most interesting features of this church are the in the details. Much of the work was done by local masons, carpenters, stone cutters, etc. For example, the pew ends, pulpit and columns are the work of Heinz Warneke, who also did work at the National Cathedral.

The pew ends are carved with religiously symbolic plants that are native to the countryside.

This is the church where Paul Mellon's private funeral took place in February, 1999.The coffin was draped in a gray and yellow horse blanket with a sheaf of wheat on top. The sheaf was his "logo" and appeared on stationary and other materials printed from his Rokeby Farm.

This is also the place where he's buried. Several years previously, his parent's remainswere relocated here and there is a small plot in the cemetery behind the church, the entire area surrounded by the somber dry stone walls. It should be noted that the Middleburg cemeteries Sharon, Middleburg Memorial and Emmanuel, all appearing to be one large resting place, do not discriminate but are considered to be mostly white.Solon, on the west end of the village since before 1900, is known locally as "the black cemetery."

When Paul Mellon died, he left $1 million to Trinity Church. The Rev. Robert Davenport, who officiated at the funeral, says, "he made generosity a skill and an art form. He took his gifts and transformed them."

Like everything else in his life, Mellon's funeral was private, attended by 165 people. The family didn't want to say it was by invitation only, but wanted to discourage a large crowd. That was in stark contrast to the April, 1997 funeral service of Jack Kent Cooke, the flamboyant owner of the Washington Redskins. The event turned into a media circus, with reporters and television satellite trucks held in check across the highway in Upperville.

"I was told this was the place to be," one person told Tyler Gore, while she stood to one side of the courtyard. There are some that see such a sober ceremony as a social situation. Definitely by invitation only, the assemblage included NFL owners, players and power players from Washington. Richard Helms, former director of the CIA, read from the scriptures. The Reverend Davenport came home to find a reporter using his phone.

While battling a lung ailment in the year prior to his death in April, 1993, Gus Watkins planned his own funeral. A retired pilot with Pan American, he and wife Torrance moved to Middleburg in 1979. "How he managed to do this, I don't know," she says.

Four black women had been flown in from New York to sing "Swing Low Sweet Chariot" as the service began. "It was absolutely fabulous. I was stunned."

As family and mourners left the church, a jazz group flown in from New Orleans, played "When the Saints Go Marching In."

As if all this wasn't enough, he had arranged for a dozen bagpipers to be on hand at the reception at their home. "They were waiting at the end of the driveway, and walked down to the house," she recalls.

And oh, one last touch. Champagne.

"He wanted champagne," she says. "No hard liquor, just gobs of champagne and ham biscuits."

Erskine Bedford, joint master of the Piedmont Hunt Fox Hounds, died in December, 1998, when his field hunter buckled under him and pounded his head into the earth. Friends placed flowers on the jump where he was killed.

Over 500 mourners flocked to Trinity Church to pay respects to a beloved gentleman, farmer and stockbroker. Fox hunting friends wore formal attire of scarlet coats and carried hunting horns. It was clearly a gathering of the brotherhood of fox hunters.

"At big funerals, when you see someone across the pew that is an old friend, there's an affirmation of 'We used to do this,'" says The Reverend Andrus. "Maybe this is why people flock to these. It's a part of life."

"He reveled in his joys and made fun of the hard times. He fancied himself a gentleman farmer, but he was also a historian, a conservationist, businessman, ambassador, partner," Shelby Bonnie said to those gathered from all parts of the country, not just the local countryside.

Among the mourners that day was Bay Cockburn, a joint master and huntsman of Loudoun Hunt West. He had been paralyzed in a non-horse related freak accident eight months previously. He was in a wheelchair dressed in hunting clothes. Once a horse lover, always a horse lover.

Following the prayers, commendation and the benediction, Erskine Bedford's body left the church. Tyler Gore drove the lead car of the procession. The hearse took the casket to Old Welbourne, his 380-acre farm not far away. Mourners followed behind, much like those who follow the hunt by car.

Four riders and more than two dozen foxhounds stood soberly along the gravel road and lead the way to the stone-enclosed historic burial site. Mourners gathered around as dusk fell. The casket was lowered into the ground, and in the distance could be heard the chilling strains of the hunting horn echoing "Gone Away," the notes blown indicating the fox has left the covert and the chase is on.

To buy these other books
by Vicky Moon
go to

www.vickymoon.com